ILLUSTRATED

ILLUSTRATED

Daily Thoughts for Your Daily Walk

JEFFREY A. JOHNSON, SR.

LIFE ILLUSTRATED: DAILY THOUGHTS FOR YOUR DAILY WALK

Cover Design by Tina Williams, Tru Essence Designs
www.truessencedesign.com

© Copyright 2009

SAINT PAUL PRESS, DALLAS, TEXAS
First Printing, 2009
Second Printing, 2010

Unless otherwise noted, all Scriptures are taken from the New International Version of the Bible.

The name SAINT PAUL PRESS and its logo are registered as a trademark in the U.S. patent office.

ISBN-10: 0-9825303-7-4
ISBN-13: 978-0-9825303-7-5

Printed in the U.S.A.

To my beloved grandmother,
Mary Lester,
who has faithfully loved me,
cared for me, prayed for me,
and has been a living illustration for my life.

And to the members of Eastern Star Church whose receptivity to my
illustrations inspires me and allows me to explain the scriptures more
clearly.

Contents

Preface

A CHALLENGE THAT NEARLY EVERY PASTOR FACES on a weekly basis is how to preach the Word of God in such a way as to make it relevant to the lives of those who will be listening to the sermon. Jesus told parables that included common items to which the people of His day could relate: sheep, goats, a mustard seed, leaven, pearls, lamps, wheat, a fig tree, etc. Because those items were so ordinary, His stories still speak to us today. Through His parables, we can learn spiritual principles and kingdom values.

In this twenty-first century, we still use stories to get our messages across. Sermon illustrations are not "filler" or "attention getters." Illustrations enable the listeners to better understand what the Bible is saying, and to envision how the text can apply to them personally. The same spiritual principles and kingdom values that Jesus taught through parables are conveyed through illustrations that also include everyday themes and common experiences.

This book is a collection of illustrations that have come from my own sermons over the past few years. I offer them to help inspire young pastors to explicate the scripture and make it plain so that their congregations can fully understand the message. I offer them to encourage those who have found it difficult to relate to what the Bible has to say. And I offer them to those who are seeking a daily reminder of God's love, faithfulness, and grace in their lives.

My prayer is that you will hear God's voice speak in a special and personal way through each devotional. Whether this is read first thing in the morning, as a timeout during a busy day, or as part of a quiet time with God before going to bed, I ask God to bless His Word to your heart and let the illustrations remain in your thoughts to instruct, edify, comfort and cheer you on your journey.

Pastor Jeffrey A. Johnson, Sr.

January 1

Since, then, you have been raised with Christ, set your hearts on things above, where Christ is seated at the right hand of God. Set your minds on things above, not on earthly things. For you died, and your life is now hidden with Christ in God.

—Colossians 3:1-3

I HAD DRIVEN MY CHRYSLER EAGLE PREMIER over 125,000 miles. The engine was still good, and the body of the car still looked good. The fuel indicator, however, was broken, and it was broken in an unusual way. No matter how much—or how little—fuel I had, the gauge always pointed to "full." So even if the tank was actually empty, with no gas in it at all, the indicator would still point to "full" because it was broken. As you can imagine, that could be a real problem. If I were not careful, I would focus on the broken fuel indicator and end up falling short of my destination. I would fail to arrive at the place I needed to be because I was looking at an indicator that was broken.

We must be careful that we are not going through our daily lives focused on a broken indicator. In the world in which we live, there are broken indicators of what is positive, of what is full. We put so much focus on cars, clothes, cash, and creature comforts that we forget about the spiritual aspects of life, which is really what fullness is all about. We forget to set the thoughts of our hearts on Jesus, salvation, the Holy Spirit, and our walk with God. So, we go through life thinking we are full when actually we are running on empty. Let's keep our focus today on that which is spiritual as our indicator of fullness. And let's make sure that we are being filled continually with God's Holy Spirit as we yield more and more to Him through prayer and through His Word.

Father, we pray that we would not be fooled by the broken indicators of our society, but rather that we would focus on the things that please You. In Jesus' name, Amen.

January 2

The eye is the lamp of the body. If your eyes are good, your whole body will be full of light. But if your eyes are bad, your whole body will be full of darkness. If then the light within you is darkness, how great is that darkness!

—Matthew 6:22-23

MY YOUNG SON WAS STICKING HIS HEAD outside the car window, looking at the front of the car on the passenger side. I asked, "Son, what are you looking for?" He said, "Dad, when you turned on the turn signal just then to turn right, there was no flashing light *inside*, so I wanted to see if the light was flashing on the *outside*." I explained to him that the flashing light on the *inside* is an indication that the turn signal is working. If it is not flashing on the *inside*, then it is not working on the *outside*.

We must all learn that God has placed His Holy Spirit inside of us, and when the light of Jesus Christ is shining *in*side, it will be reflected on the *out*side. But if the Holy Spirit is not being allowed to move freely on the *in*side, we must recognize that He is not being demonstrated properly on the *out*side either. Let us allow the light of God's Spirit to shine in our hearts so that our very lives are radiant examples of God's love to the world.

Father, we open to You the doors of our hearts. Please allow Your Holy Spirit to move in our hearts, minds, and souls on the inside so that we may be a powerful witness to others as we daily live for You. In Jesus' name, Amen.

January 3

Stand fast therefore in the liberty wherewith Christ hath made us free, and be not entangled again with the yoke of bondage.

—Galatians 5:1 (KJV)

SEVEN-YEAR-OLD ERICA WAS KIDNAPPED IN Philadelphia by men who planned to get a ransom from her parents. These men took Erica and wrapped duct tape around her hands, her mouth, and her eyes. Then they threw her in the basement of a home in her neighborhood and left her there. Little Erica was frightened, disheartened, and confused. Yet somehow, this young girl had the resourcefulness to bite through the tape on her mouth and then to bite off the tape that bound her hands. Then she was able to pull the tape off her eyes. Once she was unbound, she threw something at the basement window that broke it, and then she climbed out to freedom. She ran to a nearby house, where the neighbors assisted her and called the police. Her assailants were arrested. Later, her uncle appeared on national television holding Erica in his arms while she waved and smiled, celebrating her freedom.

There are times when the enemy of our souls will try to put us in bondage and pull us away from that which is positive in our lives—from our families, friends, and others who are trying to help us grow in our relationship with God. We need to learn how to respond as Erica did and use our resourcefulness to get out of those bad situations. Through the power of God's Holy Spirit, we must be willing to work and struggle to get free. Then we need to be willing to trust those who are trust*worthy* to help us grow and develop in Christ. We also need to call on the name of God, through His Son Jesus Christ, knowing He will free us from the things that would try to keep us in bondage. Then we, like Erica, can celebrate our freedom.

Father, we pray that in the power of the Holy Spirit, You will set us free from the things that attempt to keep us from doing Your will so that we might be pleasing in Your sight. In Jesus' name, Amen.

January 4

My flesh and my heart may fail, but God is the strength of my heart and my portion forever.

—*Psalm 73:26*

OPRAH WINFREY INTERVIEWED ELIZABETH EDWARDS, the wife of Senator John Edwards, shortly after she was diagnosed with cancer. Oprah asked her how she was feeling. Elizabeth Edwards responded that she was still experiencing a lot of pain from a broken rib. But she added that she thanked God that her rib was broken because that is what led her to go to the hospital, which led to her getting an x-ray, which led to her getting a bone scan, which led to a CT scan, which led to the doctors discovering that she had cancer—and discovering it early enough that she felt she would have enough strength to fight it in a positive way. So, she told Oprah, the broken rib was what put her in a better position to fight a bigger battle.

We all need to realize that there are times that we experience brokenness, but it is God's way of showing us some internal things that need our attention. As we address those situations, it puts us in a position to strengthen ourselves by His Holy Spirit so that we can fight the big battles that come in life.

Lord, we pray that by the power of Your Holy Spirit, You will help us to deal with the pains of life. Strengthen us as You reveal to us the areas where we need to be built up to better fight the difficulties of life. We believe that You will give us the victory. In Jesus' name, Amen.

January 5

When the storm has swept by, the wicked are gone, but the righteous stand firm forever.

—Proverbs 10:25

THE FIRST TIME I PREACHED IN MIAMI, Florida, it was right after a hurricane had hit. The pastor of the church picked me up at the airport. As we were driving into the city, we saw such terrible destruction: homes, businesses, churches, and schools, were all destroyed. In the midst of this, I saw so many palm trees that were bent over that I commented about how sad it was that so many of them were lost. The preacher said, "Oh, they haven't been destroyed." "But, look," I said, "they're all bent over." "Yes," the pastor acknowledged, "they are bent. But when the sun comes out again, they will rise back up." He explained to me that the roots of a palm tree go down deep until they find a rock. Then, the roots wrap around that rock so that they are able to stand firm during a storm. They bend, but they don't break.

We who have our lives wrapped by faith around Christ Jesus can go through the storms of life and, although they may batter us down, we will not be destroyed. When we stay in right relationship with the Son of God— not the s-u-n, but the S-o-n—we will be able to rise up and stand strong again in the power of Jesus.

Father, please help us to endure storms as they come into our lives by maintaining the proper relationship with You through Your Son Jesus Christ. Help us to remember that after the storms are over, we will rise up and stand again with strength and power. In Jesus' name, Amen.

January 6

I do not trust in my bow, my sword does not bring me victory; but you give us victory over our enemies, you put our adversaries to shame.

—Psalm 44:6-7

ONE DAY I WAS HAVING PROBLEMS WITH the brand new steamer in my office. Even though my clothes were clean, they were wrinkled and needed to be ironed. Usually, I can easily use the steamer to quickly get out the wrinkles. But on this day, I was putting forth far too much physical energy, exerting way more effort than is usually necessary to get out the wrinkles. Finally, I discovered the reason. I did not have enough water in the container to get the necessary steam from the heat. Once I filled the water container, I had so much steam coming forth that it didn't take much of my energy at all to straighten my clothes.

At times, there are situations in our lives—in our jobs, in our relationships, in our priorities— that need to be straightened out. Sometimes we find ourselves putting forth great energy and effort, only to discover that it is not getting the job done. At some point, we must come to the realization that it isn't until we are filled with God's Holy Spirit and allow Him to control our lives that we are able to get things straight. We have to stop trying to work things out on our own and trust instead in the power of God.

Father, we pray that You will help us to quit striving by our own efforts to handle the wrinkles of our lives. With Your help, we will stop trusting our own abilities and depend instead upon the power of Your Holy Spirit to get things straightened out in our situations. In Jesus' name, Amen.

January 7

"Not by might nor by power, but by my Spirit," says the Lord Almighty.
—Zechariah 4:6b

MY SON JALON USED TO LOVE TO play with the remote control when he was a small child. He would turn the television off and on, change the channel, and raise and lower the volume. He kept playing with the buttons until finally his mother and I decided we needed to take action. We found that the best way to get him to stop spending so much time with the remote control was by removing the batteries. When we took out the batteries, even though he was pushing the right buttons, nothing happened. The TV wasn't going off and on, the channels weren't changing, and the volume wasn't being affected. My son still had the right instrument, but he did not have the necessary internal power to make things happen.

We need to make sure as we go to the right schools, work for the right companies, marry the right people, attend the right church, and do the right things that we aren't simply going through the motions. We must make sure that we have the internal power of God's Holy Spirit in our lives to make the necessary changes to accomplish what God desires for us.

Father, we pray that we will fully know the presence and power of Your Holy Spirit in our lives to help us reach the goals that You have given us and accomplish the things You desire for us. In Jesus' name, Amen.

January 8

My prayer is not that you take them out of the world but that you protect them from the evil one. They are not of the world, even as I am not of it. Sanctify them by the truth; your word is truth. As you sent me into the world, I have sent them into the world. For them I sanctify myself, that they too may be truly sanctified.

—John 17:15-19

THE GECKO IS A SMALL LIZARD THAT is able to stick to almost any type of surface. It has amazed scientists for years as they have tried to figure out how this natural phenomenon works. Even if the surfaces are dirty, the geckos can stick there; but if you remove them, the dirt from the surface somehow does not end up on their feet. The gecko is able to hold on in dirty environments without taking on the dirt from their environment.

God understands that, as His children, we must go into a variety of environments—on the job, in the community, in our neighborhoods, with our family, and with our friends. Yet, no matter what environment we are in, we do not have to get dirty from that environment. Because of our relationship with God through His Son Jesus Christ, we can stay clean even though we have to live in an environment that is dirty.

Father, thank You for the ability to accomplish the things You want us to accomplish in different situations without taking on the negative aspects of that situation. Thank You, Father, that we can live in the world and not be of the world. In Jesus' name, Amen.

January 9

"My Father, who has given them to me, is greater than all; no one can snatch them out of my Father's hand."

—*John 10:29*

MY SON K. J. IS NOW ELEVEN YEARS OLD, but when I used to take him downtown as a little boy, I had to watch out for him because traffic could be so busy and dangerous. I would always tell K. J. to hold my hand as we crossed the street. He would reach up and hold my hand, but more importantly, I held his hand. If things got out of control, he might get scared and let me go, but I would never let go of him. But why would I even let him be downtown in the first place and allow him to be in the face of danger? Because that's where the museums are, where the State Capitol is located, and where the Pacers and the Colts play. He wouldn't get to experience any of these things if he didn't go there, so I let him go. But I never let go of him.

By faith in Christ, we have taken hold of the hand of God. As we walk through this life with Him, there are times we have to deal with issues that are frightening, issues that could even cause us to panic and do something foolish. But even as we are holding onto God, remember that God is also holding onto us, and no man shall pluck us out of His hand. No matter what goes on, no matter what situations we have to go through, everything will be all right—not only because we are holding onto God, but because God is holding onto us.

Father, thank You that You will never let us go. Thank You that even though our way may be frightening at times, You are right beside us, holding onto us so that You can rescue us from any danger. Thank You, God, that our security is not in our strength to hold onto You, but in Your power to hold onto us. We are safe. Amen.

January 10

The Lord will rescue me from every evil attack and will bring me safely to his heavenly kingdom. To him be glory for ever and ever. Amen.
—2 Timothy 4:18

ONE DAY YEARS AGO, WHILE MY son Jordan and I were playing catch with a baseball, Jalon, my younger son, came and positioned himself right behind me. As he stood there, I was afraid he was going to get hurt because at that time, Jordan had a lot of power but little control as he threw the ball. So I told Jalon, "You'd better move. You're going to get hurt. This ball is out of control." But he refused to move. I said again, "You need to move before you get hurt." He still didn't move. Then it dawned on me what Jalon already knew—that he was in a safe place. As long as he stood behind me, anything coming at him would have to go through me before it got to him. He was protected by my presence.

We need to realize that God is our Father and we are His children. As long as we position ourselves close to the Father, we are in a safe place. Even when life gets out of control, we know that everything is going to be all right because nothing can touch us that our Father does not allow.

Father, thank You for allowing us to be Your children, and allowing us to draw close to You. Help us to hide ourselves in You so that as life gets out of control, we are safe in Your presence. In Jesus' name, Amen.

January 11

He shielded him and cared for him; he guarded him as the apple of his eye, like an eagle that stirs up its nest and hovers over its young, that spreads its wings to catch them and carries them on its pinions.

—Deuteronomy 32:10b-11

WE STOOD AMAZED AS WE WATCHED PICTURES of the plane incident that became known as *The Miracle on the Hudson*. US Airways Flight 1549 had just taken off from LaGuardia Airport in New York City when it collided with some geese, silencing both plane engines and causing one of them to catch fire. Some of the flight attendants said the plane's cabin became as silent as a library. It appeared that the plane, its crew, and its 155 passengers were headed for disaster. But the heroic pilot Chesley Sullenberger was not giving up. Instead of resigning himself to their fate, he used his knowledge of gliding and air currents to *glide* the US Airways Airbus into a textbook landing on the surface of the Hudson River. Everyone was saved.

There are times when we find that our power is gone. We expect to soar into the heights; instead, we find ourselves plunging to certain disaster. But even in those catastrophic moments, we do not need to despair or give up. As Christians, we have God's Holy Spirit operating in our lives. Even when we are falling, God is faithful. Even when we fail to realize it, God is watching over us and guarding us like an eagle watching over its young. When we are fragile, fainthearted, and falling, God swoops down and spreads His wings to catch us and carry us to a safe landing.

God, thank You that You are with us in the midst of our moments of peril, when all seems hopeless and our own strength is gone. Thank You that when we are weak, You are strong; when we are falling, You hold us up; when we see certain disaster coming toward us, Your unseen presence intervenes and saves us. Thank You, God, Amen.

January 12

We live by faith, not by sight.

—2 Corinthians 5:7

A BROTHER SHARED WITH ME THAT HE had trusted God to pay for his daughter to go to college. He knew he could not afford to send her to the school of her choice. But because he believed God wanted her to be there, he trusted God to provide the funds. This man became disheartened, however, when he prayed, trusted God, and continued to give his tithes and offerings to God, and yet God was not responding. He expected God to answer prayer, but God was silent. My friend's faith turned to frustration. Yet, at the very moment that this man's daughter actually needed the money, God provided her with a two hundred thousand-dollar scholarship.

The man wanted the money so that he could see to meet the need; God gave a scholarship that he could not see in advance. We have all been like that. God says, "Trust," and we say, "But God…." God says, "Have faith," and we say, "Yes, God, but…." God says, "Wait," and we say, "But how long?" When will we learn to fully trust God? When will we truly take God at His word? When will our faith rise to meet His faithfulness?

God, it is with humble hearts that we come before You, asking that You forgive us for doubting You. Forgive us for the times that You have wanted to surprise us with a joyous answer to our prayer, but we took the joy out of the experience by sulking, complaining about Your timing, and fearing that You would fail us. Forgive us for being like spoiled children, instead of children who lovingly trust their Father. We look to You, God, to forgive us, and to enable us to live by faith and not by sight. In Jesus' name, Amen.

January 13

Then he told this parable: "A man had a fig tree, planted in his vineyard, and he went to look for fruit on it, but did not find any. So he said to the man who took care of the vineyard, 'For three years now I've been coming to look for fruit on this fig tree and haven't found any. Cut it down! Why should it use up the soil?'"

—Luke 13:6-7

WHEN I WAS A STUDENT AT BISHOP COLLEGE (now the site of Paul Quinn College in Dallas), my roommate was Denny Davis. Denny had a beautiful new Monte Carlo, and he liked to test the car by waiting until it was just on the verge of empty before getting gas. One night when we were out together driving around in his car, he kept waiting and waiting as the gas gauge dropped closer and closer to the "empty" mark. Finally, with a bit of common sense and a little pressure from me, he pulled off the highway to get gas. He found, however, that the gas station advertised on the big billboard along the side of the road was no longer in service. Disappointed, he remarked, "If they're going out of business, at least they could take the sign down."

Why do some of us wear crosses, get baptized, or do some of the other things symbolic of being a Christian if we are not really Christians? God is not satisfied with trees that only *look* like they are going to bear fruit. Neither is He satisfied with people who only *look* like Christians, who only *look* like they are going to bear the fruit of the Spirit. Let us make a decision to *be* Christians, not just to *look like* Christians.

God, let us never be satisfied to live hypocritical lives. Let us never be satisfied only to look as though we are Your people when actually we seek only to please ourselves. Let us never disgrace You by pretending to represent You in the world when, in fact, we are not like You at all. Forgive us, God, and make us holy from the inside out. In Jesus' name, Amen.

"…apart from me, you can do nothing."

—John 15:5b

MY WIFE ONCE HAD AN ONSTAR FEATURE in her car that was totally useless. It was intended to allow her to get directions, make reservations, unlock doors, or call for help in case of an emergency. It was a wonderful feature, but we could not use it because we had never made the necessary connection with it.

When God made us, He gave us an internal navigational system that can help us reach our destination and get what we need along the way. But in order for it to help us, we have to make the connection. If we are going through life on our own, without a personal connection with God through His Son Jesus Christ, we are disconnected from the Source of our guidance and the One who can get us safely to our destination.

God, we realize that we have been missing out on so much that You have wanted to give us. We wander around lost, we miss out on blessings, we fail to have doors open for us, and we suffer alone in the midst of the crises we face in life—all because we have never connected with You. God, we want that connection. We need that connection. We trust You for that connection. In the name of Jesus, the One who connects us to You, we pray, Amen.

January 15

"Bring the whole tithe into the storehouse, that there may be food in my house. Test me in this," says the Lord Almighty, "and see if I will not throw open the floodgates of heaven and pour out so much blessing that you will not have room enough for it."

—*Malachi 3:10*

WHEN WE PAY FOR INSURANCE, WE ARE investing our money in the assurance that if we ever have an auto accident, a fire in our home, or some other calamity, our insurance company will provide for us. We trust that they will be there in our time of need. On what do we base our confidence? Their promise. They tell us they will come through for us, and we believe them.

If we are willing to believe what some mere mortals tell us, why is it so hard then to believe God? If we believe them when they promise to help us, why can we not believe God when He promises us something? Is it not time to bring our tithes and offerings to God and trust Him to keep His promise to bless us?

Almighty Lord, You have given us all that we have. Whatever wealth, whatever possessions, whatever blessings, they all come from You. Please forgive us for not giving back to You the little You ask in return. We want now to start taking You at Your word and believing what You have told us. We promise now to commit our tithes and offerings to You, and we pray, God, that You will enable us to be as faithful in keeping our promises to You as You are in keeping Your promises to us. In Jesus' name, Amen.

January 16

"So I was afraid and went out and hid your talent in the ground."
—*Matthew 25:25a*

ON THE TV SHOW *DEAL OR NO Deal,* contestants have the opportunity to win up to a million dollars. But to do so, as they progress in the game, they must be willing to give up what they have in order to take the chance of receiving more. There is no opportunity for them to get more unless they first give up what they already have.

That same principle applies in God's kingdom. Jesus told the story of the wealthy man who entrusted five talents of money to one of his servants, two to another, and one to a third. The first two let go of what they had and invested their talents. In return, they each gained twice as much as they had been given. But the third servant was afraid and held tightly to what he had, so he gained nothing more. God expects us to exercise enough faith to invest what He gives us into His kingdom. Only then will He give us more.

Jesus, we thank You for all that You have given us. Help us to act in faith by trusting You—not to cower in fear, unwilling to do what You expect of us. Help us to let go of what You have given us—to give freely and without reservation—so that when You return, You will find the value of Your investments in us multiplied. Let our faith please You, and let fear find no place in our walk with You. In Your holy name we pray, Amen.

January 17

How great is the love the Father has lavished on us, that we should be called children of God! And that is what we are!

—*1 John 3:1*

MY WIFE AND SONS WERE FLYING BACK to Indianapolis, but when they got to the airport, Sharon realized she couldn't find her picture identification. She looked through her purse again and again, but it just wasn't there. She felt in her pockets, but it wasn't there. She was a long way from home, and now she would not be allowed to board the plane that could take her to her destination because she could not find her ID. Then one of our sons said, "Mom, look in your Bible." Sure enough, it was there. She put it there purposely because she planned to carry her Bible on the plane and knew the identification would be easy to access there.

We, too, can find our identity in the Bible. In the Bible, we learn that we are children of God, citizens of heaven, friends of Christ, saints of God, co-laborers with Christ, followers of Christ, more than conquerors…and on and on goes the description of those who have received Christ. We find great contentment and peace when we find our identity in the Bible. It is worth searching there for it.

Father, thank You for letting us know in Your Word who we are. Thank You that You didn't leave us wondering, and wandering. You let us know that we are Your children and that we are greatly loved by You. Help us to seek, through the Bible, to find our identity as we truly are in Christ. Amen.

January 18

"They will be mine," says the LORD Almighty, "in the day when I make up my treasured possession."

—*Malachi 3:17a*

IN A SMALL TOWN IN FLORIDA, AN eight-year-old girl was abducted. While teams of people went out searching for her in the streets, alleys, and fields, a police officer found the child abused, beaten, and left for dead in a dumpster.

Everything that has been relegated to the trash is not trash or garbage. Some of us may feel like trash because others have treated us like trash. We may think we are worthless, of no value to ourselves or to anyone else. But that is not the way God sees us! Just as that police officer recognized a person of value in the midst of the garbage into which she had been thrown, God sees our worth and beauty regardless of the environment in which He finds us.

God, thank You that You know when we've been cast away by others like a piece of trash, worthy only to be thrown out. Thank You for not leaving us there. You come looking for us, and when You find us, You recognize that, no matter how dirty we are or how messed up we are, we are of great value. Thank You for rescuing us out of the trash, cleaning us up, caring for us, and treating us as treasures. In the precious name of the One who saved us we pray, Amen.

January 19

I am in pain and distress; may your salvation, O God, protect me.
—*Psalm 69:29*

AN OYSTER ONLY CREATES A PEARL IF it first experiences pain. An organic particle invades the shell and causes an irritation, which prompts the oyster to produce layer after layer of a secretion that gradually surrounds the irritant to keep it from harming the oyster. Eventually, a pearl is formed at the very source of the oyster's pain.

We experience pain in the kingdom of God, but only we decide whether to use that pain to produce pearls. There are many sources for our pain—a parent who neglects us, a spouse who walks out on us, a friend who betrays us, a boss who harasses us, an illness that will not go away, a disappointed hope... so many things. Some of us respond to pain with bitterness and by putting up barriers to try to keep the source of the pain from affecting us. Those responses, however, produce only more pain. But if we let our pain prompt us to pray and to produce layer after layer of love, forgiveness, gentleness of spirit, and compassion for others, we will find that the pain meant to harm us has been transformed into a pearl.

God, let this pain that we are experiencing in our lives right now be transformed into a pearl. Give us right attitudes and a heart that pleases You even in the midst of our pain. Let us understand that it takes time for a pearl to form, and help us not to be impatient with the process. And, God, when that pearl is formed, we give it to You to be used in Your kingdom. In the name of Jesus we pray, Amen.

January 20

He regarded disgrace for the sake of Christ as of greater value than the treasures of Egypt, because he was looking ahead to his reward.

—Hebrews 11:26

IN HIS BOOK, *WHO SWITCHED THE PRICE TAGS?*, Tony Campolo tells of an incident in which someone switched the prices in a store, making things of value very cheap and making cheap things very costly.

We too often do that as well in our world. We pay a lot of money to see a celebrity perform, but we give little to a pastor who cares for our souls. We shell out a great deal to watch a team play a sport, but when teachers, who prepare our children for their future, want a pay raise, we balk. We make time to watch TV for hours every night, but say we have no time to pray or read the Word. Which kingdom are we really living in?

Once again, God, we come asking Your forgiveness. Our value system has gotten screwed up. We pay a high price for things that are temporal and that satisfy us only for a moment. Yet, we are unwilling to give anything for that which really matters, for those things that are truly precious. Remind us, God, that we are living in Your kingdom even while we are here on earth. Help us to live as citizens of heaven, and to value what You value and treasure what You treasure. In Christ's name, Amen.

January 21

"Woe to you, teachers of the law and Pharisees, you hypocrites! You are like whitewashed tombs, which look beautiful on the outside but on the inside are full of dead men's bones and everything unclean. In the same way, on the outside you appear to people as righteous but on the inside you are full of hypocrisy and wickedness."

—Matthew 23:27-28

A FEW YEARS AGO, A WOMAN IN Indiana died while having cosmetic surgery. Her husband assumed malpractice was involved and wanted to sue the doctors and hospital. It was determined, however, that his wife didn't die because the doctors did anything wrong during the surgery—she died of heart trouble. She was concerned about her outward appearance and was spending a lot of money to make sure she *looked* good, but that could not help what was happening on the inside. She was concerned about her *external* appearance, while her *internal* condition killed her.

How is our internal condition today? Are we caring for our inner person as much as for our outer appearance? Are we spending time and money (for Christian books, music, retreats, and opportunities to grow spiritually) to make sure our souls are healthy? Let's not be caught like those Jesus described in the verse for today: "...beautiful on the outside but on the inside full of dead men's bones and everything unclean."

O, God, we come to You today knowing that You can see our hearts as well as what is visible to others. Cleanse us, God, from all that is unclean within us. Motivate us to focus on the health of our eternal soul and not just on how we appear to others. May the Spirit of Christ who dwells in us take over every aspect of our inner person and bring life and health to our souls. In Jesus' name, Amen.

January 22

Let us fix our eyes on Jesus, the author and perfecter of our faith…
—*Hebrews 12:2*

WHILE WORKING DURING MY COLLEGE DAYS AS a bank teller, I was trained to identify counterfeit money without ever being shown a counterfeit bill. They taught us how to spot a phony by ingraining within us what *real* money looks like. In the same way, a number of good coaches teach their teams how to make good plays not by watching their mistakes on tape, but by watching the *right* way to play ball.

We don't become the most effective Christians we can be by focusing on our sins and our mistakes, reliving them in our minds and recounting them over and over again to God even after He has forgiven us. We become more like Christ when we keep our eyes on Him, looking at His righteousness, His love, His holiness.

Our God, we know that we cannot make ourselves better by staring at our failures, sins, and faults. Instead, help us to fix our eyes on Jesus, knowing that He alone can make us like unto Himself. Thank You for forgiving us and giving us the desire to be more like Jesus. In His holy name we pray, Amen.

January 23

My dear children, I write this to you so that you will not sin. But if anybody does sin, we have one who speaks to the Father in our defense—Jesus Christ, the Righteous One.

—1 John 2:1

MY FRIEND PASTOR SABIN STRICKLAND WAS GOING kayaking. He explained to me matter-of-factly that he expected to overturn at some point. In fact, it happens so often that learning what to do when your kayak capsizes is a routine part of the instructions on how to paddle this type of boat. While a kayak is made to move swiftly and gracefully through the water in an upright position, a kayaker knows he or she is likely to start tipping over when encountering a wave, a strong current, or other such challenge. Therefore, instructions are given to teach the person how to avoid turning over completely and how to upright the kayak if that does happen.

We are made to move through life in an upright position. We are made to withstand waves, strong currents, and other challenges. Yet, knowing that it is part of our nature to roll unsteadily when we encounter rough places, and that we may even capsize at times, God has given us instructions for how we can get our lives back in an upright position.

God, we know that You have created us to be holy even as You are holy, and You expect us to live uprightly in this world. Yet at the same time, You know that we do sin and fall short of Your expectations. Thank You that "if anybody does sin," we have Jesus, the Righteous One, to intercede on our behalf. Thank You that we do not have to remain upside down, but that because of Jesus we can continue our journey—forgiven and upright. In the name of the Righteous One we pray, Amen.

January 24

"But the Counselor, the Holy Spirit, whom the Father will send in my name, will teach you all things and will remind you of everything I have said to you."

—John 14:26

ANOTHER THING I LEARNED ABOUT KAYAKING IS that a certain stability resides within the kayak that keeps it from capsizing. It isn't something that the kayaker can see, but he or she senses when the kayak is reaching the point that it is going to tip over. The kayak is supposed to remain upright: it is built to be upright, and it can only fulfill its destined purpose when it is upright. The stability within the kayak helps to keep it upright and lets the kayaker know when it is going too far.

When the Holy Spirit resides in us, He becomes our stability. He counsels and guides us and lets us know when we are reaching the point that we are about to go too far. We must become sensitive to the Spirit within us if we are to remain upright. If we keep on going in a certain direction, or with a certain activity, when we sense within us that the Spirit is telling us to stop, we leave ourselves vulnerable to finding ourselves upside down and drowning.

Heavenly Father, we thank You for the Holy Spirit who resides in us. Thank You that He counsels, teaches, and guides us. Thank You that if we listen to Him and obey His voice, we will remain upright. Thank You that You have created each of us to fulfill a destined purpose. Thank You that Your Holy Spirit will teach and guide us safely and surely, so that we may see Your will accomplished through us. In Jesus' name, Amen.

January 25

Then I heard the voice of the Lord saying, "Whom shall I send? And who will go for us?" And I said, "Here am I. Send me!"

—*Isaiah 6:8*

AT AN AIRPORT, YOU CAN FIND MANY excited passengers just waiting to board a plane that will take them to new places, new activities, and new opportunities for growth and service. But not all those who go to an airport are there to take off themselves for a new destination. Some of them are there only to tell others to have a good trip or even just to watch the planes take off and land. They have not paid the price to get a ticket. They haven't made any preparations. They have chosen to stay where they are. Therefore, while the passengers can go through the security check, get on a plane, and go to their next destination, the others can only go back to life as usual.

Some people in church are like that. They have no intention of going anywhere spiritually. They are not willing to pay the price of going to the next level with God. They are unwilling to prepare themselves. They feel comfortable, safe, and satisfied to stay where they are. Year after year, they are content just to tell others to have a good trip. Some of those persons are even in ministry, but still not going anywhere.

Lord, give us the spirit of Isaiah, who cried out, "Here am I. Send me!" When You show us the fields ready to harvest, help us to cry out, "Here am I, Lord. Send me!" When we see the lost, the sick, and the dying, let us cry out, "Here am I, Lord. Send me!" When we see those wandering aimlessly without Christ, those in prisons, and those in despair, let us cry out, "Here am I, Lord, send me!" When we see You hungry, thirsty, naked, and a stranger, let us cry out, "Here am I, Lord, send me!" O, God, let us not be content with our own complacency, doing only what is convenient, satisfying our own comfort, but let us hear Your voice and respond with willing hearts. In Christ's name, Amen.

January 26

Rather, as servants of God we commend ourselves in every way: in great endurance; in troubles, hardships and distresses; in beatings, imprisonments and riots; in hard work, sleepless nights and hunger.

—2 Corinthians 6:4-5

WHEN I WAS A YOUNG PASTOR, I had people who helped me along, and I try to do that now for other young preachers and pastors. One day I was taking a young pastor on a walk-through of our facilities and explaining to him how we have one church in three locations, how that came about, and the background for our structure. We walked into one of our sanctuaries, and he started looking around. He was just looking and looking. I was trying to figure out what he was doing. Finally, he said, "Pastor Johnson." I replied, "Yes, what's up?" He asked, "How did you fall into all of this?" I said, "Excuse me?" He said, "How did you fall into all of this?" I responded, "Man, you don't *fall* into *this*. This is decision. This is discipline. This is determination. This is destiny."

Great athletes don't just *fall* into a championship. They make the right decisions, line their discipline up with their decisions, and then exercise the determination to achieve and the endurance to keep going—no matter what. We don't *fall* into destiny, we *walk* into destiny. We've got to make the right decisions, line our discipline up with those decisions, and then make up our minds to not stop until we get everything God has for us.

God, let us never think that we can "fall into" our destiny. Help us to know that while You provide for us, open doors for us, lead us, and empower us, there is still a work that we have to do. We still have to be obedient to Your voice. We have to choose to do the right thing rather than the easy thing. We have to sacrifice and persevere under all kinds of trials. Let us never miss what You have for us because we are unwilling to pay the price. In Jesus' name we pray, Amen.

January 27

Let us not become weary in doing good, for at the proper time we will reap a harvest if we do not give up.

—*Galatians 6:9*

GARY BRACKETT IS AN NFL MIDDLE LINEBACKER with the Indianapolis Colts. He graduated from Rutgers University but was a walk-on in college football. He hadn't been recruited; he hadn't been offered a scholarship; he didn't start out with the level of respect that comes with being recruited for a school team; and his parents had to make great sacrifices to enable him to have a chance at fulfilling his dream. But by his senior year, Brackett had not only earned a football scholarship, but he was captain of the defensive team and had been named the team's defensive Most Valuable Player. Now Gary Brackett wears a Super Bowl ring and earns millions.

Years ago, there was a poster with the caption: "Happy is the man who dreams dreams and is willing to pay the price to make them come true." We need to do more than just dream the dream. If any of our dreams are to become realities, we have to put forth the time and effort—and keep putting forth the time and effort—until we see them materialize. We can't be deterred by the fact that we haven't been given the same advantages as some people, or that we aren't given the respect we deserve, or that our circumstances are harder than others' circumstances. We must keep our goal in sight and "not become weary in doing good."

Father, forgive us for the times we've felt like quitting, and the times we have quit. Renew within us the resolve to stay on course and to do whatever it takes to get to the place for which we believe You created us. Let us not be discouraged, but give us the perseverance to continue to work in our fields until the harvest comes. In Your name we pray, Amen.

January 28

I pray also that the eyes of your heart may be enlightened in order that you may know the hope to which he has called you, the riches of his glorious inheritance in the saints.

—Ephesians 1:18

I WAS AN ADULT BEFORE I GOT my first pair of glasses. I didn't realize what I couldn't see until I began wearing glasses and then contact lenses. Until then, I thought everyone saw things as I saw them. But once I could really see, I finally realized how bad my vision had been all along.

If our family members and friends are not Christians, they may not realize how poor their spiritual vision is. They may assume, as I did, that their vision is accurate and everyone should see things as they do. Remember that we once saw things differently, too.

God, we ask that You enlighten the eyes of our hearts. Let us see people and things as You see them. If there are any areas in which we are not seeing clearly, we pray that You will spotlight those for us. For those who are still looking at life through their natural eyes, we pray that You will open the eyes of their hearts so that they might see You and then see the world and other persons even as You see them. Give us patience with them, remembering that we once saw things only from our own perspective, too. In the name of our Lord, Amen.

January 29

And you also were included in Christ when you heard the word of truth, the gospel of your salvation. Having believed, you were marked in him with a seal, the promised Holy Spirit, who is a deposit guaranteeing our inheritance until the redemption of those who are God's possession—to the praise of his glory.

—Ephesians 1:13-14

WHEN MY WIFE AND I BOUGHT OUR first house, we had to learn each of the steps of buying a house. One of the things we learned about was earnest money. You probably know that earnest money is a deposit that prospective buyers pay when they sign the contract to make an offer on a house. This deposit shows the current homeowner that they are serious about making the purchase and that they can afford to do so.

The verses from Ephesians tell us that the Holy Spirit is like the earnest money. He is the "deposit guaranteeing our inheritance." God sent the Holy Spirit to assure us that He is in earnest about our redemption and that what He has promised, He will do.

God, we thank You today for the Holy Spirit. Thank You that His presence in our lives assures us that You intend to keep Your promise to us about our future. Thank You that our inheritance is guaranteed and we need not doubt You. Let us live today in the joy of knowing that Your promises to us are true. Amen.

January 30

"Why do you look at the speck of sawdust in your brother's eye and pay no attention to the plank in your own eye?"

—*Matthew 7:3*

AN ADMINISTRATIVE ASSISTANT DROVE A PASTOR TO the church one sunny day. But from the minute they walked in, she began complaining that there was not enough light in the sanctuary. She saw the custodian and told him that he needed to find a way to bring more light into the church. The custodian resolved the problem by telling her to take off her sunglasses.

Some people think something is wrong with the church, when the problem is not in the church but in them. Whenever we start becoming critical of the pastor, the leaders, and others in the church, we need to check to see if the problem is in us rather than in them. Do we have on fault-finding glasses that we need to remove? Are we wearing glasses of pessimism so that we see everything in a negative light? Or does it just make us feel better about our own sins, faults, and failures if we focus instead on the weaknesses of others?

God, we are so grateful for the church—for people with whom we can worship, fellowship, and grow in You. When we begin to complain about this or that within the church, remind us to stop and think about which glasses we are wearing. Help us to know that most often the problem is not in someone else but in ourselves. Let us be brave enough to face this, honest enough to acknowledge this, and humble enough to confess this. In Jesus' name, Amen.

January 31

And we also thank God continually because, when you received the word of God, which you heard from us, you accepted it not as the word of men, but as it actually is, the word of God, which is at work in you who believe.
—1 Thessalonians 2:13

I AM SURE YOU ARE NOW ACCUSTOMED to seeing medicine with a notice on the bottle saying it is time-released. A time-released medicine can be taken at one time, but its power is not released inside the body until the person needs it. When it is the right time, the medicine is released and it goes to the exact area in the body that is sick and needs healing.

The Bible works like that. When we store the Word of God within us, it is released to address a particular need at exactly the time that we need it. That's why we must keep taking in the Word whether we feel that we need it that moment or not. Even a portion of scripture that doesn't seem to mean much to us at the time we read it will surprise us by coming back to our minds sometime later on—at just the time we need for it to minister to us.

Beloved God, thank You that You know what we need and, if we will let You, You will put within us in advance that which You know we will need sometime down the road. Help us to receive scripture not as the word of men but the Word of God, and help us to store it within our hearts, trusting You to release its power at just the moment we need it. In Christ's name we pray, Amen.

February 1

At the window of my house I looked out through the lattice. I saw among the simple, I noticed among the young men, a youth who lacked judgment.

—Proverbs 7:6-7

SOLOMON WAS SETTLED SAFELY INSIDE HIS HOME. He didn't need to be concerned about what was going on outside, yet he was. He watched through the window from where he could see what was happening in the streets, and he used his knowledge of the streets to warn others about the dangers lurking there. As we read on in Proverbs 7, we learn that he saw a young man seduced by a promiscuous woman, and he warned other young men not to be taken in by such a woman.

Even though we are safe in the kingdom of God, we need to be concerned for those vulnerable ones who are still in the streets. We need to be aware of what is going on in our world and be willing to let God use us to try to keep others from falling prey to the temptations that await them as they walk through this world. Being a Christian gives us no reason to sit smugly in our homes while we wait for Christ's return. While we are still in the world but not of it, we need to care for others within our own spheres of influence.

God, forgive us for the times that we have been content to bask in Your love, joy, and peace, not caring about those outside the walls of our homes and the walls of our churches. Help us to watch out for those who are vulnerable, along with the ones lacking in judgment. Help us to care enough about them to try to use our influence in a gracious manner to teach them to walk in Your ways. In Christ's name we ask, Amen.

February 2

Follow my example, as I follow the example of Christ.

—*1 Corinthians 11:1*

ONE YEAR, MY FAMILY AND I WERE at a praise gathering in a parking lot. This is an event that our church sponsors every year. While I was walking around among the people, I noticed that K. J., my youngest son, kept shadowing me. When I moved forward, he moved forward. When I moved backward, he moved backward. When I stooped down, he even stooped down. Not only was he shadowing me, but I *had* a shadow that day, too, because I was standing in the sun. Therefore, my son was experiencing whatever I experienced because he was standing in my shadow.

On a spiritual plane, I have a shadow because I am standing in the Son. My son, who follows me around and imitates my every movement, will get as close to Jesus or as far from Him as I get because he is standing in my shadow. Who is standing in your shadow? Let's be sure that we can say with Paul, "Follow my example, as I follow the example of Christ."

God, it humbles us when we think that others could be following our example. We know we haven't always been as close to You as we truly want to be. And we know that there are times when our example hasn't looked like the example of Christ. Forgive us, God, and help us to stay in the light of the Son so that anyone walking in our shadow will find himself or herself walking toward Him. In Jesus' name we pray, Amen.

February 3

Make a joyful noise unto the LORD, all ye lands.

—Psalm 100:1 (KJV)

WHEN THE PITTSBURGH STEELERS LOST A 2005 game to the Indianapolis Colts, their quarterback Ben Roethlisberger accused the Colts of piping in fake crowd noise to keep his players from hearing the calls. Coach Tony Dungy pointed out his team didn't need to bring in any fake noise. The Colts were undefeated, and the fans of an undefeated team know how to *make* noise!

Why is it that when it comes to worshiping God, we are often so quiet and reserved? No one had to tell the fans to stand and make a joyful noise when Coach Dungy came onto the field. They didn't have to be *persuaded* to cheer or clap their hands. Surely, we can be just as enthusiastic when we are in the presence of the One who leads us to victory after victory.

Lord, we recognize today that we have a reason, a right, and a responsibility to praise You. It is with great joy that we thank You today for all of the battles You have fought for us and for all of the victories You have won for us. We praise You, we magnify You, we exalt You! In Your name we pray, Amen.

February 4

And the lord said unto the servant, Go out into the highways and hedges, and compel them to come in, that my house may be filled.

—Luke 14:23 (KJV)

ONE OF THE FIRST LESSONS IN FISHING is that you have to go where the fish are. You can't stay away from the water and expect the fish to come to you. Some Christians consider themselves too holy to go into the natural habitat of the fish to find the fish; instead, they expect the fish to somehow find them.

When I go to conferences, people are often handing me their business cards. Some of them introduce themselves as evangelists and tell me they would like to speak at my church. I don't understand that. Evangelists should be out in the world evangelizing, not in the church preaching to a bunch of evangelicals.

God, we're mixed up. We aren't going out to find the lost; we're expecting the lost to find us. Instead of being out in the highways and hedges compelling others to come into the house of God, we stay within the walls of the church and preach about the unsaved outside. God, give us a new passion for those who don't know You. Let us no longer be comfortable sitting in Your house without them. Amen.

February 5

Therefore do not be partners with them. For you were once darkness, but now you are light in the Lord. Live as children of light.

—Ephesians 5:7-8

A FRIEND'S CAR CAUGHT FIRE IN HIS garage one day. It happened when he was using jumper cables to try to start a car that had a dead battery with another car that had a good battery. He accidentally connected the positive post of one car battery with the negative post of the other. The result was that the car blew up.

Anytime we Christians try to connect ourselves with some negative stuff, something's going to blow up. How many lives have blown up when Christians thought they could sin just a little bit—just a little bit of clubbing, just a little flirtatious affair, just a little bit of drugs, just a little overeating, just a little lying, just a little…. But before they knew it, the negative overcame the positive, the darkness overcame the light, and their lives blew up.

God, let us not become smug in our Christian walk. Help us not to think that we can avoid Your instructions and everything will still be okay. Help us to know that there are consequences for trying to connect the positive in us with the negative in the world. Save us, God, even from ourselves. In Jesus' name, Amen.

February 6

For we are to God the aroma of Christ among those who are being saved and those who are perishing.

—*2 Corinthians 2:15*

WHEN I FIRST CAME TO EASTERN STAR Church as the new pastor over twenty years ago, one of the members came up to me one Sunday and whispered that he had smelled the odor of some marijuana in "his" area. A few weeks later, he reported smelling alcohol. He must have thought that I would investigate to find out who the culprits were, rebuke them, and cast them out of the church like Jesus did to the moneychangers from the temple. But what his information told me is that we had someone in our midst who needed Jesus, and it was my hope that the person would keep coming back until he or she got to know Him personally.

We can't win people to the kingdom of God if we aren't willing to overlook the smell of the world that is on them. We Christians have a smell, too. It is the "aroma" of Christ. Just as we spray air freshener in order to overcome a bad smell in a room, our presence should smell so sweetly of the aroma of Christ that those who are perishing—those who smell like the world—will be attracted to the fragrance and be drawn to Christ.

God, shame on us when we forget what we smelled like before You washed us in Your blood and cleansed us from our sin. When we smell the smells of the world on others, help us to desire to reach out to them and love them just as they are, even as Christ loved us when we came to Him. In Your name we pray, Amen.

February 7

With God we will gain the victory, and he will trample down our enemies.
—Psalm 60:12

DESPITE THE QUALITY OF HIS CHARACTER, AND despite taking the Buccaneers to the playoffs four times in six seasons, Coach Tony Dungy was fired by Tampa Bay in 2001. However, he was quickly picked up by the Indianapolis Colts. With the Colts, he became the first African American coach to win a Super Bowl. With the Colts, he signed a three-year extension contract in 2005 for five million dollars. With the Colts, he gained the respect he deserved. But all of this happened only after he changed teams.

We know when we "change teams" and get on the Lord's side, everything will be all right. Too many of us keep struggling and fighting to be winners, but all we get is failure, disappointment, and disrespect. That's because we are on the wrong team. God can't bless us as long as we are working for the opposing team. Let's be sure we're living for God and trust Him to give us victory.

God, we acknowledge today that we have been playing for the wrong team. We have been playing for a team that promised us much, but gave us little; for a team that was willing to drop us even though we have great potential; for a team that does not recognize our value. Thank You, God, that You are just the opposite. You keep Your promises; You desire to use us even though You know we are imperfect vessels; and You thought we were worth so much that You sent Your Son to redeem us. God, we choose to be on Your team forever. Thank You for choosing us. Amen.

February 8

"The wind blows wherever it pleases. You hear its sound, but you cannot tell where it comes from or where it is going. So it is with everyone born of the Spirit."

—John 3:8

HAVE YOU EVER FLOWN A KITE? YOU know what it is like to run with the kite, string in hand, holding tight while you wait for a gust of wind to carry the kite into the air. On one of our family vacations, I was flying kites with my sons and accidentally dropped the string to a kite I was flying. Quickly, it went way up out of my reach. It was free to go wherever the wind took it.

We sometimes think that the person holding onto us is keeping us up, but actually that person may be holding us back. If we look to another person to keep us bolstered, to keep us soaring, we will find that person's arms are not long enough to get us to where God wants to take us. We need to break away from the hold that people have on us and let God's Spirit help us to soar wherever it pleases Him to take us.

God, it is exciting to think that You are guiding us by Your Holy Spirit. We don't know where You may take us, but we want to be where it pleases You. Help us to break loose from all those who would hinder us, and enable us to begin to soar in Your Spirit. Amen.

February 9

"The knowledge of the secrets of the kingdom of heaven has been given to you."

—*Matthew 13:11*

THERE WAS A PREACHER WHO LIKED TO put together jigsaw puzzles. He found it both challenging and relaxing to sit quietly and look for pieces that would fit together, and slowly watch the picture form as he attached one piece after the other. One day, however, he emptied a puzzle box of all the pieces and spent quite a long time turning each piece face-up, trying to match some of the same colors, knowing they would likely fit together at some point. But when this man went to get the box so he could see the picture of the puzzle, he couldn't find the box. He looked and looked but just couldn't find it. It was so frustrating that even though he had all the pieces, he couldn't put the puzzle together because he didn't have the picture to go by. He didn't know what it was supposed to look like.

In Matthew 13, Jesus has given us a picture of what the kingdom of heaven looks like: "The kingdom of heaven is like a man who sowed good seed in his field" (v. 24). "The kingdom of heaven is like a mustard seed…." (v. 31). "The kingdom of heaven is like yeast…." (v. 33). "The kingdom of heaven is like a treasure hidden in a field…." (v. 44). "…the kingdom of heaven is like a merchant looking for fine pearls" (v. 45). "…the kingdom of heaven is like a net that was let down into the lake and caught all kinds of fish" (v. 47). One parable at a time, Jesus lays out the pieces of the picture of the kingdom.

Lord, we thank You for revealing to us what Your kingdom looks like. It is so different from the world in which we live that we would not be able to envision it for ourselves apart from You. Help us to put the pieces together so we can learn the "secrets of the kingdom" that You have given us. And most importantly, help us to live as citizens of that kingdom. In Christ's name, Amen.

February 10

I have hidden your word in my heart....

—*Psalm 119:11*

I USED TO GO TO SCHOOL IN Dallas and still have friends there, so when I am there to preach in one of the churches in that city, I usually rent a car and drive around to visit some of the people and places I know. One time, I drove to the hotel where I was staying and gave the valet the keys to my rental car. When I was ready to leave the hotel the next morning, the valet brought my car around. I got in and got ready to drive away. But as I looked down on the seat, I noticed that something was missing. The valet had retrieved the wrong car. I knew it was the wrong one because I had left my Bible in my car the night before, and now it was gone. It looked like my car, but it was not mine because the Word was not in it.

We need to have the Word in us. As an adult, I wish I had stored more in my memory from classes I took in high school and college. I could really use some of that knowledge now. When we read the Bible or hear the Word preached or taught, we may not feel that it is relevant for that moment in our lives, but we need to store it up now so that we can draw on it later on when we do need it.

God, help us never to take Your Word for granted. Let us understand that the Bible is one of the key ways You have chosen to communicate with us. Let us never leave Your Word sitting on a shelf collecting dust, and let us never turn off our attention as Your Word is being preached. Help us to hide Your Word in our hearts that we might "hear" it again in the moment we need it most. Help us to know something is missing if the Word is not in us. Amen.

February 11

...that I might by all means save some.

—1 Corinthians 9:22 (KJV)

RECENTLY, I WAS LISTENING TO "(SITTIN' ON) the Dock of the Bay." When Otis Redding recorded that song back in 1967, people listened to it then on their eight-track players. When I listened to it the other day, I heard it on my iPod.

Because we live in an iPod society, we need to learn to communicate the gospel using methods that allow people to hear the message today. It's the same old story, but we need to be open to finding new ways of presenting it. Some Christian rap artists, for example, have been able to use rap to communicate with some young people who would never listen to a sermon. Let's not mistake the methods for the message. The methods can be changed, but the message stays the same. The methods are transitory, but the message is eternal.

God, keep us from becoming so rigid that we prevent You from inspiring us afresh and anew. Help us not to confuse what we cannot change with what we must change in order to win people to Christ. Let us be ever open to Your creative ways of reaching out to win others to You. In Jesus' name, Amen.

February 12

You were taught, with regard to your former way of life, to put off your old self, which is being corrupted by its deceitful desires; to be made new in the attitude of your minds.

—Ephesians 4:22-23

WHEN THE INDIANAPOLIS COLTS BEGAN THEIR 2006 season, their defense was so weak that they felt the sting of the critics game after game. In fact, they were so bad that they became identified as one of the worst defenses in NFL history. But during the playoffs, the Colts made a dramatic turnaround. The sportscasters asked Coach Tony Dungy if they had been working on new plays, or trying new strategies, or what it was that made the difference. He replied, "We didn't change any plays at all. All we changed was our attitude."

Too often, our attitudes bring about our defeat. God has placed within us all we need for victory, yet our attitudes can keep us from succeeding. As today's verse says, we need to put off our old selves and be made new in the attitudes of our minds.

God, we come to You today, asking that You help us put off our old attitudes of discouragement, defeat, and despair, and put on new attitudes of faith, trust, and confidence in You. We know that You have not set us up for failure, but too often our own bad attitudes keep us from enjoying the victory that You want us to have. Help us now, God, to be made new in the attitudes of our minds. In the name of Christ, we pray, Amen.

February 13

…giving thanks to the Father, who has qualified you to share in the inheritance of the saints in the kingdom of light.

—*Colossians 1:12*

SAM WALTON, FOUNDER OF WAL-MART, WAS ONCE the richest man in the world. When he died, his fortune was estimated at around a hundred billion dollars. Upon his death, his children immediately became wealthy. This had nothing to do with what *they* had done, but it was because of what their father had accomplished that they received a great inheritance.

We have an inheritance in the kingdom of God. It has nothing to do with what we have accomplished. We cannot earn this inheritance. We simply *receive* it when we receive Christ by faith, and His Father becomes *our* Father. By sending His Son to forgive our sins, God qualified us to share in the inheritance of the saints.

God, what You have done, what You have given us in Christ, is so awesome that we have a hard time receiving it. It seems too much for us, for we know how unworthy we are. Yet, You have given us such a great inheritance, and it was the death of Jesus that qualified us to receive it. We will not allow such a costly gift to be given in vain. We do receive it from Your hands, and with hearts of gratitude, we say thank You, Lord. Amen.

February 14

Come, let us sing for joy to the LORD; let us shout aloud to the Rock of our salvation.

—Psalm 95:1

WHEN BARRY BONDS HIT HIS 756TH HOME run, setting a new baseball home run record, he immediately threw his hands in the air in victory. The fans in the stands went wild in celebration. His team was cheering. Fireworks began to go off. All of this happened, yet the run wasn't even official until he rounded all the bases and came back to home plate. None of those present that night waited for him to get home before they began celebrating. They didn't wait for the run to show on the scoreboard. They knew it was a home run, so they immediately began cheering.

Jesus hit a home run on Calvary. It was there that He won the victory over sin and there that He ensured our eternal salvation. Even though the game isn't over yet and, and even though He hasn't finished His "play" yet, we have reason to celebrate. We're just running the bases now because the victory is already ours. Let's not wait a second longer before we start celebrating.

*God, in the name of Jesus, we come to You, praising You, and thanking You that victory is ours. It is ours **now**! We don't have to wait until heaven to start the celebration. Jesus has already opened the way. He has already redeemed us. He has already won! Thank You, God! Thank You, God! Praise Your name! Amen.*

February 15

For you, O God, tested us; you refined us like silver.

—Psalm 66:10

WHEN SILVER GOES INTO THE REFINER'S FIRE, the fire destroys the waste and removes impurities. The silver always comes out different from the way it went in.

When we look at the pure image of Jesus and see His love, His compassion, His holiness, we often pray to God to make us more like Jesus. We want to express His love to the world. We want to show His compassion to those we encounter through life. We want His holiness because we know, like Isaiah, that "all our righteous acts are like filthy rags" (Isaiah 64:6). Yet when trials and hard times come to develop and refine us, we forget what we asked for. We cry out to God to get us out of the mess we're in, and we wonder why God has seemingly turned on us. When we feel the burning of the Refiner's fire, however, we need to know that God hasn't left us, He's leading us. He's taking great care to remove the impurities so that we will come out of our trial different from the way we went in. We will come out being more like Jesus.

Father, help us to remember that You are the Refiner. It is You who are in control of the fires that burn in our lives. Fire is painful and we want it stopped, but You know that without the fire, the trials, we will never change. God, we thank You that we can trust You in the midst of what we're going through. No matter who started the fire, You are using it to make us more like Jesus. Teach us to be patient, God, and help us to rest assured that the silver that comes forth will be worth the wait. In the name of the One we can trust, Amen.

February 16

"The LORD who delivered me from the paw of the lion and the paw of the bear will deliver me from the hand of this Philistine."

—*1 Samuel 17:37*

WHEN WE WORK OUT AT A GYM, the weights we start out with seem so heavy. It takes all the strength we've got to lift them. But then as we continue, we find it takes less energy on our part to lift those same weights. It isn't because the weights have become lighter; it's because we have become stronger.

Before David was placed in the position of fighting against the giant Goliath, he had been a shepherd. In that role, he had to kill a lion one time and a bear another time because they came to attack his flock. It was because he knew he could conquer a lion and he knew he could conquer a bear that he was confident he could conquer a giant as well. Slaying Goliath was a defining moment for David, but it would not have come had he not first faced the lion and the bear. Whatever we are facing in our lives, we need to be strong and overcome that which is trying to defeat us spiritually. We will find that every *little* battle will make us stronger and better equipped to face the next one.

God, we know that You don't allow us to slay giants until we've first learned to deal with the smaller challenges. We know that You don't have us do something requiring great strength until we've first built ourselves up in the faith by handling smaller matters. Thank You that we will grow stronger. Thank You that we will conquer our enemies. In Jesus' name, Amen.

February 17

"He that is faithful in that which is least is faithful also in much: and he that is unjust in the least is unjust also in much."

—Luke 16:10 (KJV)

MOST PEOPLE KNOW THAT TIGER WOODS' FATHER was his coach. From the time he was two years old, Tiger not only liked to play golf, but he exhibited extraordinary skill. His father Earl began to teach him the sport. As Tiger was growing up, Earl Woods continually made him play with people at a higher level than he was. When asked how he knew when to take his son to the next level, his father replied that it was only after he dominated the level on which he had currently been playing.

God wants us to handle achievements at the level we're on before He will take us to a higher level. Some of us *think* we're ready for the next level when we haven't yet mastered the level we are on right now. God doesn't usually make us a leader until we become a good follower. He doesn't usually give us a lot of money until we have proven we can handle the little we have. He doesn't usually send us to preach before crowds until we've been faithful to witness to our neighbor next door.

God, we're too often like the child who insists he or she can handle "it"—a pet, a cell phone, dating, a car—whatever "it" is. But as parents, we have not yet seen the sense of responsibility, the faithfulness in caring for other things, and the maturity we need to see in our child before granting that request. As our Father, we know that You also wait for us to be ready. You want to see that we are faithful in that which is least before You entrust us with much. Teach us to be faithful and to grow in the areas in which You want to take us to the next level. We ask this in Jesus' name, Amen.

February 18

"...*pray continually;*"

—*1 Thessalonians 5:17*

IN GREENWOOD, INDIANA, TWO POLICE OFFICERS WERE trying to put an eighteen-year-old in custody when the young man pulled out a nine-millimeter gun and shot at both of them. The first officer got hit and required surgery, but the second officer's police radio caught the bullet meant for him. That officer was able to go home. His means of communication, which he kept close to him while serving, protected him.

Prayer is our means of communication with God. While we are serving God, we need to keep our means of communication close to us. Too many people say hello to God in the morning and then go about the rest of the day without hearing His voice. We need to learn to call upon Him continually throughout the day. We'll be thankful when we realize how many times prayer protects us—keeps us from saying or doing the wrong thing, keeps us from thinking the wrong thought, keeps us in the place where God wants us, and keeps us close to the One who is our Protector.

Father, thank You for the privilege of calling upon Your name continually throughout each day. Thank You that You are never too busy or too tired to listen. Thank You that You always care about whatever is on our hearts. Thank You that You actually enjoy hearing us call upon You. We love You, God, and we are just grateful in this moment that You guide us, protect us, and speak to us even as we speak to You. In Your holy name we pray, Amen.

February 19

For I am the LORD, your God, who takes hold of your right hand and says to you, Do not fear; I will help you.

—Isaiah 41:13

A FRIEND WITH A NEW LEXUS SHOWED me features that allow the car to do for him what he can't do for himself. For instance, his car has an advanced parking guidance system that allows him to take his hands off the steering wheel while the car parallel parks itself perfectly. In addition, he can press a button in his car, and the lights in his home will go on so he doesn't have to drive up to a dark house. And, of course, his car has a global positioning system that enables him to be able to find his location on a screen and get directions to his destination.

There are things that are difficult or impossible for us to do for ourselves. Knowing this, God put the Holy Spirit within us to help us. The Holy Spirit helps us get in and out of tight spaces that we could not do without Him. He provides light along the way, both to illumine our path and to keep us from being afraid. And the Holy Spirit guides us, shows us the way, and gets us safely to our destination.

How thankful we are, Lord God, that You didn't just make us and then leave us to fend for ourselves. Instead, You placed Your very own Spirit within us to help us, walk with us, and guide us safely as we make our way in this world. We trust You today to guide us to where You have chosen for us to be. Help us along the way by doing for us those things that we cannot do for ourselves. We love You today, God. Amen.

February 20

But my God shall supply all your need according to his riches in glory by Christ Jesus.

—*Philippians 4:19 (KJV)*

ROCK STAR MICK JAGGER HAD REACHED THE pinnacle of fame and wealth, yet at the Super Bowl halftime show in Detroit, Michigan, he was still singing, "I can't get no satisfaction." That is a song he and Keith Richards wrote in 1965. Forty years later, he was still singing the same tune.

While he obviously sang the song at this event because of its continued popularity with Rolling Stones fans, it does illustrate a point. What the world offers can't bring satisfaction, no matter how much we get. If it doesn't satisfy us one year, we can continue on the same path for the next forty years and still find ourselves dissatisfied with life and living without a purpose.

God, thank You that You are able to supply all our needs, and You do so in a way that truly satisfies. In our past, we have tried to find satisfaction in other people, in keeping busy, in food, in new jobs, new homes, material goods…in so many things. But it wasn't until we met Jesus that we knew deep inside what it means to be satisfied. Thank You for that satisfaction; thank You for shalom. Amen.

February 21

I tell you, now is the time of God's favor, now is the day of salvation.
—2 Corinthians 6:2b

THERE IS A TALE THAT SAYS SATAN had a business meeting with his demons in hell. They sat around brainstorming about the best way to keep people from turning to God. Some were in favor of lying about God, saying that He was just a figment of their imagination. Others suggested they tell people that God used to exist but now He had died, so they could no longer count on Him to help them. A lot of thoughts were considered, but Satan himself came up with the idea they settled upon: "Let's tell them that God is real; that they do need Jesus; and they do need to be in a church—but they need to make that decision another time."

Deep inside, we know God exists. There is something in our spirits that tells us there had to be a Creator—Someone behind all that we see in nature and especially in the remarkable mind-soul-body makeup of human beings. If we've read or heard the gospel—that Christ died for us, was resurrected, and is coming back for us—something about that rings true within us. In our heart of hearts, we believe in Jesus. But if Satan can keep us from acting upon that belief—from knowing Jesus personally, from drawing closer to God, from receiving Christ as Lord and Savior, and from joining a church where we will learn more about God—the enemy of our souls will win. If we let him, he will keep us procrastinating until we die.

God, we do believe in You. We know that You love us and that Jesus died for us. We receive Christ into our lives and commit ourselves to Him, trusting Him for forgiveness of our sins and for eternal salvation. We also trust that He will be with us moment by moment and day by day to communicate with us, to draw us close to Himself, and to lead and guide us for now and all eternity. In Jesus' name, Amen.

February 22

My son, if you accept my words and store up my commands within you, turning your ear to wisdom and applying your heart to understanding, and if you call out for insight and cry aloud for understanding, and if you look for it as for silver and search for it as for hidden treasure, then you will understand the fear of the LORD and find the knowledge of God.

—Proverbs 2:1-5

WHEN MY WIFE GOES GROCERY SHOPPING, SHE often comes home with as many as twenty bags of groceries. But when she brings all that food home, we don't sit down and eat it all right then. We store it up for later on, when we will be hungry and need it.

Many of us, upon reading a scripture or listening to a sermon, think to ourselves, "Well, that doesn't relate to me. I'm not feeling it." So, we let our minds wander to other things and we pay no attention to what we are reading or hearing. Now, if we threw out all the groceries we couldn't eat immediately when my wife brings them home, we wouldn't have anything to fill us when we become hungry. So, too, do we remain spiritually hungry if we don't hide away and store up the Word of God within us for the times that we are hungry to hear from God.

Father, we realize that too often we have taken Your Word for granted. We have let it go in one ear and out the other without reflecting upon it and without storing it in our memory bank so that we can draw on it later on when we need a word from You. Please forgive us for taking for granted that we will always be able to get a fresh word when we need it. Forgive us for the times when we have responded foolishly or unlike You because Your Word was not within our hearts to give us direction. God, from now on, when we read or hear Your Word, help us to receive it and to hide it away in our hearts and our minds so that it will be there for us when we need it. In Jesus' name, Amen.

February 23

But as for me, I watch in hope for the LORD, I wait for God my Savior; my God will hear me. Do not gloat over me, my enemy! Though I have fallen, I will rise. Though I sit in darkness, the LORD will be my light. Because I have sinned against him, I will bear the LORD's wrath, until he pleads my case and establishes my right. He will bring me out into the light; I will see his righteousness. —*Micah 7:7-9*

IN THE MOVIE *SUPERMAN RETURNS*, LEX LUTHOR NEARLY defeats Superman by stabbing him with kryptonite, the one element that weakens him and could kill him. Superman falls into the ocean. After being rescued, he makes his way toward the sun because it is from the sun that he gets his strength and power to overcome his enemies.

There are times when our enemy seems to defeat us. He tempts us in an area of our weakness, and we fall. But we do not stay down! Though we fall, we will rise. Though we are in darkness for a moment, the Lord Himself will be our light. The Son Himself, the very One against whom we have sinned, will plead our case and bring us again into His light. No matter how great our fall or how dark it is in that moment, there is hope in the Lord. He will bring us out again into the light—forgiven, restored, and standing in His righteousness.

O God, against You and You only have we sinned. We thought we were strong, but suddenly the enemy attacked us where we were weak. Now, he stands over us, gloating in his power and in our defeat. But God, we thank You that we are not without hope. We thank You that there is forgiveness with You. We thank You that You do not leave us in that fallen state. Thank You that we will rise again because Jesus rose again. Thank You that He is a cleansing, renewing, and guiding Light in whose light we can stand. Thank You that our strength and power are in the Son and He will enable us to defeat the enemy. In His holy name we pray, Amen.

February 24

But you, O Sovereign LORD, deal well with me for your name's sake; out of the goodness of your love, deliver me. For I am poor and needy, and my heart is wounded within me. With my mouth I will greatly extol the LORD; in the great throng I will praise him. For he stands at the right hand of the needy one, to save his life from those who condemn him.

—Psalm 109:21-22, 30-31

HUNTING DOGS ARE TRAINED TO CHASE DEER, but the only ones they can catch are the wounded deer. Healthy deer can leap high and outrun their pursuers, jumping fences and moving swiftly through dense forests to get away. But a wounded deer does not run as fast or jump as far, and, inevitably, it will be found by pursuing dogs.

There are a lot of dogs in this world, and not all are of the four-footed variety. Two-footed dogs behave a lot like the hunting dogs. They may try for a little while to chase after a healthy victim but soon realize it is of no use; that person will be able to get away from them quite readily. With the wounded, however, it is another story. Those who have been wounded by past encounters with dogs have been left hurt, vulnerable, and lacking self-esteem; therefore, they are easily captured. If we are in that state, we need to beware of dogs.

God, our encounters with others have left us wounded. We thought we could trust that person who said, "I love you." We believed, trusted, loved…and were left wounded. Now, God, other dogs are after us. Protect and deliver us from the dogs that pursue us. Save us from those who hurt, criticize, and seek to do us further harm. Heal our wounds from the past. We don't want to remain easy targets for dogs. We want to be healthy again—not vulnerable. Thank You that You stand beside the needy, beside us, today. We praise You because You will save us from those who condemn us. You will deliver us from those who are feeling smug as they encircle us, assured that we will be their victims. Thank You, God, that out of the goodness of Your love, You save us. Amen.

February 25

And when the men of that place recognized Jesus, they sent word to all the surrounding country. People brought all their sick to him and begged him to let the sick just touch the edge of his cloak, and all who touched him were healed.

—Matthew 14:35-36

DR. DOOLITTLE IS A FICTIONAL CHARACTER IN a series of children's books who is able to communicate with animals. Since the stories were published, mostly in the 1920s, they have been adapted into plays, musicals, and movies. In a remake starring Eddie Murphy as Dr. Doolittle, an owl comes to see him one night and complains that she has a twig stuck in her wing that she can't get out. Dr. Doolittle treats her, and she goes on her way. But the next day, a bunch of other animals start showing up at his doorstep— all because the owl told others of what he had done for her.

Is this not the way it should be with Jesus? Shouldn't people be rushing to find Him because they hear from us what He has done? Shouldn't they be coming one after another because they have heard that Jesus will help them? If they are not hurrying to Jesus, could it be that we have not been faithful in sharing with others what Christ has done in our lives? Are we content to receive salvation, healing, deliverance, and everything else that is ours in Christ, and then go on our way without telling anyone else of Jesus—without letting them know where they can find Him and without seeking Him on their behalf as well?

God, it is in shame that we come to You today. We recognize that we have not been faithful in telling others about Jesus and all He has done for us. We got what we needed from Him and then went on our way, oblivious to the needs of those around us. Please forgive us, God. Cleanse us from caring only about ourselves. Deliver us from egoism, and cause us to bring others to You. In Jesus' name, Amen.

February 26

"Lazarus, come out!"

—John 11:43

A CAR DEALER IN A SMALL TOWN WAS ROBBED and his twelve-year-old son killed. The thieves slit the man's throat, buried him in a shallow grave, and left him for dead. But the man dug his way out, made his way to the nearest house, and was rushed to a hospital where he was cared for. The police found and brought to justice the offenders who had brought so much evil upon him and his family.

From time to time, we all have to deal with cutthroats—folks who deliberately hurt us and walk away, expecting us to die from our injuries. This man provides an example for us about dealing with them. When someone says or does something to crush us, we need to refuse to let that person kill our spirits. Even though we may feel as if we've been buried alive and there is no hope, we can't give up. We have to dig our way back to the place where we can breathe again—back to the place where we can find a brother or sister who can help us. We must get ourselves into a church, a counseling office, or wherever we can find healing for our wounds. We can't let a cutthroat end our lives.

O, God, You know there are times that we have been brutally assaulted by someone who then walked away and left our spirits so wounded that they assumed we would never recover. But God, we thank You that even in those dark moments, You were there with us; You did not leave us alone. Thank You, God, that even now, if we find ourselves in a shallow grave of despair, covered over with the dirt of dejection and depression, You call us by name and say, "_____, come out!" You did not intend for our spirits to die while our bodies are yet alive. Give us courage to dig our way out, as well as the courage to believe that we will yet live again. In Your loving Spirit we pray, Amen.

February 27

"You intended to harm me, but God intended it for good..."
—*Genesis 50:20*

THERE IS A FOLLOW-UP TO THE ACCOUNT shared yesterday. You may have wondered how it was possible that a man with his throat slit could have survived such an ordeal. The reason the man did not bleed to death from having his throat cut is because the dirt that was thrown over him to bury him became the very means of his deliverance. The dirt stopped the bleeding. The very thing that the murderer had meant to him for evil, God had used for his good.

What is it that has been thrown at you lately? What is it that someone said or did to hurt you? Don't get discouraged. That very thing is what God will use in some way for your good. Our God is a God of transformation. Even as He transforms us, He also transforms those things that were intended to do us harm. They become instruments that work for our good. He did that for Joseph, He did it for this man whose throat was cut, and He will do it for us as well.

God, we praise You that You are a God of transformation. You take that which is intended to harm us and turn it into an instrument that will bring our healing. Thank You that You are God even of the details. When someone thought he or she was sealing our fate, You were there, turning their efforts into something that would ultimately work for our good. Thank You for caring for us in such an intimate and personal way. Amen.

February 28

Our salvation is nearer now than when we first believed.

—*Romans 13:11*

A DESPERATELY DESPONDENT WOMAN KILLED TWO OF her three children and then killed herself, all because she was depressed because she couldn't buy new school clothes for her children. When the grandmother learned of what had happened, she was especially heartbroken because she realized the irony of this situation. She had known that her daughter was depressed because of ongoing financial problems and other troublesome situations, and that her daughter was feeling like a failure as a mother because she couldn't provide her children with clothes, as she saw other parents buying for their children at the start of the new school year. The grandmother, therefore, had already bought new clothes and put them in the closet to surprise her daughter and grandchildren. If this woman had waited a few more minutes, she would have seen her situation turn around.

There are times when all of us feel especially discouraged and feel that we are failing in one area or another. We cannot, however, allow our circumstances to dictate our actions. We must remember that our God is greater than our circumstances. In a moment, in a twinkling of an eye, He can change our situation and turn our sadness into singing. We can't give up. We can't let ourselves give up on God. We have to keep on going, knowing that at any time we are going to see what He has been doing behind the scenes.

Lord, You are our Shepherd, and we know that shepherds care for their sheep. They watch over them to protect them, and take them to where they can find pasture to graze in and water to drink. Even now, God, when we are tempted to take matters into our own hands, we hear Your voice and we believe. Your presence gives us hope. We have faith that You are still in control, and we trust You. Thank You for Your great love to us, O God. Amen.

February 29

What a wretched man I am! Who will rescue me from this body of death? Thanks be to God—through Jesus Christ our Lord!

—*Romans 7:24-25*

PASTOR THERON WILLIAMS TELLS THE STORY OF A little bird who refused to fly south for the winter, and instead stayed in Indiana until it got so cold that its wings froze. It fell to the ground and couldn't move. To add insult to injury, a horse came along and relieved itself right on top of the frozen bird. The bird said, "Look, God, I know it's my fault that I'm in this situation. I know I should have flown south when You told me to. I know I deserve to freeze to death. But, God, did You have to let that horse add that final humiliation to my situation?!" As the bird lay there complaining to God, the manure from the horse melted the ice that had immobilized the bird, delivering him from bondage and freeing him to continue living.

We may find ourselves right now in a mess of our own making. We knew we should be making a different choice. We knew God was saying to do one thing, but we insisted we knew better. So we're lying here right now immobilized, feeling the shame of our situation, and seeing no way of escape. Let's remember that God comes to us even when we don't deserve Him. Jesus died for such a time as this.

To you, O Lord, I lift up my soul; in you I trust, O my God. Do not let me be put to shame, nor let my enemies triumph over me.... For the sake of your name, O Lord, forgive my iniquity, though it is great....Turn to me and be gracious to me, for I am lonely and afflicted. The troubles of my heart have multiplied; free me from my anguish. Look upon my affliction and my distress and take away all my sins.... Guard my life and rescue me; let me not be put to shame, for I take refuge in you. Amen. (Psalm 25:1-2, 11, 16-18, 20)

March 1

In the morning, O LORD, you hear my voice; in the morning I lay my requests before you and wait in expectation

—*Psalm 5:3*

THE GENERAL STORES OF OLD DIDN'T HAVE everything sitting on the shelves in nice, neat little packages for customers to come in and pick up. Many of the common items—from sugar to pickles—had to be scooped out of a barrel or bin; measured, counted or weighed; and put into an appropriate container for the customer to carry home. There's a story of a little boy who went into such a store to purchase ten cents' worth of raisins. The raisins were in a barrel at the front of the store, and they were sold for ten cents a handful. The little boy could easily have reached in, gotten his handful, put the raisins in a bag, paid his money, and left. Instead, he waited for the store owner to finish with other customers and then let him know what he wanted. You see, the little boy knew that the store owner's hands were much bigger than his hands. He was going to get more for his money if he let the owner reach into the barrel and scoop out the raisins.

God's hands are bigger than ours. If we insist on getting things ourselves, we may not realize that we are getting less than we would have if we allowed God to give us those things that we need. Even though waiting on God requires patience, we will find our needs more fully satisfied than if we do it ourselves.

God, Your hands are bigger than ours. If we insist on getting what we want in our own power, at best we will get less than what You can give us. At worst, we will get something You don't even want us to have. We choose, therefore, to leave our needs and cares in Your hands. Teach us to be content to wait upon You, knowing that You will never be too late and Your provisions will never be too little. In Jesus' name, Amen.

March 2

He that spared not his own Son, but delivered him up for us all, how shall he not with him also freely give us all things?

—*Romans 8:32 (KJV)*

A WEALTHY MAN WHOSE ENTIRE ESTATE WAS being sold at auction after his death stipulated in his will that the portrait of his son had to be purchased first before anything else could be sold. On the day of the auction the portrait was shown to the crowd, and the bidding opened. The auctioneer asked for a high figure as a starting bid; but when no one bid on the portrait, he lowered the opening price, and then lowered it again. There were many fine pieces in the estate that the people were eagerly waiting to bid on, but no one wanted the portrait. Finally, the auctioneer just told the crowd, "Look, the owner of this estate stipulated that nothing else was to be sold until the portrait of his son was purchased." When someone in the crowd then purchased the portrait for one dollar, the auctioneer closed the auction. As the crowd sat there in disbelief and became angrier by the second, the lawyer for the deceased man came forward. He explained that according to the man's will, whoever got his son got everything else, so the entire estate went to the one who had bid one dollar.

We have a heavenly Father who has offered us His Son. He is ours if we only receive Him. Some folks, however, are so intent on getting *things* that they don't want to be bothered with Jesus. They don't realize that the peace they are looking for is in Him; the joy they are seeking is in Him; the love that they want is in Him. Whoever gets Jesus gets everything else God has to offer.

Father, we thank You for the gracious way in which You care for us and meet our needs. Help us to remember that Whom we get is more important than what we get. Remind us that in Christ, we receive all things. Apart from Him, we have nothing, even if we believe we have all things. Help us today to seek Jesus. In His name, Amen.

March 3

Let us not give up meeting together, as some are in the habit of doing, but let us encourage one another—and all the more as you see the Day approaching.

—Hebrews 10:25

WHEN MY WIFE SHARON GOT BACK FROM Augusta, Georgia, she told me about an awesome seafood restaurant there that she had tried. I asked her how she happened to find it. She said that she and our son J. Allen, whom she was visiting there, drove past the restaurant several times since it was on the way to his college. She decided it must be a good place because whenever they drove by, they saw customers carrying out bags of food after they had finished their meals there. She was right. She and J. Allen went there and had a wonderful meal. Because their portions were so generous, they had food to take home with them.

That is not unlike church. We go to church empty-handed, get full spiritually, and still have something to take home with us—something we can even share with someone else. Some individuals think today that they don't need church and can commune with God alone. Yes, they *can* commune with God alone, and He delights in our spending time alone with Him. But God has also ordained the church as a meeting place for His people, and there are blessings we can receive in the company of other Christians that we simply cannot receive alone. God has designed it that way.

God, help us to know that attending church is important, not just for us but also for others whose lives we will touch. You never want us to be satisfied with getting only what we need for ourselves but also getting enough to share with others as well. Help us, God, to continue to meet together with other Christians to encourage one another and to welcome new folks into our midst and into Your presence. Amen.

March 4

"You will seek me and find me when you seek me with all your heart."
—*Jeremiah 29:13*

ONE DAY, OUR GARAGE DOOR OPENER WOULDN'T work. I called the repairman and told Sharon that he would be coming over while I was at the church. When I called her later in the day, she told me that the repairman had come, but the door opener wasn't broken. Of course, I immediately started telling her that it *was* broken. I had flipped the switch several times, and it still didn't work. She said, "No, it didn't work, but it wasn't broken." She went on to say that the problem was that the door opener wasn't plugged in. Again, I started telling her that it *was* plugged in; I knew enough to at least check that out when the door didn't open. I had looked up at the outlet, and I could see the plug there. She said that the repairman had taken a closer look: he discovered that even though the plug was there *at* the outlet, it was not plugged *into* the outlet.

It's not enough to be *at* the place of deliverance; we also have to be *in* the place. A lot of us go to church thinking that something miraculous is supposed to happen just because we are there *at* the church. But it isn't enough to simply be *at* church. We have to be *in* church—in right relationship with God, in fellowship with other Christians, and actively involved in ministry. We have to be fully engaged and fully plugged in so that the church will be a place of power in our lives.

Lord, deliver us from a spirit of complacency that allows us to be satisfied simply to be at church. Give us the desire to be fully engaged and fully plugged into the worship services, the fellowship, the teaching, the preaching, the ministries of the church, and even the giving of our tithes and offerings. Help us not to be deceived in thinking that we can simply be at church and find the same power as those who are in church. In Christ's name we pray, Amen.

March 5

Do not merely listen to the word, and so deceive yourselves. Do what it says.
—James 1:22

THE LATE DR. FREDERICK G. SAMPSON, NOTED pastor and chaplain to the U. S. House of Representatives, said he realized one day that there were cleaning places on each of the four corners where his church sat. On one corner was a car wash for cleaning cars; on another, a laundry for cleaning clothes; on the third corner, a beauty salon for cleaning hair; and on the final corner, the church for cleaning souls. He observed that in three of the four places, people had something dirty about them when they went in, but they came out clean. A person went into the car wash with a dirty car and came out with a clean car. A person went into the laundry with dirty clothes and came out with clean clothes. A person went into the beauty salon with dirty hair and came out with clean hair. Yet people with dirty souls went into the church and came out just as dirty as when they went in.

Upon pondering this, Dr. Sampson figured out the difference. The difference was that in the car wash, the laundry, and the beauty salon, all those who went in followed instructions. They put their car into neutral and took their foot off the brake at the car wash. They put in the appropriate amount of money and soap at the laundry. They sat back and let the beautician shampoo their hair at the beauty shop. But at church, the people went in, heard what they needed to do to become clean, and walked out without doing a thing. God help us not to be hearers only but doers of the Word!

God, You have been faithful in speaking to us. You have told us what You want us to do. Help us not to be hearers only, but doers of Your Word. Help us not to walk out of Your presence just the same as we walked in. Teach us to do Your will, O God. In Jesus' name, Amen.

March 6

"You are a garden fountain, a well of flowing water streaming down from Lebanon."

—Song of Solomon 4:15

THE SEA OF GALILEE AND THE DEAD Sea have one of the same water sources: the melting snow from Mount Hermon. The Sea of Galilee is clear, cool, and refreshing—a place where fish flourish, birds live in abundance, and people are refreshed. But nothing can live or grow in the Dead Sea. The difference is that the Sea of Galilee receives the water and then releases it to continue flowing, but the Dead Sea only takes in and never gives out.

We see that same pattern in the lives of Christians today. Some Christians are always growing and full of life, and they are a source of refreshing for others. Other Christians are consistently downcast, focusing on the negative, and they easily drag others down with them. The difference is the same as that of the two seas. The thriving Christians are those who continue taking in and giving out. There is a flow in their lives that keeps them fresh and alive. The failing Christians are those who take in but never give out. They receive from God—blessings, knowledge, and material goods—but they keep what they get for themselves. Their failure to share with others results in their failure to thrive.

God, we see in the metaphor of the seas that we need to give out if we are to stay fresh and alive. We do not want to be like the Dead Sea, living only for itself and not being a source of life for any living thing. We ask You to help us get rid of all of the obstacles that keep the Water of Life from flowing freely through us. Use us to deliver the fresh Water of Life to others. In Jesus' name, Amen.

March 7

"The Spirit of the Lord is upon me, because he hath…sent me to heal the brokenhearted…, to set at liberty them that are bruised,"
—Luke 4:18 (KJV)

A FRIEND OF MINE LEARNED THAT THE WART THAT appeared on his foot didn't come from walking barefoot on the floor at the YMCA, as he had surmised. His doctor told him that when children have warts, these skin growths may retreat into their bodies and come out later in different places when they are adults. Warts are minor irritations in comparison to the impact of repressed negative emotions. Children can keep their emotions bottled up inside of them when they don't feel they can express them openly. When they experience abuse, neglect, fear, or other negative experiences or relationships, they may not have any way of dealing with those situations— no counselor, no adult in whom to confide, no safe place to talk about them. It may appear as though the negative feelings go away over time, but often they are just repressed and come back in other relationships when they are adults.

Thankfully, we have a Savior who came to heal our broken hearts and free us from our woundedness. All of the pain we suffered, our lost ability to trust, our difficulty in communicating—Jesus can heal us and help us to recover and be free to live and love again.

Lord Jesus, we come to You now, asking that You heal our broken hearts and free us in areas where we have been wounded. You know the pain, the fear, the confusion, and the anger that we buried years ago. The emotions continue to work below the surface to prevent us from receiving the blessings, the relationships, You have for us today. Begin that healing process within us. We don't know what all it will take for You to make us whole again, but we give ourselves fully to You, trusting You to do in us what You were sent to do. In Your loving name we pray, Amen.

March 8

Let us run with patience the race that is set before us.
—Hebrews 12:1 (KJV)

PASTOR ERIC WIGGINS' WIFE CAMILLE TOOK SO long getting home from the grocery store one day that he was becoming concerned about her. When she finally arrived, he was relieved but noticed that she parked really crooked in the driveway. When she came in the house, she explained that something in the car had broken—which they later learned was the tie rod, the part that helps the steering mechanism. When she started driving home, she realized the car would only make right turns, so she had to figure out how to get home only making right turns.

Some of us may feel it's taking us a long time to get to our destinations because we are required to keep making "right" turns. We may see others taking shortcuts, turning in directions that are not right, and yet they seem to be making so much better time. But we have to keep running with patience—*running*, so that we will make it to our destination; *with patience*, so that we will keep going right. We must keep going on the path God sets before us even though it may *look* like another path might be faster.

God, You know we get anxious and frustrated sometimes. We want so much to reach a place we know You have appointed for us, but we have to keep going the right way. We see others going their own way—sometimes right and sometimes wrong—and yet they seem to be moving ahead faster. God, help us to remember that You will never allow us to be late when we are running at Your pace for us and in the direction You have set for us. Give us patience to do things Your way and in Your timing. Amen.

March 9

...we take captive every thought to make it obedient to Christ.
—*2 Corinthians 10:5*

A DOG MUST BE HOUSETRAINED BEFORE THE owner will allow it to move about freely throughout the house. Sometimes when training a new pet dog, the owner will keep it in a kennel for a period of time, letting the animal out only for times of supervised activity while the owner teaches it boundaries and the rules of the house. Once the dog learns submission and obedience, then it can have total freedom in the house.

The same is true of our thoughts. As long as we let our thoughts go wherever they want to go and focus on anything they like, we have a real problem on our hands. Our thoughts will be causing damage to our hearts because they will draw us away from God. We must hold every thought captive and learn to make each one of them obedient to Christ.

God, we acknowledge that we let our thoughts run wild at times. We allow them to go places You do not want them to go and focus on things that are off-limits. We confess that we have failed to rein in our thoughts and make them obedient to You and Your Word. Forgive us, God, and help us with every thought to please You. In Jesus' name, Amen.

March 10

Finally, brethren, whatsoever things are true, whatsoever things are honest, whatsoever things are just, whatsoever things are pure, whatsoever things are lovely, whatsoever things are of good report; if there be any virtue, and if there be any praise, think on these things.

—Philippians 4:8 (KJV)

IN AN AMERICAN INDIAN STORY, AN AGED man explained to a young man that when one wants to be righteous, there is both a good dog and an evil dog inside of him. He explained that they are both fighting inside him for control of his mind. "Which dog, then, is winning?" he was asked. He replied, "The one I feed the most."

There is a war between good and evil, obedience and sin, raging within each of us. If the force of righteousness—that which delights in God's law—is going to win, we must feed our minds on things that are true, honest, and pure. We must feed our minds on the Word of God, listen to good sermons, and read Christian books to become filled with that which nurtures our souls.

Father, help us to feed our minds on those things that are good and positive, and help us to grow in Your ways. In Jesus' name we pray, Amen.

March 11

So God created man in his own image, in the image of God he created him; male and female he created them.

—Genesis 1:27

WHILE I WAS AT A CAR WASH, some brothers started to have an intellectual discussion. They began talking about freedom of speech. But as I listened, I realized they were simply justifying their right to use the "n-word" and to call themselves by other derogatory names. Finally, I couldn't just listen anymore; I *had* to tell them to stop living down to the level of those names others have called us in the past. Why should we adopt negative images that someone else forced upon us in times past? I pointed out that we weren't the ones to make up those words and we need to stop internalizing them.

We are made in the image of God—every one of us. On the day that God created humankind, he looked upon what he had created and said it was "very good." We cannot let anyone other than our Creator define who we are. We must stand against any name that would dishonor or demean that creation of Almighty God.

God, You know how people sometimes use negative terms in describing those of us who are female, African American, or from other racial or ethnic groups. Some of us even adopted those terms ourselves, thinking that the stigma would wear off if we used the terms to be funny or cool. But we realize now that those words make a difference to You. It was Your love and power that made us, and You made us in Your image. When we call ourselves by those negative terms, we are calling You by those names as well. Forgive us, God. We never intended to disrespect You. We didn't understand. But now that we do, we confess our sin, ask Your forgiveness, and will stand against that practice from this moment on. In Jesus' name, Amen.

March 12

I know what it is to be in need, and I know what it is to have plenty. I have learned the secret of being content in any and every situation, whether well fed or hungry, whether living in plenty or in want.

—Philippians 4:12

SOMEONE ASKED JOHN D. ROCKEFELLER, "HOW MUCH money is enough money?" He replied, "Just a little more." Money can be illusive because, for some people, there is never enough. That means their entire lives can be spent in pursuit of something that will never satisfy them.

How would we respond to that question? Can we say with the apostle Paul that we have learned the secret of being content "whether living in plenty or in want"? Who is better off: the person who has great wealth yet is never satisfied, or the person of modest means who abides in contentment?

Father, let us remember that You supply all of our needs. Whatever Your hand supplies is enough to satisfy us. Help us not to spend our lives striving for more. Help us instead to learn the secret of contentment. Amen.

March 13

Why spend money on what is not bread, and your labor on what does not satisfy? Listen, listen to me, and eat what is good, and your soul will delight in the richest of fare.

—Isaiah 55:2

I HEARD ABOUT A MAN WHO WAS walking in the mall and found a nice suit. Then he asked himself, "Do I want this suit?" He decided to keep walking and that if he came back to it, it would mean that he really wanted it. What kind of logic is that? If we don't really need something and aren't sure that we really even want it, why should we talk ourselves into buying it?

Isn't it time that we concentrate on getting those things that are good and that delight our souls? Just because we like something and can afford it, that does not mean we have to have it. How do we determine how we spend our money? Is it simply based on what we want? Perhaps we need to determine what it is that will be "good" for us and delight our souls.

Father, we acknowledge that we have fallen prey to this world's system: "Get all you can; can all you get; and sit on the can." Forgive us for seeking yet one more thing simply because it pleases us for the moment. Forgive us for being directed by our desires rather than what You desire for us. Forgive us for buying yet another suit. In Jesus' name, Amen.

March 14

When he was accused by the chief priests and the elders, he gave no answer. Then Pilate asked him, "Don't you hear the testimony they are bringing against you?" But Jesus made no reply, not even to a single charge—to the great amazement of the governor.

—Matthew 27:12-14

PILATE THOUGHT JESUS WAS WEAK BECAUSE HE refused to defend Himself. Pilate thought He should be offering excuses, explanations, and arguments in His defense. But Jesus was exhibiting meekness, not weakness. Meekness is power under control.

When we are walking in Christ, people may misunderstand us as well. They won't understand when someone is shouting at us and we don't shout back. They won't understand when someone says something unkind to us and we don't say something unkind back. They won't understand when someone is blaming us for something and we don't frantically try to justify our actions. A weak person would react in fear and would *have* to respond in order to try to save face. A meek person, however, can *choose* to behave as he or she deems appropriate. Weak people don't understand those who are meek.

O Lord, let us recognize that the meekness of Jesus is a great example to us. Help us always to respond in meekness, even if it means we will be misunderstood. Help us to know that it is the meek who are strong. In the name of the One we follow, Amen.

March 15

Jesus gave them this answer: "I tell you the truth, the Son can do nothing by himself; he can do only what he sees his Father doing, because whatever the Father does the Son also does."

—John 5:19

WATCHING LAILA ALI IN HER SOUTH AFRICA match against Gwendolyn O'Neil was reminiscent of watching her father Muhammad Ali in his glory days. Laila knocked out her opponent in just fifty-six seconds in the first round. She even *sounded* like her famous father when she said tongue-in-cheek afterward that she *wanted* to make the fight go at least two rounds for the sake of the spectators, but she just didn't know how great she was. Not only her father's talent but also his spirit was passed on to her.

Jesus tells us that if we have seen Him, we have seen the Father. He tells us that we are to follow in His steps. Let's recognize that when we walk after Jesus in the same way that He walked after the Father when He was on this earth, we too can possess the same characteristics and the same Spirit. Let's live in such a way that others see and hear our Father when they see our actions and hear our voices.

Our Father, we truly want to live in this world as You want us to live. We want others to see You and hear Your voice through us. Let Your Holy Spirit so fill and indwell us that we will do Your will in Your way, and that others will be drawn to You. In the name of Your Son, Amen.

March 16

"But seek first his kingdom and his righteousness, and all these things will be given to you as well."

—Matthew 6:33

IN HIRING THE NEARLY TWO HUNDRED EMPLOYEES at Eastern Star Church, I have never once asked an interviewee about his or her car, house, or clothes. I'm not interested in the external things because they aren't important in determining what they will be able to do for the church. It is what's on the inside that gets them in. But, *after* they are employed, these individuals can use their income to *buy* a nice car, house, and clothes. It's their inner lives that open a way for them to address their external circumstances.

There are some persons who go through life trying to get ahead, trying to position themselves for promotions, trying to get their foot in just the right door so that they can improve their status in life. They are so focused on the external that they neglect their inner lives. Then they are upset when someone else gets what they wanted, and they just don't understand how that could have possibly happened. In God's kingdom, if our focus is on the spiritual matters, the material things just follow naturally.

God, too often we have focused on getting what we want and what we think we need without regard for who You want us to be. Help us to turn our thoughts and attention away from external things and focus on our walk with You. Make us over, dear God, from the inside out, we ask in Jesus' name. Amen.

March 17

Whoever trusts in his riches will fall, but the righteous will thrive like a green leaf.

—Proverbs 11:28

DID YOU EVER STAND ON TOP OF a building and wonder what would happen if you drop a stone toward the ground? Of course not. We know what will happen. The stone will fall. There is nothing to wonder about because we know about the law of gravity. Gravity works because it is a law, an immutable principle.

God's Word works because it also is an immutable principle. If the Bible says, "Do this, and this will happen," we don't have to wonder about that. We don't have to question it. We know it is true, so we need to adjust our own actions and behavior in keeping with that principle. If God's Word says we will fall if we trust in our riches, we had better be putting our trust in God instead of our wealth. We had better be trusting in Him rather than in our own ability to care for ourselves. We can challenge it if we want, but the law will prevail.

In all honesty, God, there are probably times that we wish we did have a bit more flexibility in terms of the way we live our lives because there are times when we think we know what's best for ourselves. Your Word says ___, but we think that maybe we know better in this or that particular instance. But every time we act upon our own reasoning rather than upon Your Word, we fall. You have given us free will so we can challenge Your principles if we want, but Your Word always prevails. We're sorry, God, for being so dense and so stubborn. Help us to begin to take You at Your word as never before and realize that there are rewards for doing things Your way. Amen.

March 18

Do not conform any longer to the pattern of this world, but be transformed by the renewing of your mind. Then you will be able to test and approve what God's will is—his good, pleasing and perfect will.

—*Romans 12:2*

I HAD SUCH A FRUSTRATING EXPERIENCE one day. I had pulled up to a gas station because my car was on empty. I swiped my debit card and punched all the right buttons, but the gas didn't come out. I started over and punched the buttons again; still nothing happened. I went into the station to report that there was something wrong with the pump, but the attendant assured me that was not the case. Irritated, I was beginning to think there was something wrong with him, too. Probably thinking I was just not punching the buttons correctly, he came out to the pump to take a look. What we both discovered then was that there was not a problem either with the pump or with my ability to punch the buttons. The problem was with the hose: it was twisted. The gas couldn't flow through the channel because there was a kink in the hose.

Some of us have been blocking the flow of God into our lives because we have a kink in our mindset. Rather than letting the mind of Christ be within us, we are thinking according to the mindset of this present age, and it's screwed up—it's twisted. We need to let the Holy Spirit come in and renew our minds, so they will be lined up with the mind of Christ.

O God, we come to You realizing that our thinking has been twisted. Without even realizing it, we have allowed the world's values, attitudes, and ways of thinking to take root in our minds. It happened so gradually that we didn't realize it until now when, as we are looking for You to flow through us to others, we see that that isn't happening. There is nothing wrong with You, and nothing wrong with those "others." The problem is that our thinking is twisted, and we need for You to come and get us straightened out. Come to our aid, God. We need You. Amen.

I sink in the miry depths, where there is no foothold. I have come into the deep waters; the floods engulf me.

—*Psalm 69:2*

DR. TIMOTHY WINTERS, PASTOR OF BAYVIEW BAPTIST Church in San Diego, tells the story of a little boy who seemed to be having a good time splashing around in the water. He was flapping his hands, kicking his feet, ducking under and then coming up, and squirting water out of his mouth. Then an old man passed by and saw a "No Swimming" sign, so he called out to the boy and said, "Come on out of there! You're not supposed to be swimming in there!" "I'm not swimming," the boy called back, "I'm drowning!"

Some of us may look like we're swimming—in our relationships, in our finances, in our work—but we know the truth. We aren't swimming: we're drowning. From the outside, we may appear okay. Perhaps we even appear that we are fully in control because we have a lifestyle envied by others. But the fact is that unless we get some help fast, we're going to go under and not come up.

God, help us not to be so proud that we would rather die than acknowledge that we are drowning. We may look successful to others, but You know the areas in which we are failing and floundering. Please, God, we need for You to reach out and save us from our present situation. We are drowning, but we look to You to rescue us. In Christ's name, Amen.

March 20

While Jesus was in one of the towns, a man came along who was covered with leprosy. When he saw Jesus, he fell with his face to the ground and begged him, "Lord, if you are willing, you can make me clean." Jesus reached out his hand and touched the man. "I am willing," he said. "Be clean!" And immediately the leprosy left him.

—Luke 5:12-13

A FEW YEARS AGO, I BROKE MY ankle playing basketball. When I went to the doctor, he was trying to figure out just where it was broken, so he touched it here and felt it there. Each time he touched my ankle, I winced and made a face, and pulled back because it hurt. It was sensitive to touch. But the doctor said, "If I don't touch it, I can't heal it."

Some subjects—our finances, relationships, parenting skills, and service to God—are sensitive to touch, but if God doesn't touch the place that is hurting, He can't heal it. If the man covered in leprosy had tried to conceal his disease by covering his body up in long robes and hiding in the shadows, he would have remained sick. But his willingness to expose his problem and let Jesus touch him allowed him to receive healing.

You know, God, that we sometimes don't want to face the fact of our own areas of weakness or dis-ease. And we surely don't want anyone else to point them out to us! But, God, we do know that they are there. We do realize there are areas of our lives that are sensitive because they are broken. We see that the man covered in leprosy was so desperate for healing that he begged Jesus to make him clean. God, forgive us for the pride that has caused us to try to conceal our areas of brokenness. Today, we acknowledge that we need Your touch, and we beg You to make us clean. Amen.

March 21

"Will a man rob God? Yet you rob me. But you ask, 'How do we rob you?'
In tithes and offerings."

—*Malachi 3:8*

NOT TOO MANY YEARS BACK, SOMEONE WAS ripping off various churches in Indianapolis, where our church is located. When the person was caught, his picture was put on the front page of the local newspaper's City-State section under the bold headline: "STEALING FROM GOD."

There were probably not just a few pastors who felt like sending the newspaper a copy of their church's pictorial directories to print under the same headline. Every Sunday, some of us rob from God by not tithing. We may read in amazement about a man who would actually go in and steal something from a church, of all places, but some of us do it on a regular basis and don't think twice about it.

God, we know that ignorance is no excuse, but we really haven't considered that failing to tithe is stealing from You. Even though Your Word is so direct about it, we've just seen our failure to tithe as a personal choice, a temporary action because of our personal financial crisis, or an issue we've simply not even really thought about at all. God, we would never go into a church and walk out with something that belongs to You, yet that's what we've been doing on a regular basis for years. We walk in with money You have put in our pockets, and even though You've only asked for a portion of it back, we have walked out with it all. God, we repent for stealing from You and ask Your forgiveness. Even in this moment, we recommit our finances to You and covenant with You to bring our tithes and offerings to You each time You are so gracious to give us provision from Your hand. In Jesus' name, Amen.

March 22

Even to your old age and gray hairs I am he, I am he who will sustain you. I have made you and I will carry you; I will sustain you and I will rescue you.

—Isaiah 46:4

I WAS SITTING WITH MY FAMILY AT A PARADE ONE DAY when another family came and sat down on the bleachers in front of us. This caught my attention because the father was carrying his daughter on his back. She was not a little girl whom we might typically see a father carrying; she looked like she was about twelve or so. But then I noticed that the girl had a cast on her leg, so that explained why her father was carrying her.

As I watched, it struck me that God is like that father. When we're broken, He carries us to our destination and makes sure that we are in our assigned place. He does that because He is our heavenly Father and He loves us. We have to make sure, however, that it is God whom we allow to carry us. The person we allow to carry us when we're broken determines our destination. Not everyone will care that we follow God's will for our lives or understand that we are created for a special purpose and have a destiny to fulfill. If we let the wrong person carry us, we may find ourselves moving away from the plan God has for us.

Heavenly Father, we thank You that You love us when we are broken. You know Your plans and purposes for us, and when we have been injured and cannot walk, You offer to carry us to our destinations. In those times when we are wounded, lonely, and vulnerable, help us not to put ourselves in the hands of someone who does not have our best interests—our spiritual destiny—at heart. We offer our broken selves to You, O God, and trust You to see us to the place appointed for us. Amen.

March 23

Search me, O God, and know my heart; test me and know my anxious thoughts. See if there is any offensive way in me, and lead me in the way everlasting.

—Psalm 139:23-24

IF I WERE TO GO OUT TO our church parking lot and see someone looking under the hood of *my* car to find out what is wrong with *his or her* car, I wouldn't understand that. If another person's car does not start and that individual is tinkering with *my* car to try to get his or her own car to start, that wouldn't make sense. That person would need to look inside his or her *own* car to find out what is wrong.

When something isn't working in our lives, we need to look inside *ourselves* to figure out the problem. So often, however, the first thing we do when something is going wrong is to look at others. We have trouble getting along with someone, so we look for faults in the other person to figure out what the problem is. We throw a temper tantrum, so we look at the person we've shouted at to discover the flaw within him or her that has triggered this totally uncharacteristic behavior on our part. We find our marriage isn't working, so we try to figure out what's wrong with our spouse so we can *fix* it. It's time for us to accept responsibility for what is happening in our lives and let the Holy Spirit search us and reveal to us any "offensive" ways.

Search me, O God, and know my heart; test me and know my anxious thoughts. See if there is any offensive way in me, and lead me in the way everlasting. Amen.

March 24

"Guard the good deposit that was entrusted to you—guard it with the help of the Holy Spirit who lives in us."

—2 Timothy 1:14

WHEN I USED TO PLAY BASKETBALL, IF the ball went flat, we had to find the needle, connect it to the air pump, put it in the slot of the ball, and pump it to get air back into the ball. We had to look outside of the ball to get what it needed *inside*. Today, however, infusion basketballs have on the *inside* all they need to repair themselves. If they go flat, a micropump on the inside of the ball can be released to pump the ball up again.

We have the Holy Spirit within us to empower us when we "go flat." We do not have to look outside—to drugs, alcohol, unhealthy relationships, money, or just keeping busy—to try to build ourselves up. We need to remember that the Holy Spirit is right there inside of us to help us. When our lives seem flat, we need to call upon Him to bring life back into our deflated situations.

Holy Spirit, we thank You that You dwell right inside of us. We don't have to go outside looking for help when our problem is on the inside. We trust You now to pump fresh life within us. Breathe upon us with Your holy breath that we might once again be filled with You and be ready to be used of God. In Jesus' name we ask, Amen.

One day Jesus was praying in a certain place. When he finished, one of his disciples said to him, "Lord, teach us to pray, just as John taught his disciples."

—*Luke 11:1*

FIRST SAMUEL 23:9 SAYS, "WHEN DAVID LEARNED that Saul was plotting against him, he said to Abiathar the priest, 'Bring the ephod.'" An ephod is a garment that is representative of what the priest would use to get in touch with God. When David asked the priest Abiathar for an ephod, he was asking for that which would empower him and enable him to communicate directly with God.

As a pastor, I cannot be present with every member of my congregation every time each person needs to hear from God. That is impossible for me or any minister of the gospel. It was impossible even for the priests of old. David knew, however, that the ephod was what the priest wore when he needed to communicate with God, so David asked the priest for the ephod. Jesus' disciples, recognizing that they, too, needed to know how to talk with God directly, asked Jesus to teach them to pray. Each individual needs to learn how to seek God for himself or herself. It is not enough to know someone who can communicate with God for us; we need to know how to communicate with Him ourselves.

Our Father which art in heaven, Hallowed be thy name. Thy kingdom come, Thy will be done in earth, as it is in heaven. Give us this day our daily bread. And forgive us our debts, as we forgive our debtors. And lead us not into temptation, but deliver us from evil: For thine is the kingdom, and the power, and the glory, forever. Amen.

March 26

But David said to Saul, "Your servant has been keeping his father's sheep. When a lion or a bear came and carried off a sheep from the flock, I went after it, struck it and rescued the sheep from its mouth."

—1 Samuel 17:34-35

IN PENSACOLA, FLORIDA, A YOUNG BOY WAS ATTACKED by a shark. The shark bit the boy's arm and was dragging him out to sea. Upon realizing what was happening, the boy's uncle ran from the beach and jumped into the water, rescuing the boy and retrieving his arm from the very mouth of the shark. The uncle had been relaxing on the beach, but when the boy yelled, "He's got me!" the uncle left his comfort zone and did what needed to be done to rescue the boy.

I wonder how many of us today are listening to the cries of young people who have been attacked by Satan and are being carried out farther and farther into lives that lead only unto death. When one of them calls out, "He's got me!" is there anyone willing to leave the quiet solitude and safety of the beach and go out and do battle for the sake of this young person who is being carried off by the enemy?

God, we think about how David responded when a lion or bear came and attacked one of the sheep that was in his care. He didn't make excuses or procrastinate: "The rest of the sheep need me here," "God will take care of him," or "I'll just wait and see what happens; if he really needs me, I'll go." He immediately went running after that sheep. God, let us not be complacent about the young people who are under attack in this day and age from the enemy of their souls. Give us the love and passion that You feel for them, and the courage and willingness to run after them in the name of Jesus to bring them into the safety of Your fold. In Your holy name we pray, Amen.

March 27

Then I heard the voice of the Lord saying, "Whom shall I send? And who will go for us?" And I said, "Here am I. Send me!"

—Isaiah 6:8

KEVIN COSBY, AN EXPERIENCED SKYDIVER, WAS once asked, "How many times have you jumped?" His response was, "Never. But I've been pushed 175 times."

That, unfortunately, is how some of us get into ministry. We aren't like Isaiah, who simply overheard God expressing a need for a worker and responded, "Here am I. Send me!" We are more likely to respond, "Here she is, God. Send her!" Many of us are like Jeremiah. When God said to him, "Before I formed you in the womb I knew you, before you were born I set you apart; I appointed you as a prophet to the nations," Jeremiah replied, "Ah, Sovereign Lord, I do not know how to speak; I am only a child" (See Jeremiah 1:4-6.)

Dear God, it is with shame that we come to You today. We remember those moments when we heard Your voice telling us to go here or go there, to say this or say that, or to do the work of ministry in one way or another. But we did not respond. We were too busy, we had too many things we wanted to do first, or we had too many priorities competing with Your will for our lives. Forgive us, God. Please let us hear Your call to us afresh and anew, and help us to respond as quickly to You as we want You to respond to us when we call upon Your name. Let us feel Your heart and become Your instruments in this world. In the name of the One who set the example for us, Amen.

March 28

...a great door for effective work has opened to me, and there are many who oppose me.

—*1 Corinthians 16:9*

A PASSENGER ON A GREYHOUND BUS FROM LOS ANGELES to San Francisco took a pair of scissors, walked from the back to the front of the bus, and cut the bus driver's throat. The court ordered a psychological evaluation, but that seemed a bit unnecessary. It should be obvious that something is wrong with a person who cuts the throat of the one helping him get to his destination.

Yet, we see that happening in churches all the time. Pastors around the country lay down their lives day after day and week after week for their congregations. They make sacrifices, face spiritual battles, continually pray for those in their churches, and seek messages from God to help them find direction. Yet, there are people in those very congregations who stand in opposition. Perhaps not literally, but by their words, there are some who even "cut the throat" of the one who is there to help them. By their critical spirits, their gossip, and even their slander, they bring harm to the very one who has been ordained of God to guide them spiritually.

God, we pray today for all those in our churches who, directly or indirectly, are opposing the very person whom You have appointed to help them find their destiny in this life and their destination in the next. Whatever it is within them that motivates them to do and speak harm instead of help, we ask that You deal with it. Open their eyes and let them see what they are doing, not only to their pastors, but also to themselves and their brothers and sisters in Christ. Help them to be instruments for good rather than for evil. Let us not fool ourselves. In Jesus' name, Amen.

March 29

And he said unto them, Come ye yourselves apart into a desert place, and rest a while: for there were many coming and going, and they had no leisure so much as to eat.

—*Mark 6:31 (KJV)*

WHEN GREEN BAY PACKERS' RUNNING BACK JASON BROOKINS heard the coaches tell him to turn in his playbook at the end of his first preseason, he packed his SUV and went home. When he didn't show up for the next team meeting, the coach contacted his agent, who told him that Brookins thought he was cut from the team so he went home. But the coach explained that the playbooks are always collected at the end of preseason so that they can be modified and new plays added.

There are times when God may call for our playbooks. There may be a pause in our playing. God may want to show us some new tactics to use in fighting spiritual battles. He may want to show us additional ways we can work together with our teammates to be a stronger force. He may want to modify some of the things we are currently doing that aren't working so that we can gain ground in areas in which we have been defeated. We can't give up and leave when God does this in our lives. He is not setting us aside; He is setting us up for greater victory!

Our God, we remember today the times that we've been discouraged and thought that You had given up on us. We saw our failures and weaknesses, and felt like walking away because we thought You didn't want to use us anymore. Thank You, God, for showing us that there are times when You bring us apart to give us a fresh word, to show us better ways of living life and serving You. Thank You, that those times don't mean You are finished with us. Instead, they mean that You have found something within us worth cultivating. O, God, thank You for not giving up on us. We wait today upon You, God. We wait today upon You. Amen.

March 30

For the Scripture says, "Do not muzzle the ox while it is treading out the grain," and "The worker deserves his wages."

—1 Timothy 5:18

SOLDIERS DON'T PROVIDE FOR THEIR OWN NEEDS. Everything is provided for them so that they can be free to focus on fighting the battles.

The same should be true for pastors. They should not have to concern themselves about meeting their own needs. How effective can they be in fighting spiritual battles, if they are always having to figure out how to provide for their families' needs or how to get the resources they need to minister as God is telling them to minister? Moreover, pastors should receive more than just bare necessities because they are generals, not privates. They bear the weight of responsibility for the spiritual battles in which their churches are engaged.

Lord, help us not to be stingy with those whom You have chosen to lead us. Help us to remember that as we care for the needs of our pastors, we free them to care for our needs. Let us be generous with those who are called to serve within the church, knowing that even as we minister unto them, we minister unto You. In Jesus' name, Amen.

March 31

For for this cause pay ye tribute also: for they are God's ministers, attending continually upon this very thing. Render therefore to all their dues: tribute to whom tribute is due; custom to whom custom; fear to whom fear; honour to whom honour.

—Romans 13:6-7 (KJV)

PASTORS ARE LIKE SHARECROPPERS: AFTER THEY DO the work, they get a share of the crop. They don't *own* the land; but since they sow, plant and reap, they should receive a portion of that which is gained from their work.

It is interesting that even when a church prospers, some congregations want to continue to pay their pastors what they were making when they first arrived and the church was in a downhill spiral. They don't take into account the fact that God has used this man or woman of God to grow His house and bless His people.

Lord God, why is it that we are so generous in the world and so stingy at church? Why is it that we are willing to spend a lot of money to hear a musician entertain us in a concert, but unwilling to give freely to the pastor who helps to fit us for the kingdom of God? Why is it that we exalt celebrities who live worldly, immoral lives yet criticize the pastor who is living a holy life before us? Why is it that we will buy this and buy that to satisfy ourselves, but complain when the pastor makes a request that will help us win more people to Christ? God, sometimes we just don't understand ourselves. Forgive us for misguided priorities and affections and let us line up our concerns with Yours. In Christ's name, Amen.

April 1

Come near to God and he will come near to you.

—James 4:8

AN OLD COUPLE DRIVING DOWN THE STREET saw a young couple in a car in front of them. The young man and woman were all snuggled up close to each other. In contrast, in the other car, the old lady was sitting way over against the door on the passenger's side. Seeing the young couple, she said to her husband, "I remember when we used to sit close together, and you used to hug me like that." The old man responded, "I'm still in the same place."

While that little story may make us smile, when it happens between God and us, it isn't so funny. Reflecting upon the relationship we used to have with God, we miss the closeness and intimacy—the way it felt as though God was right there beside us. But today, there is distance. We've lost something precious. We miss the intimacy with Him. Well, the fact is, God hasn't moved, we have. It's time for us to draw near again to Him, and we will find that He will come near to us. Even though we're the ones who moved away, He will graciously come to meet us as we head back in His direction.

Lord God, we miss what we once had with You. We miss the sweetness and closeness of our relationship with You. We don't want to continue with this distance between us. We want to feel the joy of Your presence again and hear the whisper of Your voice. Lord, right now, we come to You. Amen.

April 2

The weapons we fight with are not the weapons of the world. On the contrary, they have divine power to demolish strongholds.

—2 Corinthians 10:4

MY FRIEND DAVID PAGE, SENIOR PASTOR OF New Baptist Church in Indianapolis, used to be in the military. He told me that if soldiers have to fight at night in foreign territory, they are issued special equipment. They receive night-vision goggles to see in the dark. But these alone are not enough. Just being able to see would still leave them vulnerable. Therefore, they also get a radio so that they can stay in communication with their commander and receive orders and directions to know what to do and where to go. The radio would be worthless, however, if the enemy could jam the frequency, so the soldiers are also given a special frequency at which to operate, one with which the enemy cannot interfere. Yet, even with all this it is still possible to get lost at times because the terrain is so rugged and the territory so unfamiliar. But even if they get lost, everything is still going to be all right because the Army always gives them a compass.

We are soldiers in God's army, sent out to do battle against spiritual forces. We are equipped through the Holy Spirit with "night-vision goggles"—the ability to continue to see a vision even in dark situations; a "radio"—the Holy Spirit speaking within to direct and guide us; "special frequencies" so that the enemy can't hear what we're saying; and, in case we do get lost in unfamiliar territory, a "compass"—the Bible to help us get our bearings.

> *God, we know that, whether we want to be or not, we are in the midst of spiritual warfare. We are in battles for our minds, battles for our souls, and battles for those we love. Help us, God, not to just be happy about the weapons we've been given, as though we are children playing with toys, but to recognize the value of each one and to use each one for the kingdom's sake. Amen.*

April 3

Be very careful, then, how you live—not as unwise but as wise.
—Ephesians 5:15

SOMETIME AGO, IN INDIANA, A WOMAN WHO had escaped from prison got rearrested after having been free for thirty-five years. She was able to elude those who went after her for so many years by doing a combination of three things: changing her identity, cutting off all ties to her previous life, and developing all new relationships. Through those actions, she essentially became a new person.

That woman was very smart. She knew how to stay free from bondage. We would do well to employ those same actions in order to remain free from the things that have held us in bondage. The key is making a complete break from our past. We can't go back and forth between a life of freedom and a life of bondage—today, living as one who has been delivered from sin; and tomorrow, doing the same old things, going to the same old places, and hanging with the same old crowd. If we want to remain free, we must stay free from those things that would pull us back into our old lives.

God, we thank You that unlike the woman who was rearrested, we aren't trying to live a new life on our own. You indeed have made us brand new: old things have passed away and all things have become new. Sometimes, however, people in the world are wiser than people in Your kingdom. That woman knew she had to stay free of her old life in order to remain in freedom. We, on the other hand, sometimes try to keep a little of the old life while maintaining our freedom in the new life. We can see now, however, that those ways are not going to work. Entanglement in our old life will keep us from enjoying the freedom that You intend for us. Help us, God, to decide once and for all that we are going to live like the new persons You have made us. Thank You for our freedom in Christ. Amen.

April 4

So teach us to number our days, that we may apply our hearts unto wisdom.
—Psalm 73:26

IF YOU ARE FORTY YEARS OLD BUT fearful of returning to school because you will be forty-four years old when you graduate, how old will you be in four years if you don't go back to school?

Some people live as slaves to time in many ways. They have a sense of being driven by time. They have to do everything, and they have to do it all right now. They begin having sex as a young teen. They have a baby before graduating from high school, they are married by eighteen, they are divorced by twenty-one, and they become grandparents by thirty-five. Somewhere along the way, they lose themselves and spend the rest of their lives mourning the loss of that life they thought they would have. Others behave as though time will stand still for them, so they wait their whole lives to begin living. They can't find the perfect mate, so they don't get married. They are afraid of not succeeding, so they don't go to college. They have a dream of what they want to be, but they find every reason imaginable for not going after it. God gave us this life to live and to live to the fullest. We can't let our warped concepts of time keep us from becoming all that God intends for us. We need to embrace that dream—that calling on our lives God has put within us—and take the next step that will lead to its fulfillment.

Lord, You are the One who gave us the concept of time for this life, and You are the same One who puts dreams in our hearts and a calling into our spirits. We know these are compatible. We need for You to show us how to live in Your perfect will even though that means restructuring our priorities and restructuring our thinking. We want to do Your will, O God. Please motivate us and direct our steps, we pray in Jesus' name, Amen.

April 5

Then Jesus told his disciples a parable to show them that they should always pray and not give up.

—*Luke 18:1*

A NEWSPAPER STORY TOLD OF A SEVENTY-YEAR-OLD man who had been married for fifty years when his wife went into a coma. He hoped and prayed for her recovery. Day after day, he sat by her bedside, wondering if this would be the day she would wake up. But finally, after six months, he became so discouraged that he committed suicide. One week later, his wife came out of the coma.

We recognize the tragedy and irony of that incident, yet we can relate to the man's frustration and despair. We too are faced with situations that seem hopeless. We may be in a financial bind, our marriage may be in trouble, our children may be in crisis situations, or we too may be facing a major health issue. There are so many things that can bring us to the point of feeling like giving up, but we need to keep hanging in there. We need to keep trusting God that He *will* work it out. Whatever we have to go through, God will help us and give us strength. But if we give up, we deem Him powerless and miss the opportunity to see Him work on our behalf.

Father, when the path seems agonizingly long and the road seems so hard that we feel we have to just stop, when our hearts feel that they can't take it anymore, and we are tempted to give up, remind us of who You are. Help us to remember that You are the One who hung the worlds in space. You are the One who parted the Red Sea. You are the One who brought Lazarus back to life. You are the One who healed all manner of disease. You are the One who provided the coin to pay Peter's taxes. You are the One who saved us and gave us new life. Let us not fail to trust You even in this trial that confronts us. In Jesus' name, Amen.

April 6

I pray also that the eyes of your heart may be enlightened in order that you may know the hope to which he has called you, the riches of his glorious inheritance in the saints, and his incomparably great power for us who believe.

—Ephesians 1:18-19

I WAS TALKING ON THE PHONE ONE day with a friend when I heard the beep telling me another call was coming in. I put him on hold but found that when I answered the second line, it was the same person on that line as well. He explained that his cell phone upon which he had initially called was very nearly out of power so he had switched to his home phone, which was grounded.

Some of us may be realizing that our power is running out, and we need to switch to a power source that will not run out. Some folks run on the power of money, drugs, fame, position, relationships, or feverish activity. All of these things are limited; they will run out. We need to make sure we are empowered by the Holy Spirit, who is eternal and therefore able to keep us going forever.

Holy Spirit, thank You for empowering us. You enable us to keep going and to keep doing all that our Father wants us to do. We are so grateful that Your resources for us never dry up and we never look to You in vain. We thank You. In Jesus' name, Amen.

April 7

Even so faith, if it hath not works, is dead, being alone.

—James 2:17 (KJV)

GOD REQUIRES BOTH FAITH AND WORK. IT TOOK FAITH for Adam and Eve to believe that by putting little seeds into the ground, they would end up with full-grown plants. It took work because God gave them only seeds that they had to plant and cultivate. It took faith for Noah to build an ark when the sun was shining. It took work because God gave Noah trees, not the ark itself. It took faith for Moses to believe that the waters of a sea would part if he simply held up his staff. It took work to hold up the staff God gave him.

God does not move in our lives in a way that makes us lazy or complacent. God doesn't give us everything ready-made. He often simply gives us what we need in the short term in order to get what we need in the long term. The job-seeker who sits at home waiting for an employer to knock on his door is going to be waiting in vain. The mother who wants a loving, caring family but gives her children no nurturing, no guidance, and no discipline is going to be sadly disappointed. The diabetic who wants to be well but refuses to take his insulin or watch his diet will be lying in a hospital bed, wondering what went wrong. Our faith, no matter how great, will never make up for our failure to do what we know to do.

God, we recognize that our Christian walk is always a balance between faith and works, between believing and doing. Help us to remember that You worked for six days before You sat down to rest. Sometimes, we want just to rest continually and expect You to do all the work. Help us as we reorder our thinking and realize the critical importance of being obedient in doing what You tell us to do with what You have provided for us. In Your holy name we pray, Amen.

April 8

"The man with the two talents also came. 'Master,' he said, 'you entrusted me with two talents; see, I have gained two more.'"

—*Matthew 25:22*

WELLINGTON MARA, CO-OWNER OF THE NEW YORK Giants, died in 2005 at age eighty-nine. He had spent a lifetime maintaining the Giants as a profitable championship team. Tim Mara, his father, had bought the team for five hundred dollars when Wellington was nine years old. The young boy served as ball boy for the team that year and continued during his youth to shine shoes, run errands, and do whatever he could to help the team. In 1930, Tim Mara split the interests of the ball team between Wellington, then fourteen, and his older brother Jack. The younger brother worked his way from one position to another until he became president and co-chief executive officer. Over the years, he turned that five-hundred dollar purchase into a team worth a billion dollars. He took what his father gave him and developed it.

What has our heavenly Father given us? How many talents? How many gifts? How much money? What resources? What work? What relationships? What ministry? What calling? When we face Him someday, what will we say to Him about that which He entrusted to us? What will we have to present back to Him? Will we have doubled His investment in us, or even more? Or will we be ashamed and have only excuses to offer Him?

Heavenly Father, we thank You for that which You have given us, and we want to acknowledge that we have not developed that to its fullest. We are sorry for all of the excuses that we have offered over the years to try to justify our failure to develop that which You have given us. Please forgive us. Today, while there is yet time, we want to rededicate to You ourselves and that which You have given us. May we see growth and development in all of the areas in which You have imparted something to us. May we not be ashamed when we stand in Your presence to give an account. We pray in Jesus' name, Amen.

April 9

Those who live according to the sinful nature have their minds set on what that nature desires; but those who live in accordance with the Spirit have their minds set on what the Spirit desires.

—*Romans 8:5*

ONE OF MY SINGLE FRIENDS WAS BOASTING to me one day that a beautiful woman had sent him a picture of herself on his cell phone. It made him feel good each time he opened his phone and saw her face. But a few days later, he was complaining to me about that same picture because he couldn't figure out how to delete it. It had become a problem to him because she was getting into his head. Every conversation he had on his phone was colored by her image. At first the picture was only in his hand; he saw it only when he looked down at his cell phone. But after a while, because he saw the picture so often, it got into his head and he couldn't get free of it. Finally, however, he was delivered from that image when someone else sent him a new picture that displaced hers.

There are some pictures in our minds that we need to replace with Jesus. The pictures we carry with us are so varied. Some of us have pictures in our minds of beautiful women or handsome men that, at first, we just enjoyed imagining, but now we can't seem to get away from them. Others of us carry mental images that bring us anger or deep sadness because they represent people who have mistreated us and hurt us deeply. Still others of us have motion pictures in our minds—movies of what we would like to do to our enemies. We can't think away our thoughts. We have to let Jesus come into our minds so that our thoughts and images of Him displace those other pictures.

God, we confess to You this day that we have images in our minds that do not belong there. We have images that cause us to lust and sin, images that keep us from experiencing Your joy and peace, images that tempt us to behave in ways that are unlike Christ. God, we come to You today, asking Your help in getting rid of these images. Help us to live in accordance with Your Holy Spirit and to set our minds on things of the Spirit. In Jesus' name, Amen.

April 10

I would like you to be free from concern. An unmarried man is concerned about the Lord's affairs—how he can please the Lord. But a married man is concerned about the affairs of this world—how he can please his wife—and his interests are divided. An unmarried woman or virgin is concerned about the Lord's affairs: Her aim is to be devoted to the Lord in both body and spirit. But a married woman is concerned about the affairs of this world—how she can please her husband. I am saying this for your own good, not to restrict you, but that you may live in a right way in undivided devotion to the Lord.

—1 Corinthians 7:32-35

I AGREED TO PREACH RECENTLY IN CHICAGO FOR ONLY two nights. The church wanted me to stay longer, but as a married man, I have a wife and children about whom I am concerned.

Paul said he would like the Corinthians to be "free from concern." Both married and single folk have concerns, and both have great joys. Both also have only twenty-four hours in each day. But one of the benefits of being single is often having more flexibility in the use of time. That isn't always true, of course, such as with single parents or singles caring for elderly parents, but most singles don't have so many other persons' agendas to take into consideration. They should value this period in their lives and not let others try to force them into marriage or make them feel bad if they are not married. Being single is not a sickness, and getting married isn't a cure.

Lord, we thank You right now for our marital status whether we are single or married. We pray that those who are single will treasure this time in their lives and their possibility of having an undivided devotion to You. Help those of us who are married not to neglect our families while serving others, and not to neglect You while serving our families. Give us wisdom, we pray. Let us remember that whether we are single or married, we are Yours. In Jesus' name, Amen.

April 11

To the church of God in Corinth, to those sanctified in Christ Jesus and called to be holy, together with all those everywhere who call on the name of our Lord Jesus Christ—their Lord and ours.... it is better to marry than to burn with passion.

—*1 Corinthians 1:2, 7:9*

PASTOR THERON WILLIAMS HAS POINTED OUT THAT it is possible to be hot and holy. These verses illustrate that. First Corinthians 1:2 points out that this letter was written to a sanctified church, to those called to be holy. Yet in 1 Corinthians 7:9, Paul speaks of those who should marry rather than burn with passion. There were individuals in the church at Corinth who were sanctified and called to be holy who were burning with passion.

Being hot does not mean one is unholy. Some people testify boastfully, "When I accepted Christ, God took away all of my fleshly desires." No, He didn't! If you no longer have any sexual desire, you need to see a doctor because there's something wrong. We just need to learn to handle our passions, because being hot does not make us unholy.

God, our Creator, You know how we are made because it is You who made us. You know the wonderful gift You gave us that draws us into a relationship of intimacy. Rather than denying that gift, help us to receive and use it as You intended. In Christ's name, Amen.

April 12

He who conceals his sins does not prosper, but whoever confesses and re-
nounces them finds mercy.

—*Proverbs 28:13*

THERE IS A STORY TOLD OF A Mother Sadie, who taught the children of her church in Sunday school year after year for decades. Week after week, she told her class that she didn't need anybody but Jesus. She considered that her testimony: "Nobody but Jesus." One Sunday, she was yet again saying to her class, "I don't need anybody but Jesus," when one of the boys spoke up: "That's right. Just the other day I saw Jesus climbin' out of Miss Sadie's bedroom window."

This story is obviously intended to make us smile, but there are real people who live their lives in deception. Maybe they are not as blatant as Mother Sadie, but they still are trying to pretend that their lives are godly, while, in fact, they are enjoying their sinful activities. But God says that we find mercy by confessing and renouncing our sins. We may fool others, and sometimes we even begin to fool ourselves; but God is no fool, and He sees what we hide from others.

God, You know that we want to live righteous and holy lives. We also want to prosper in our relationships, family life, finances, work, areas of ministry, and all that we do. But this verse today says that those who conceal their sins don't prosper. We recognize that we have been praying for prosperity, but our behavior has prevented that from coming to us. We do confess our sins in this moment, and we ask You to strengthen us to be able to stand when the temptations come again. Thank You, God, for Your mercy. Thank You so much, God, for Your grace. In Jesus' name, Amen.

April 13

The wife's body does not belong to her alone but also to her husband. In the same way, the husband's body does not belong to him alone but also to his wife.

—1 Corinthians 7:4

MY WIFE IS AN EXCELLENT HOMEMAKER AND a great cook. There have been times when she has prepared a four-course meal for me, and then I have had to leave to go to a meeting right after eating. On my way to the meeting, I may pass by a whole bunch of restaurants—really good restaurants that could normally tempt me—but I don't even think about stopping because I'm already full.

Husbands, take your fill at home. No matter how appetizing something looks, if your wife isn't the one serving it, consider it as poison because Proverbs 5:5 says of an adulteress that "her feet go down to death; her steps lead straight to the grave." And wives, remember that if a man's needs are met at home, he won't consider stopping anywhere else along the way. A woman who thinks of sex as a means of manipulation, something she can withhold to get her own way, is a foolish woman. From five-star restaurants to fast food drive-ins, there are a lot of places available to get hungry diners to stop and eat.

God, help us remember that sex is a precious gift from You; let us never treat it as something cheap that we can handle as we please. Let us remember that our bodies belong not only to ourselves but also to the spouse with whom we are in a lifelong covenant. Let us find pleasure in seeing that person satisfied, and help us to love one another even as Christ loves the church. In Jesus' name, Amen.

April 14

We always thank God for all of you, mentioning you in our prayers. We continually remember before our God and Father your work produced by faith, your labor prompted by love, and your endurance inspired by hope in our Lord Jesus Christ.

—1 Thessalonians 1:2-3

AT A WASHINGTON STATE HIGH SCHOOL FOOTBALL game, cheerleader Cali Kaitschmidt got tackled by the team she was there to support. She went to adjust the front of the school banner just as the team came bursting through the back of the banner to run onto the field. The team ran over one of their own supporters because they didn't see her.

We must make sure we are seeing the supporters in our lives. Unfortunately, we tend to overlook those who are closest to us—those who are our greatest blessings. We don't intend to ignore them, take them for granted, or even push them out of the way as we rush onto the field to provide care and ministry to others. But we somehow no longer see them as we once did. We have forgotten their love, their works of kindness, and their enduring faithfulness to us. Let's remember and thank God for our supporters.

Father, we have allowed ourselves to get so caught up in ourselves— and even in what You are doing in our lives—that we have pushed aside or pushed down those who are always there for us. God, we think of our spouse, friend, child, pastor, teacher, supervisor, coworker—that person who encourages and supports us. Even before we ask, he or she anticipates our needs and stands ready to help. Forgive us for taking that individual for granted. We pause today to remember what a gift he or she is to us, and we say thank You. Help us to begin anew to show this one how much he or she means to us. Amen.

April 15

Now to him who is able to do immeasurably more than all we ask or imagine, according to his power that is at work within us,...
—*Ephesians 3:20*

I WAS IN MIAMI, WAITING IN THE lobby of a four-star resort for the valet to retrieve my rented car so that I could go to South Beach for dinner. After an excessively long delay, the valet came and told me the car had a flat. Already late and not wanting to take any longer than necessary, I told him I would change the tire rather than having to wait for an auto service to come fix it. So I set about to change the tire but soon discovered that the spare tire didn't fit. Very frustrated by now at the loss of time and the fact that the rental company hadn't equipped the car properly, I called them to report my predicament. They didn't do what I expected of them, however. They didn't come and fix the flat so I could drive that car. Instead, they brought me a sweet, brand new Mustang convertible to replace it!

If you are single and in a relationship that has gone flat because it was a bad fit, don't keep working on it yourself. Call upon God. He won't just try to make something work that was never intended to fit. Instead, He will bring you a new relationship that is sweeter and better than the one you were trying to make work.

Wow, God! How many times we have worked and struggled, and spent time trying to get something that was never intended for us in the first place. How many times, we've been frustrated and disappointed when something didn't work out, and all the while, You had something better in store for us. We trust that You know our needs better than we know ourselves, and we believe that You are able to do "immeasurably more than all we ask or imagine." So, God, we leave our greatest needs and our deepest concerns, in Your hands, and we watch in faith to see what You are going to do. In Christ's name, Amen.

April 16

"Remain in me, and I will remain in you. No branch can bear fruit by itself; it must remain in the vine. Neither can you bear fruit unless you remain in me. I am the vine; you are the branches. If a man remains in me and I in him, he will bear much fruit; apart from me you can do nothing. If anyone does not remain in me, he is like a branch that is thrown away and withers; such branches are picked up, thrown into the fire and burned."

—John 15:4-6

WHEN I WENT TO PREACH IN ATLANTA recently, I flew in a plane at thirty-five thousand feet. When my wife and I got on a cruise ship, we went from Florida to the Bahamas. When I am in a car, I can go eighty-five miles per hour, or more if I want. Now, on my own, I can only jump a few feet. On my own, I can't run anywhere close to eighty-five miles per hour. On my own, I couldn't begin to swim the distance from Florida to the Bahamas. But inside a plane I can go high, inside a car I can go fast, and inside a ship I can go far.

The secret to success in life is being inside Christ. Whenever we try to do things in ourselves—that is, our own strength, our own effort, our own ingenuity, our own resources—we will find that we fall short, far short. But when we are operating in Christ, we will be amazed at how high, how fast, and how far we can go.

Jesus, we are thankful that You have invited us—even cautioned us—to remain in You. We know our own weaknesses and limits. But, we thank You that as we remain in You, You can do amazing things in and through us. We are excited today, Lord, as we anticipate what great surprises You have in store for us. Our faith is no longer in ourselves, but in You. In Your holy name we pray, Amen.

April 17

Jesus answered, "I am the way and the truth and the life. No one comes to the Father except through me."

—John 14:6

PEOPLE TURN TODAY TO TELEVISION TO HEAR others' opinions. That's such a mystery to me. The newscaster stops after announcing the death of Michael Jackson to ask the proverbial man on the street how he thinks the pop icon died. That man doesn't know anything more about the situation than I do, and I know nothing that hasn't been told to me on the news. A woman pours out her heart on one of the TV talk shows, telling the intimate secrets of her relationship with her husband, and then the host turns to the audience and asks their opinion about what the woman should do. Why should this poor, wounded soul care about what John Doe or Jane Smith thinks about her situation? Then there are the fiery political pundits who make a fortune telling those in their own particular political camp what they want to hear. Millions of viewers watch TV every day, listening to the opinions of other people.

When Absolute Truth speaks, it doesn't matter what someone else's opinion is. This same Jesus who identified Himself as "the truth" said thirty times in the book of Matthew, "I tell you the truth…." Isn't He the One to whom we should be listening? Even the experts and our best friends don't know what He knows about us, our situation, or our future. Shouldn't we be listening to *Him?*

Jesus, we acknowledge today that You indeed are the Truth. You know all things. We need to hear Your voice today. We need Your wisdom, Your direction, Your thoughts. Speak to us, O Lord. Amen.

April 18

Then Jesus told his disciples a parable to show them that they should always pray and not give up.

—Luke 18:1

SUPERMODEL PETRA NEMCOVA WAS STAYING AT A resort in Thailand in 2004 when a tsunami struck. The catastrophic wave was so immense that it killed over two hundred thousand people in eleven countries. Petra's life was in danger as well. In fact, she only survived the ordeal by clinging to a tree for eight hours until the water subsided and she could be rescued. She was delivered because she held on.

We need to learn that lesson as well. We often start out with great resolve, but when we begin to get tired and the challenge wears on and on, we start giving up in our hearts. We begin to think, "I might as well just let go; I can't hold out any longer." "This is probably just a waste of my time. I'm going through all of this and in the end, I'm going to be defeated anyhow." "I should have known this would happen to *me*. Nothing good ever happens to me; I don't know why this should be any different." "God, why did You let me down?" Jesus' word to His disciples was that they "should always pray and not give up."

We confess, O God, that we have sometimes allowed ourselves to be defeated because instead of praying, we began complaining. Rather than talking to the One who could deliver us, we talked to ourselves. Instead of holding on, we let go. But God, we don't intend to let go this time. In Your name and by Your strength, we declare that we will hold on and not give up. We watch and we wait for Your deliverance. Amen.

April 19

Then God said to Noah, "Come out of the ark...."

—Genesis 8:15-16

THE STORM THAT CAUSED THE FLOOD FOR which Noah built the ark lasted only forty days. But Noah did not get to resume life as normal after forty days. It was an entire year before the earth dried out and became livable again. There was nothing Noah could do to make it dry out any faster. He had to simply stay in the ark until God told him it was time to come out.

We may have experienced a storm of some sort in our lives—trouble on our job, trouble with our marriage, trouble with our children—that lasted for a relatively short period of time. But even now, our situation still isn't livable as it is. We have to wait for God to "dry it out." If we emerged now, we would get stuck in the muck and mire, and we would find no food or water to sustain us. We must have patience, even as Noah did, knowing that the One who quieted the storm will continue to work to make our situations livable again.

Thank You, God, that You provide an ark of safety for us even during the most turbulent storms. Thank You that we can remain in that ark until our lives become livable again. During this time of waiting, You will continue to provide for our needs and to keep us safe. We may not be where we want to be right now, God, and we are not where we look forward to being someday, but we thank You that even now, You are "drying things out" for us. You are preparing our circumstances so that when we emerge from this place, we will be able to grow and thrive once again. Thank You, God, for Your timing and Your ways. Amen.

April 20

Do you not know that in a race all the runners run, but only one gets the prize? Run in such a way as to get the prize.

—1 Corinthians 9:24

RUNNER MICHAEL JOHNSON SET NUMEROUS WORLD RECORDS at Baylor University and in multiple Olympic and world championship events. He credits his record in the 400-meter to the four P's: push (off at top speed), pace (in the backstretch), position (coming into the third curve), and pray (down the homestretch to the finish line).

The same strategy works well in our life's race. We should push off at top speed, determined to run this race like someone who intends to win and not be defeated. We need to pace ourselves in the backstretch, which is where the advice from Hebrews 12:1 comes in: "Let us run with perseverance," or as it says in the King James Version, "Let us run with patience the race that is set before us." Remember that our position is *in Christ*. Last, but definitely not least, pray!

God, teach us to run this race so that we will have victory. We look forward to the day when we see You waiting for us at the finish line and we can say with the same confidence and joy as Paul, "I have finished the race." In Christ's name, Amen.

April 21

Do not fret because of evil men or be envious of those who do wrong; for like the grass they will soon wither, like green plants they will soon die away. Trust in the LORD and do good; dwell in the land and enjoy safe pasture.
—Psalm 37:1-3

WHEN NOW-RETIRED MICHAEL JOHNSON USED TO RUN, he often ran in lane three or four. This made it look as though he was always behind until he got to the final stretch; then he said he would realize that because the lanes were staggered, it only looked like he was behind. In actuality, he was ahead of the rest.

We needn't be envious of those who seem to be doing well by cheating or taking advantage of others. We shouldn't get upset if we feel that others are moving ahead of us by doing things that God won't allow us to do. We just need to keep running, keep persevering, keep trusting God, and keep obeying Him. As we near the end, we'll find that we're exactly where we need to be to come out victorious.

God, we thank You today that You see all that goes on. Sometimes, life in this world just feels so unfair. We see others get ahead by doing things that are opposed to Your Word and Your kingdom principles. It's hard to stay in our lanes, where we feel we are so far behind that we can never catch up. But, God, just as Michael Johnson learned, we do believe that we will come to a point that we can see we are not lagging behind as we thought. Instead, we will realize that we even have the lead. We trust You today for victory. In Christ's name we pray, Amen.

April 22

Shouts of joy and victory resound in the tents of the righteous: "The LORD's right hand has done mighty things!"

—*Psalm 118:15*

YEARS AGO, WHEN HE WAS A LITTLE boy, my son Jordan came into my room while I was getting dressed and noticed the hockey game on TV. He asked me who was winning. I told him that I didn't know because I had just turned the game on and hadn't seen the score yet. While I continued what I was doing, he watched the game for a few seconds and then said, "Daddy, I know who's winning. *That* team is winning," and he pointed to those in a particular uniform. I asked him, "How do you know that they are winning?" "Because they are the ones who are cheering and excited," he replied. Even though he knew almost nothing about the game and the scores hadn't been shown on the screen, the winning team was obvious even to this little boy because one team was excited and the other wasn't.

We as Christians should reflect that we're part of the winning team. When people look at us, can they tell we are winning? Do we look happy? Are we cheering? Are we praising the One who is giving us the victory? Can anybody tell that we aren't losing? Let's declare our faith in the One who is fighting our battles for us.

Our God, we do praise You today. We rejoice in You, and we bless Your holy name! In You alone, O God, we have victory. Because of You, O God, we see our enemies defeated. Let our countenance today be that of a people on the winning team. May our joy be so evident that others will be drawn to the One who has given us that joy. We praise You, O God, because of all the mighty things You are doing in our lives. Praise You, Jesus, Amen.

April 23

Let us draw near to God with a sincere heart in full assurance of faith, having our hearts sprinkled to cleanse us from a guilty conscience and having our bodies washed with pure water. Let us hold unswervingly to the hope we profess, for he who promised is faithful.

—Hebrews 10:22-23

A YOUNG GIRL GREW UP IN A home where she was continually made to feel guilty. Guilt and the fear of God were tools used by her parents to keep her from exhibiting even normal childlike behavior. Guilt was a constant feeling because everything she did, according to her parents, was sinful, and God was going to punish her. Eventually, she could do nothing without feeling that God's wrath was hanging over her. Now, as an adult, it is hard for her to accept forgiveness and to believe that she is no longer guilty in God's eyes.

Maurice Watson, pastor of Beaulahland Baptist Church in Macon, Georgia, calls our feeling of guilt "illegitimate guilt" if we continue to feel it after we have confessed our sins and believed God for forgiveness. I've found that many Christians are walking around under the burden of illegitimate guilt. This is where our faith comes in. We have to accept salvation by faith, not by feeling. We have to believe that God always tells the truth and that His Word is true: "If we confess our sins, He is faithful and just to forgive us our sins and to cleanse us from all unrighteousness" (1 John 1:9). It doesn't matter how we feel at this moment; God is faithful and our sins are forgiven. Our guilt was laid on Christ, and He paid the penalty for our sins: "So if the Son sets you free, you will be free indeed" (John 8:36).

God, we can go through the rest of our lives trying to atone for our sins by feeling guilty, or we can believe in You and in Your Word and trust that we are forgiven through the blood of Jesus Christ. Because He has set us free, we are free indeed—not only from the penalty of our sins but from our guilty consciences as well. We receive what You have promised and by an act of our faith this day, we walk with a clear conscience, which is a gift from You. Amen.

April 24

And they were all amazed at the greatness of God.

—*Luke 9:43*

WHILE I WAS FLYING ACROSS THE OCEAN one day, God pointed out to me that His love is as vast as that ocean. I was in awe of that thought when God interrupted to amaze me even more. He said that beyond His love being as immense as the ocean, I needed to remember that I was only seeing the *surface* of the water. God's love is as *deep* as the ocean, too!

The late J. B. Phillips, British Bible translator and clergyman, wrote a book a number of years ago entitled, *Your God Is Too Small.* That title could be true for most of us. Some of us limit God to what we can see; or we limit God to what we can do ourselves; or we limit God by the circumstances we face. We need a new revelation of God. We need to see God in all of His vastness and His glory. Our limited view of God limits our faith in Him.

God, we know in our hearts today that we do not have a true picture of You in the vastness of Your presence, the greatness of Your power, and the depths of Your love. We are seeing You as too small. Open our eyes and let us see You as You really are; help us not to limit You because of our own limitations. In Jesus' name, Amen.

April 25

"Bring the whole tithe into the storehouse, that there may be food in my house. Test me in this," says the LORD Almighty, "and see if I will not throw open the floodgates of heaven and pour out so much blessing that you will not have room enough for it."

—Malachi 3:10

A FRIEND OF MINE WAS VISITING A church in Virginia. During the worship service, someone from the congregation went up to the pastor, handed him something, and whispered in his ear. The pastor then announced that forty dollars had been found in the women's restroom. After a very grateful woman claimed her money, the pastor observed, "Whenever you leave money at the church, you don't lose it."

This is a good lesson for us. We can't outgive God. The more we give, the more He pours out a blessing upon us. God even invites us to test Him on this. When we take Him at His word and care for the needs of *His* house, He takes care of the needs of *our* house—abundantly!

God, we are ashamed when we think of the times that we held our money tightfisted in our hands and refused to give the tithes and offerings that we knew You wanted from us. Not only does that make us ungrateful; it also makes us fools. Instead of trusting You to take care of our needs, we tried to do that ourselves. We now realize how foolish it was to depend on our meager income when You were offering to bless us so much that we wouldn't have room enough to receive all that You wanted to give us. Forgive us, Father. Amen.

April 26

We were therefore buried with him through baptism into death in order that, just as Christ was raised from the dead through the glory of the Father, we too may live a new life.

—Romans 6:4

AN INDIANA UNIVERSITY STUDENT WAS CRITICALLY INJURED in an auto accident. One news report even said that the young woman was actually dead but that she was being kept on life-support systems till relatives arrived. She wasn't dead after all, but she was definitely in very critical condition. But during that time she lay there in a hospital bed with death looming, a surgeon arrived on the scene who was able to help her. The young woman came back from her ordeal and lived.

God, too, knows how to give us comebacks. We may sometimes be at a point that we feel like we are on life support. We may feel as though we've already died—spiritually, emotionally, and mentally—but our bodies just haven't given up yet. Yet no matter how bad it seems or how bad it actually gets, God can still bring us back from our ordeal and make us live.

God, we know that You raised Jesus from the dead; You raised Lazarus; You raised Jairus's daughter, and so many others. Now, we need for You to come and raise us. We are sad in spirit, we are mentally confused, and we are emotionally depleted. Our bodies are like empty shells. Please come and raise us up. Give us a comeback, we pray. In Jesus' name, Amen.

April 27

And it was so, that when Solomon had made an end of praying all this prayer and supplication unto the LORD, he arose from before the altar of the LORD from kneeling on his knees with his hands spread up to heaven. And he stood, and blessed all the congregation of Israel with a loud voice, saying, Blessed be the LORD, that hath given rest unto his people Israel, according to all that he promised: there hath not failed one word of all his good promise.

—*1 Kings 8:54-56 (KJV)*

ONE DAY MY GARAGE DOOR WASN'T OPENING, and I couldn't figure out why. I checked the remote and looked over the doors, and everything seemed okay. But then I got down on my knees and I could see that the sensors were out of alignment. Once I realigned the sensors, the door worked again just fine.

Some of us need to get on our knees and realign ourselves with God. It's amazing what we can see clearly on our knees that we miss when we are standing upright. In our scripture passage for today, the first thing Solomon did after spending time on his knees was to stand and praise God. While he was on his knees, he recognized that God had given rest to his people and that "there hath not failed one word of all his good promise." He had realigned his image of God with the reality of God and realized his God was worthy of praise.

Lord, we kneel in Your presence today, seeking to be realigned with who You are in our lives and with who You want us to be. Let us see our relationship as You see it, and let us be lined up in right relationship with You. Realign anything in our lives that is not as it should be. Thank You that we, too, can stand and praise You for Your faithfulness and for keeping all of Your promises. In Your holy name we pray, Amen.

April 28

Keep me safe, O God, for in you I take refuge.

—*Psalm 16:1*

WHEN HE WAS A LITTLE BOY, MY oldest son J. Allen was afraid of the dark. We would put him to bed in his room, but sometime during the night, he would make his way to our room and curl up in bed with my wife and me. Now, I realized quickly that scenario was just not going to work, so I tried to figure out what he was thinking. I said, "Son, why is it that you say you are afraid of the dark, and yet you are willing to get out of your bed, walk down a long dark hallway, enter our dark room and climb into our bed? It's still dark in here. Why aren't you afraid in our room?" He answered, "Because you are there."

If we could only have that childlike trust in our heavenly Father. No matter how dark it gets in our lives, if we can only get to our Father, we know it's going to be okay. We may be afraid for a moment, but we know we're headed in the right direction when we're going toward our Father. We know we won't be afraid any longer once we're in His presence.

Father, thank You that we do find refuge in You. Thank You that You keep us secure and You let us know we don't have to be afraid when we are in You. Even as a little child, we can curl up and sleep, knowing that whatever happens, our Father can handle it. Help us to trust You, even as a little child. In Your precious name we pray, Amen.

April 29

As you know, we consider blessed those who have persevered. You have heard of Job's perseverance and have seen what the Lord finally brought about. The Lord is full of compassion and mercy.

—*James 5:11*

I WAS INVITED TO THE JANUARY 2007 AFC CHAMPIONSHIP game between the Indianapolis Colts and New England Patriots. I was seated at the fifty-yard line in a nice suite with a great view, perfect climate, and good company. But by halftime, we were losing 21-3, and I wanted to leave. It was painful to watch the Colts losing so badly, and I didn't want to sit there and watch it play out minute by excruciating minute to the end. It was only halftime, but I thought the game was over. I stayed only because I didn't want to offend the one who so generously gave me the ideal tickets. In the second half, however, the Colts came back, scored thirty-five points, and won the game! I almost missed it because I thought it was over before it was over.

Some folks have given up on life before it is over. When facing difficulty, they just wanted to be out of their misery. So, instead of trusting God and staying put, they sought escape through drugs, alcohol, adultery, gluttony, overwork, suicide, or a host of other means. What's so sad is that they have taken themselves out of position so that they cannot see the second half of the game. They will never know that God had planned a comeback. They will never know that, even when it looked like they were defeated, God had already secured their victory.

God, You know how painful our current situation is. You know that we are in agony. You know that we want to run away and hide from what seems like certain failure and defeat. But, You have given us ideal seats in this life, and we don't want to offend You by copping out. So God, show us this comeback. Show us Your victory. Show us Your deliverance. We are in Your hands and we wait for You. Amen.

April 30

Perseverance must finish its work so that you may be mature and complete, not lacking anything.

—*James 1:4*

WE LIVE IN A MICROWAVE SOCIETY WITH a microwave technology that has produced a microwave mentality. We use words and phrases such as "already done," "heat and serve," "instant," "quick," "in a hurry," and "done in a jiffy." We know nothing about "simmer," "slow cook," "bake," or "cook over low heat." If something takes more than seconds to prepare, we look for an alternative.

We bring this microwave mentality into our spiritual lives without even realizing it. God *can* do the instantaneous. He *can* create a universe in seven days. He *can* heal someone in an instant. He *can* say the word, and the seas calm down. But that isn't the way God usually works in our lives. Especially when God is working on our character development and our spiritual formation, He takes His time. It takes time to turn Abram into Abraham, Jacob to Israel, and Saul to Paul. We need to learn to wait upon the Lord in our jobs, our relationships and our daily walk with Him.

God, You know we don't want to pray for patience because we don't want to have to go through what we would have to go through to get it. But God, we do trust You that this process, which does take time, is for our good. We thank You that You are at work within us and around us to make us mature and complete, not lacking anything. When the trials get rough and seem to go on and on, help us to remember the goal and let You do Your work in us. We love You, God. Amen.

May 1

I seek you with all my heart; do not let me stray from your commands.
—*Psalm 119:10*

DR. TONY EVANS, SENIOR PASTOR OF OAK Cliff Bible Fellowship in Dallas, Texas, tells about a loggerhead sea turtle that gave birth on a beach and then became disoriented. Instead of going back into the water, it began walking away from the sea. Fortunately, a ranger saw what was happening and knew that if the turtle continued to distance herself from her natural habitat, she would die. Springing into action, the ranger flipped the turtle over, attached a chain to it, and, using a jeep, dragged it out into the sea. Since the sea turtles can weigh 300 pounds or more, that was no small feat.

Sometimes, God provides a similar rescue for us. We may complain and be confused because we feel like our life is turned upside-down and we don't understand why this is happening to us, but God has our best interest at heart. He is merely getting us headed again in the right direction.

God, thank You for not allowing us to continue to stray in the wrong direction. Thank You for doing whatever it takes to get us back on track again. Keep us in the place where we can find nourishment, grow, and continue to produce. In Jesus' name, Amen.

May 2

So Joshua said to the Israelites: "How long will you wait before you begin to take possession of the land that the LORD, the God of your fathers, has given you?"

—Joshua 18:3

IT IS MORE COMMON NOW IN RESTAURANTS for those who take orders and bring food to the table to be called *servers* instead of *waiters*. This is an appropriate change because the new term is much more descriptive of what these persons actually do. *Waiting*, in that sense, has always meant *serving*—not just standing or sitting around, pausing and doing nothing.

Whenever we wait on the Lord, we are using an action verb. Joshua saw that the Israelites were simply *waiting* and doing nothing, so he challenged them: "How long will you wait before you begin to take possession of the land that the Lord. . .has given you?" God may be asking that of us today. What has He given to us that we need to take possession of? How long have we been just standing by and doing nothing while God's provision is right there waiting for us to receive it?

Lord, forgive us for calling our laziness "waiting on God." Spur us to get up and start taking possession of all that You have for us. Let us remember that "waiting" is "serving," and help us to seek ways to serve our God. Amen.

May 3

Your beauty should not come from outward adornment, such as braided hair and the wearing of gold jewelry and fine clothes. Instead, it should be that of your inner self, the unfading beauty of a gentle and quiet spirit, which is of great worth in God's sight.

—1 Peter 3:3-4

ONE YEAR WHEN OUR SON JALON WAS in grade school, he volunteered to take candy to a Valentine's Day party in his class at school. His mother went out and bought lots of candy at a popular discount department store. However, he apparently wanted to make some sort of an impression that year because he wanted her to take the candy from that discount store bag and put it in another bag. He was embarrassed by a discount store bag and wanted to mask it.

How many times do we try to mask who we are? Rather than actually changing ourselves on the inside, we simply change our outward appearance and think we're fooling people. Now, there was nothing wrong with the candy my wife bought for Jalon's class. It was good, popular name-brand candy. But for some of us, we are hiding greedy, bitter, angry, un-Christlike spirits in beautiful dresses or fine suits. We need to work on making the inside as beautiful as the outside.

God, we confess that we sometimes try to look good on the outside while we know that there are qualities and attitudes on the inside that we need to change. Forgive us for trying to look like something we're not. Let the beauty of Jesus be apparent within our spirits. In His name we pray, Amen.

May 4

The LORD had said to Abram, "Leave your country, your people and your father's household and go to the land I will show you. I will make you into a great nation...." So Abram left, as the LORD had told him...Abram was seventy-five years old when he set out from Haran.... Abraham was a hundred years old when his son Isaac was born to him.

—Genesis 12:1-2, 4; 21:5

ABRAM SPENT TWO AND A HALF DECADES without children before becoming the "father of the faithful." God promised him when he lived in Haran that He would make him a great nation if he was obedient in going out as He told him. So, Abram obeyed God and went forth in faith into his destiny, into his promise. Yet, twenty-five years elapsed before he received what God had promised.

How long are we willing to wait upon the Lord? Abram wasn't patient, either. He tried to help God accomplish His promise by having a child with someone who could easily have children, with someone who didn't need anything special from God to produce a son. But that was not the child God promised, and Abram was still Abram when Ishmael was born. It wasn't until God had prepared Abram and could change his name to Abraham that He could fulfill His promise and His purpose. It was only then that Isaac was born. Rather than focusing on trying to get God's promises to come true, let's focus on letting God make us who we need to be so that His promises can be fulfilled.

God, it blows our minds when we realize that we are speaking with the very same God with whom Abraham spoke, the very same God who was at work in the life of Abraham, the very same God who said, "I will. . ." and did. God, we know that You, being that very same God, can keep promises to us as well and can bring us into our destiny. Transform us, God, from Abrams into Abrahams. In Jesus' name, Amen.

May 5

"In my distress I called to the Lord, and he answered me. From the depths of the grave I called for help, and you listened to my cry."

—Jonah 2:2

ALL PRO DAD SPOKESPERSON, NBC FOOTBALL ANALYST, and former coach of the Indianapolis Colts Tony Dungy has a son who can't feel pain. Jordon has a rare congenital disorder that allows him to feel things, but not the sensation of pain. Without that ability to feel pain, he doesn't know if the water is too hot before he steps into a shower, if he is getting a blister from new shoes that aren't yet fitting properly, or if he has a headache or abdominal pain that needs attention.

Pain serves as a warning signal for us. It lets us know that something isn't right and we need to make a change immediately before we do further harm to our bodies. If we are healthy and normal, we don't like pain, but pain is actually a great blessing to us. Even spiritually, pain can cause us to stop offending behavior, change bad attitudes, and draw closer to God.

Lord, let us always remember that we can call upon You when we are in pain. If pain causes us to seek You, it is working together for our good and not for evil. In Jesus' name, Amen.

In God I trust; I will not be afraid. What can man do to me?

—Psalm 56:11

WHEN MY CHILDREN WERE YOUNG AND I took them to the doctor for immunizations, they couldn't understand when I would ignore the look in their eyes that said, "Daddy, stop him! Daddy, don't let him hurt me!" Sometimes, I would even help the doctor by holding them down so that he could give them the immunizations they needed. My sons couldn't understand then what I was doing, but as their father, I had to do what was in their best interest.

Our heavenly Father may sometimes seem to be allowing things that we don't understand. From our perspective, He does not appear to be doing the right thing—the thing that is in our best interest. But we have to know that we can trust Him. No matter how things appear, we know that God is worthy of our trust.

Father, help us to remember that You love us, and even when we don't understand, we can trust You. Help us to remember that You see what we don't see and You know what we don't know. Help us to trust You so that we won't be ashamed one day for thinking we knew best. In Jesus' name, Amen.

May 7

Therefore I will boast all the more gladly about my weaknesses, so that Christ's power may rest on me. That is why, for Christ's sake, I delight in weaknesses, in insults, in hardships, in persecutions, in difficulties. For when I am weak, then I am strong.

—*2 Corinthians 12:9-10*

I RECENTLY LEARNED THAT WHEN GOLF BALLS were originally manufactured, they were smooth. It was discovered, however, that dented balls traveled farther. So now, all golf balls are made with the characteristic little dents, or "dimples," in them.

We may think that if life were just smooth and we had no "dents" to experience, we would just sail along perfectly. But God knows better. He knows that lives without any dents don't go as far. So, the next time we experience another "imperfection" in our "perfect" life scenario, let us remember that God has allowed it to help us go farther.

God, we trust that what we see as flaws in the flow of our lives are instead the very things that will make our lives go farther and help us to reach our destination. We thank You even for those dents—that they don't appear randomly but are ordered in perfect precision by the One who knows exactly how our lives are to flow. In the name of that One we pray, Amen.

But they did not listen or pay attention; instead, they followed the stubborn inclinations of their evil hearts. They went backward and not forward.

—*Jeremiah 7:24*

OUR BODIES ARE DESIGNED TO GO FORWARD, not backwards. Our eyes look ahead of us, our ears hear from the front, and our feet are pointed to go forward. It is a natural thing that we should move forward. Whenever we see someone walking backwards, that person stands out and looks awkward because it is not the way our bodies were intended to move.

We need to keep moving forward toward our destiny. Just as it is true in the natural realm, it is true in the spiritual realm as well. Your destiny is never behind you! If you intend to reach the purpose of God for your life, you have to keep moving ahead.

God, there are a lot of things that could make us want to go backward instead of forward. There is fear of the unknown, laziness, a longing for an easier time, a slip back into the things we did before we committed our lives to Christ, and a host of other things. But You never intended us to walk backwards. You have plans and purposes for our lives, and we can only find them as we walk forward into our destiny. Help us, O God, to keep heading forward. In Jesus' name, Amen.

May 9

But the pot he was shaping from the clay was marred in his hands; so the potter formed it into another pot, shaping it as seemed best to him.
—*Jeremiah 18:4*

I WAS COMING BACK INTO TOWN AFTER being away preaching. When I talked on the phone to my wife Sharon, she told me I was going to get stuck in the driveway. She said there had been a really heavy snowstorm, and the driveway was covered under the snow. She said she didn't get stuck in her vehicle, but she was sure I would get stuck in mine. When I got there, I tried to prove her wrong. While I was at the end of the driveway, I lined up my car with the garage doors, and I floored it—and I got stuck. Even rocking the car, I couldn't get unstuck. So, how did Sharon get through when I couldn't? She has an SUV that has the capability to change to four-wheel drive.

As I thought later on about that incident, the Holy Spirit told me that He can give us the capability of changing when we're facing obstacles so that we can get through them while others get stuck. He is the potter, and we are the clay. God can make us and remake us as seems best to Him.

Father, we find comfort in knowing that You can change us. You can transform us so that whatever situation we face in life, we can be more than conquerors. You can give strength to the weak; can make us walk straight if we're prone to walking crooked; and can empower us when we are powerless within ourselves. Help us to get through our current situations either by changing the circumstances or by changing us. Amen.

May 10

At dusk they got up and went to the camp of the Arameans. When they reached the edge of the camp, not a man was there.

—2 Kings 7:5

THE VERSE FOR TODAY COMES FROM AN Old Testament story about four men with leprosy who were between the proverbial rock and a hard place. They reasoned that if they stayed where they were, outside the gates of the city, they would die. If they went into the city, because of a famine in the land, they would still die. So they decided they might as well go to the camp of their enemy and surrender. If their enemy spared their lives, they would live; if their enemy killed them, they would die—but at least they would have done something. What they didn't realize is that at the very time they got up and started moving, God dealt with their enemies and scared them all away.

How long will we let fear keep us bound in indecision? How long will we let fear make us immobile? We need to trust that when God shows us a way out, even if it is through the camp of our enemies, He can deal with those enemies. But as long as we sit still in fear and do nothing, He waits as well. Let's remember that it was at dusk that the men with leprosy got up and started moving, and it was at dusk that God scared away their enemies.

God, give us the courage to act upon our faith. We say we know that "it is He who will tread down our enemies," but we never give You that opportunity. We try to play it safe. We sit still and sometimes die in that situation because we are afraid to move forward in faith. Give us courage, God, to trust You. In Christ's name, Amen.

May 11

Very early on the first day of the week, just after sunrise, they were on their way to the tomb and they asked each other, "Who will roll the stone away from the entrance of the tomb?"

—*Mark 16:2-3*

AS THE WOMEN WERE WALKING TO THE tomb to finish the burial process for Jesus, they were wondering who would roll the stone away for them. They didn't know how they were going to fulfill their purpose, but they were walking toward it anyway. To their amazement, when they arrived, they found the stone had already been rolled away.

We may experience that in our own lives as well. We may be facing a formidable obstacle that lies between us and our purpose, our mission. But while we're wondering about it, trying to figure out how we're going to handle it, God has already got it worked out. We just need to keep heading in that direction in faith.

God, thank You that You are not dependent upon us to do everything that needs to be done in the fulfillment of our destiny. You have countless resources at Your disposal and people everywhere who are willing to serve You. Let us be like the women who went to Jesus' tomb—not knowing how they were going to accomplish their purpose but continuing to move to the place they needed to be. Amen.

May 12

And without faith it is impossible to please God, because anyone who comes to him must believe that he exists and that he rewards those who earnestly seek him.

—*Hebrews 11:6*

WHEN PLANS WERE MADE FOR THE FIRST meeting of New Beginnings Fellowship Church, our congregation's second church plant, a local school was the only viable place for that meeting to be held. At the 9:30 service at Eastern Star Church on Sunday, then Associate Pastor James Jackson, who had been named pastor of New Beginnings, announced there would be a meeting at the new location on Thursday. But he added that the school board, which had yet to approve the use of the school, didn't meet until Tuesday. The announcement was made in faith, without knowing how the vote would turn out just two days prior to the scheduled meeting at that location. But to his great surprise and delight, a woman present at the 9:30 service sent word to Pastor Jackson that she was on the board and would endorse their request, helping to ensure that the vote would go in his favor.

God works it out while we're walking it out in faith. Pastor Jackson *could* have waited until after the vote and then have tried to find a way to get word to all those who were joining him at that meeting, but then he would have missed the opportunity to please God. And he would have missed the blessing of knowing that God had planted a key person in his midst that morning who would be an instrument He would use to bring about the answer to his prayer. We miss so much when we avoid opportunities to live by faith.

God, teach us to live by faith, that we may please You and receive blessings of delight. Amen.

May 13

The LORD commanded us to obey all these decrees and to fear the LORD our God, so that we might always prosper and be kept alive, as is the case today.

—*Deuteronomy 6:24*

IN 2007, A SPACE SHUTTLE ATLANTIS LAUNCH was delayed because of a problem with fuel sensors. Some argued it would be okay to break the rules and launch anyhow, but the ones who won the debate argued that the safety system was there for a reason: if the fuel ran low, the engine shut down and everything could fall apart.

Some of us ignore God's safety system in the Word. We try to take off in education, business deals, and relationships—only to find that everything falls apart because we are violating the safety rules. Frequently in the Bible, God says, "If you…then I…." Some of us try to claim what God has promised without first doing what He has commanded.

God, forgive us for expecting Your blessings without first following Your instructions, Your commands. Teach us to obey You and follow Your guidance so that we may truly find life and prosperity. In Jesus' name, Amen.

May 14

What the locust swarm has left the great locusts have eaten; what the great locusts have left the young locusts have eaten; what the young locusts have left other locusts have eaten.

—Joel 1:4

THE KING JAMES VERSION OF THIS SCRIPTURE uses different names in place of "locusts" each time: the palmerworm, the locust, the cankerworm, and the caterpillar. But the footnote in the New International Version says the translators aren't sure what each of the four different words stands for, so it just uses "locusts" each time. Regardless exactly what they were, the point is that they were all small intruders. Any one worm, locust, or caterpillar could easily be stepped on and squashed. But when they come in swarms as a vast army, we can't handle them.

A lot of little things can destroy all we have. If we don't deal with the little things one at a time and allow them to build up, they will wreak havoc in our lives. For example, if we let the sun go down on our anger one night, the next morning we will be a little disgruntled. If we go to bed angry night after night without resolving the conflict, one morning we will wake up enraged out of all proportion. We need to deal with the little things before they become unmanageable and take over our lives.

Dear God, we confess that we have been letting a lot of little things build up over time. Whereas once we were simply perturbed, now we are furious. Whereas once we thought we would someday like a car similar to what our friend bought, now we are green with envy because he has it and we don't. Whereas once we enjoyed an occasional splurge by eating an ice cream cone, now we have gained over fifty pounds and our freezers, refrigerators, and cupboards are loaded with all sorts of sweets. The locusts have taken over, God, and we need Your power to overcome them. Please help us. In Christ's name, we pray, Amen.

May 15

Know then in your heart that as a man disciplines his son, so the LORD your God disciplines you.

—*Deuteronomy 8:5*

J. ALLEN, MY OLDEST SON, IS TWENTY years old, and a senior in college. He has done well in school, has a bright future ahead of him, and is a good young man. But he is who he is at twenty because of the discipline I gave him when he was four and five.

Just as we correct our children now so that they can gain long-term positive benefits, so God disciplines us as well. God wants us to succeed in life, He has a purpose and plan that He wants to work out in our lives, and He wants us to be Christlike and to do good things in this world. But in order for us to be equipped to handle what is yet to come, God has to discipline us in the now.

Father, thank You for loving us enough to take time to discipline us. We certainly don't enjoy it; it is painful and unpleasant. But, God, we know that it is for our good, and we know that You discipline us in love. Help us to learn quickly the lessons You need to teach us along the way so that we can be prepared for all that You have planned for us. In Jesus' name, Amen.

May 16

"They gave Moses this account: "We went into the land to which you sent us, and it does flow with milk and honey! Here is its fruit. But the people who live there are powerful, and the cities are fortified and very large.... We seemed like grasshoppers in our own eyes, and we looked the same to them."
—*Numbers 13:27-28, 33*

A WOMAN IN INDIANAPOLIS WAS VERY DISTRAUGHT because she couldn't get a home improvement loan. Just a few weeks later, however, she came to church overjoyed and praising God. One of seven tornadoes that hit Indianapolis did severe damage to her home. Now her insurance has taken care of her home improvements.

Sometimes things don't happen the way we want or hope; sometimes we must first go through difficulties to receive our blessing. The Israelites had no doubt envisioned themselves simply walking happily into the land God had promised them. They didn't know there would be giants in the land that they would have to overcome before they could live there.

God, by nature we want easy roads and paths of joy. But You have never invited us to live in a fairy tale. You have called us to serve You in a real world with real challenges, and we must often overcome difficulties to get to our blessings. Help us not to lose heart or fail to keep pressing through when our blessings are delayed. Help us to know that You are bringing us into our destiny even though we have to first go through a tornado or get rid of some giants that are scaring us. It is in Your name and by Your power that we go forward. Amen.

May 17

But the LORD provided a great fish to swallow Jonah, and Jonah was inside the fish three days and three nights.

—Jonah 1:17

TWO YEARS AGO, A HOUSE CAUGHT FIRE in Muncie, Indiana. It played in the news as a human interest story because there were some teens and young adults asleep in the basement, and a dog in the house woke them up and saved their lives. One of the people interviewed said the dog didn't just wake him up, however—it *bit* him!

Sometimes God will let a "dog" bite us to keep us from being destroyed. Being bitten may hurt momentarily, but it keeps us from being destroyed. Sometimes God may even "provide" a great fish to swallow us up to keep us from going our own wayward path. God will provide whatever His children need to keep them from destruction.

God, we thank You for dogs that bite us and for fish that swallow us whole. Whatever it is that we need to keep us fully alive, we thank You for providing that for us. Amen.

Jesus said to them, "I tell you the truth, unless you eat the flesh of the Son of Man and drink his blood, you have no life in you."

—*John 6:53*

IN 2008, A WINDOW WASHER FELL FORTY-SEVEN stories, nearly 500 feet, from a skyscraper in Manhattan, and he survived. His doctors said it was even likely that he could walk again. Even though he experienced a lot of brokenness, the doctors were able to keep him alive by giving him twenty-four units of blood and additional units of blood plasma.

The blood of Jesus can allow us to live as well. According to Romans 3:23, we have all fallen short of the glory of God, but Jesus Himself told us that we can have life through His blood that was shed for us on Calvary. Can you imagine any reason why the window washer would have refused to receive the blood that allowed him to live? Why then would we reject the blood of Jesus that is offered to us so that we can live?

God, we thank You today for the blood of Christ that cleanses us from all sin and gives us eternal life. It is with deep humility and gratitude that we receive such a precious gift from Your hands. Amen.

May 19

Then Jesus declared, "I am the bread of life. He who comes to me will never go hungry, and he who believes in me will never be thirsty."

—John 6:35

JESUS CHOSE BREAD TO REPRESENT WHO HE IS. What would we choose to represent who we are? What do we represent to our spouses and our children? To them, are we money? Clothes? A house? A car? What do we represent to others? Are we a television? A job? A party? A ballgame?

Jesus chose to be represented by something that could be internalized to provide nourishment and strength. What would our choice provide for others?

God, when we think of Jesus as the bread that can be eaten to keep us from ever going hungry, it does cause us to wonder what people see in us. It causes us to stop and think even more deeply about how we want to be identified by them. Help us, God, to have something to offer others that is life-giving and enduring. In Christ's name, Amen.

May 20

For if, when we were God's enemies, we were reconciled to him through the death of his Son, how much more, having been reconciled, shall we be saved through his life! Not only is this so, but we also rejoice in God through our Lord Jesus Christ, through whom we have now received reconciliation.

—*Romans 5:10-11*

I LOVE TO EAT AT FIVE-STAR RESTAURANTS. When you first walk in, a maitre d' or a couple of hostesses greet you warmly. One of them escorts you to your seat. As soon as you are seated, someone comes and unfolds your napkin for you. If you drop a crumb on the table, someone comes almost immediately and wipes it off. Your water glasses are kept filled. And when you order, the server tells you all about each entrée: where the meat or fish came from, what size it is, how it is prepared, etc. You are told everything, except only rarely the name of the chef who prepared it.

Some of us act as if we're working in a five-star restaurant. We may tell people what university or seminary we went to, what job we hold, how much money we make, or fine qualities about ourselves, but too seldom do we tell people that it was Jesus who prepared the way of salvation for us and that it is through Him that we experience this abundant life.

God, let us never forget to tell others about Jesus. Let His name come quickly to our lips, and may we praise Him continually for all He has done. In His name, Amen.

May 21

For since the beginning of the world men have not heard, nor perceived by the ear, neither hath the eye seen, O God, beside thee, what he hath prepared for him that waiteth for him.

—*Isaiah 64:4 (KJV)*

WHEN I ASK MY SON K. J., WHO is eleven, to go into the kitchen and fix a plate of food for me, I can trust him to put the food on a plate and bring it to me. I am fully aware, however, that it was my wife Sharon who *prepared* the meal, and there is a difference between serving it and preparing it.

We need to keep in mind Who has *prepared* things for us. Our boss may recommend us for a raise, but it is God who *prepared* it. Our company may offer us a promotion, but it is God who *prepared* it. A university may give us a scholarship, but it is God who *prepared* it. Let's never confuse the server with the One who *prepared* what we needed.

God, we thank You today for all of the good things You have prepared for us. We have appreciation for those from whom we directly receive a blessing, but our overflowing gratitude and praise is reserved for You because it is Your hands that prepare it. Amen.

May 22

When the LORD your God brings you into... a land with large, flourishing cities you did not build, houses filled with all kinds of good things you did not provide, wells you did not dig, and vineyards and olive groves you did not plant— then when you eat and are satisfied, be careful that you do not forget the LORD, who brought you out of Egypt, out of the land of slavery.

—Deuteronomy 6:10-12

ALZHEIMER'S IS A TERRIBLE DISEASE THAT CAUSES a person to forget a little at a time until finally the person can't even remember his or her own children.

Some of us have spiritual Alzheimer's disease. Little by little, we forget the things Jesus has done for us until finally we think we've gotten that degree, we've gotten that job, or we've gotten that spiritual gift all by ourselves.

God, we remember today all the good things You have done for us. We are thankful for the way Your hand has provided for all of our needs and fulfilled so many of our desires. O God, let us never forget the One who has cared for us, delivered us, and watched over us all our days. Amen.

May 23

Come near to God and he will come near to you.

—James 4:8

IT'S INTERESTING THE WAY THAT WORDS CHANGE in meaning over time. Today, when we say, "You're tripping," it doesn't mean you have physically gone away on a trip. It means that even though you're right in front of me, your reasoning and rationale are so far out that you are not even relating to me. Sometimes we say someone *is* "a trip." That obviously doesn't literally mean that a person has turned into a journey but that he or she is acting funny, a little bizarre. To say someone is "gone" can mean that he or she is high on drugs or alcohol.

Some of the journeys we go on are not always geographical. Some of our longest journeys are spiritual, emotional, or psychological. That's why we can say someone is distant from us. He or she can be physically standing right next to us; but mentally, emotionally and/or spiritually, we aren't connecting. We need to stop tripping with God. Some of us may be sitting right there in church every Sunday and yet be distant from Him. We may even be going through the motions of praying or reading the Bible every day, and yet we aren't connecting with God at all.

God, we have no desire to be tripping with You, to be distant from You, or to be a trip in Your eyes. We want a closer walk with You. Even now, we draw near to You once again and thank You for the promise that You will draw near to us as well. Amen.

See, I have refined you, though not as silver; I have tested you in the furnace of affliction.

—*Isaiah 48:10*

REFINERS TAKE SILVER WITH ITS DROSS, WASTE and impurities, and put it into a fire where all of these are burned off, and the pure silver comes forth. Fire destroys and develops—that which is worthless scum is destroyed, and the silver itself is perfected.

God has a purification process just like the refiner of silver. He burns the worthless, the unrighteous, the impure out of us; and when we come forth from the furnace of affliction, we come out refined, developed, and ready to be used.

God, You know how painful the furnace of affliction is for us, yet we know how needful it is. Thank You that You never take us through heated situations in order to harm us, but You allow them in order to make us better. And thank You, God, that You never keep us in the furnace even a second longer than is necessary for our good. We trust You. In Jesus' name, Amen.

May 25

Wash away all my iniquity and cleanse me from my sin.

—Psalm 51:2

MALACHI 3:2 SPEAKS OF THE LORD AS being not only like a refiner's fire but also like fuller's soap. A fuller was a person who cleaned the wool of the sheep to make it usable to be spun into thread and woven into cloth. The fuller's soap was a caustic alkali that was used in the cleaning process. The fuller would put the cleansing agent into water, rub the garment together, and beat it on rocks to get it clean. It was the friction combined with the cleansing agent that got the stains out and made the wool fit to use.

 Whenever we start going through some friction, we need to consider that God may be taking the blood of Jesus and creating friction in our lives in order to take out some stains. While it may be a painful process, it should not upset us spiritually because it means that God is getting ready to use us. God has a purpose for us and is preparing us for His use.

Lord, thank You for considering us usable in Your kingdom. Thank You that this process of friction that we are experiencing is not meant to wipe us out, but to make us ready. Thank You for the blood of Jesus that does cleanse us from all sin, and thank You that there is no stain too deep for Him to remove. In Christ's name, Amen.

May 26

For you were like sheep going astray, but now you have returned to the Shepherd and Overseer of your souls.

—*1 Peter 2:25*

THERE WAS A LITTLE DOG NAMED TOUGHIE who got lost on the south side of Indianapolis. Her master took good care of her, but she somehow strayed away. She was finally found by someone who noticed that she was lost, dirty, and alone. The person put Toughie in a van and took her to the Humane Society. There, they found that her master had put a microchip in her shoulder so that if she was ever lost, she could be returned to him. When she was with her master and things were good between them, he had put something into her that would bring her back to him if she ever strayed.

How much more did our heavenly Father put His Holy Spirit within us so that if we should stray, the Spirit would convict us and cause us to return to God!

Holy Spirit, we thank You for Your faithfulness in drawing us back to Yourself. We thank You that You continually remind us of who we are and Whose we are. Thank You for convicting us when we start to go astray and not letting us get lost from Your sight. Amen.

May 27

And we, who with unveiled faces all reflect the Lord's glory, are being transformed into his likeness with ever-increasing glory, which comes from the Lord, who is the Spirit.

—*2 Corinthians 3:18*

WHEN A COUPLE WHO ARE SEPARATED OR divorced tell me they are going to get back together, I want to be happy for them, but I can't unless they can give me a good answer to a question that I have to ask them. I ask them, "What has changed?" If nothing has changed, if everything is the same as it was when they were together, getting back together is meaningless. It won't last. A heart, a disposition, a mindset, a behavior pattern—something—has got to change if they are going to make it together.

That same question is appropriate for someone who says he or she is going to get back together with God. God is the same yesterday, today, and forever, so He isn't changing. We have to let Jesus change us so that we can be one with God.

Father, we thank You that, as Your disciples, we are always changing. You transformed us when we first came to Christ, and all things became new. But daily, as we walk with You, meditate upon Your Word, and spend time talking with You, You continue to make us more and more like Jesus. Thank You for Your transforming power at work in our lives. Amen.

May 28

One man gives freely, yet gains even more; another withholds unduly, but comes to poverty.

—Proverbs 11:24

AS WE HAVE INCREASINGLY BECOME A MORE litigious society—everybody wanting to sue everybody in court—prenuptial contracts have become more common. Two people say they want to become one in marriage; however, they want to make sure that if anything happens to the marriage, their half of the "one" gets a better deal. So they vow to love and honor each other all the days of their lives, but they have a legal agreement that says they will each hang on to whatever he or she had before the marriage.

Some of us want God to sign a prenuptial agreement. We may be willing to give God our time and our talents, but we want to hang on to our money. A prenup normally means that somebody who has something is trying to protect his or her large resources. In our case, how could we possibly sign a prenup with God? We have nothing. God is the one who owns everything. Everything we have has come from Him.

God, cause us to be ashamed of ourselves for not wanting to give back to You what is rightfully Yours anyhow. You are so gracious and give to us so freely. Yet when You ask us to give You a mere tithe and offering from all that we have received, we try to say we can't afford to do that, or we offer one-tenth of what we have and not a penny more. God, teach us that our stinginess will lead to poverty—not only of money, but of spirit as well. Forgive us, God, we ask in Jesus' name, Amen.

May 29

"But go, tell his disciples and Peter, 'He is going ahead of you into Galilee. There you will see him, just as he told you.'"

—*Mark 16:7*

I WAS WATCHING THE GREEN BAY PACKERS playing against the Seattle Seahawks during Green Bay's first game in the second round of the playoffs. Ryan Grant, a running back with the Green Bay Packers who had played with Notre Dame, was starting as a rookie. He fumbled a ball at the beginning of the game and Seattle scored. During the Packers' second series, Grant fumbled again and Seattle scored. It was 14-0, and it was Ryan Grant's fault because he kept dropping the ball. The next series, the quarterback, Brett Favre, handed the ball right to Ryan Grant. This time he held onto the ball. He rushed more than two hundred yards for a franchise record. He also scored three touchdowns and crossed the goal rushing for another franchise record. Green Bay ended up winning the game 42-20 and went on to the next level of the playoffs, and it was all because of Ryan Grant. He had his greatest victories and got the advantage of going to the next level *after* he kept dropping the ball. This is because after he dropped the ball, he didn't drop his head. He went to the sidelines, got instructions from the coaches, received encouragement from his teammates, and then went back out determined that even though he had dropped the ball the first two times, he was going to hang on to it the next time.

God will give us the ball again. God is the God of another chance. After Jesus rose from the dead, He knew how bad Peter would feel because of his denial of Him. So, when He sent for His disciples, He mentioned Peter by name so that Peter would know he was still in the game.

God, we thank You today that You don't abandon us when we mess up. Even when we try so hard, sometimes we still fail to do, say, or be what we know You want of us. We feel so ashamed and so sorry in those moments. Thank You, God, that in those very moments, You call us by name and say, "Come on. Let's go on." Thank You, God, for such great love, grace, and forgiveness. Amen.

May 30

Those whom I love I rebuke and discipline. So be earnest, and repent.
—Revelation 3:19

A FEW YEARS AGO, A CRUISE SHIP was attacked by pirates off the coast of Somalia. If they had been able to capture the ship, they could have held it and the passengers for ransom. The captain of the cruise ship, however, did not stop moving. Instead, he implemented his security system and changed course.

That's how we should handle our troubles. Our salvation is secure in Jesus Christ; but since we are those whom God loves, He does rebuke and discipline us when we do wrong so that we will repent. Repentance is a matter of changing direction. Later on, I learned that the name of the cruise ship attacked was *Spirit*. Likewise, when we're moving in the Holy Spirit, everything is going to be all right.

God, as we read that verse for today, we know that it is Your love prompting You to let us know we need to change course in specific areas of our lives. Help us not to keep going in the same direction and find ourselves in deeper trouble. We repent, God, even now and determine, with Your help, to turn around and follow close after You. In Jesus' name, Amen.

May 31

For although they knew God, they neither glorified him as God nor gave thanks to him, but their thinking became futile and their foolish hearts were darkened.

—*Romans 1:21*

I WAS HAVING TROUBLE ONE DAY RECEIVING a fax from my assistant Lisa Rattler. I checked to make sure that there was paper in the fax machine, and everything looked okay. But then I noticed a message on the fax machine reading, "Paper Jam." Even though the machine had paper, something was twisted or crooked on the inside, so nothing was coming out.

Sometimes our own minds get twisted, and we become crooked in our thinking. In those areas, we need to be adjusted in order for us to be productive once again.

God, we seem not to be producing anything right now. We know we should be flowing with ideas for serving You, doing good to others, and growing in our relationship with You. But instead, there is nothing coming forth. We ask, therefore, that You adjust us. Remove whatever may be keeping us from operating as we should, and let us get back on track so that we may fulfill that for which we have been created. In Christ's name, Amen.

June 1

The Spirit of God has made me; the breath of the Almighty gives me life.
—Job 33:4

WHEN MY KIDS WERE LITTLE, THEY played a lot of electronic games. I was playing with them one day when the game froze up. I was ready to give up, thinking it was broken and had to be thrown away. But one of my sons took the disc out, blew on it, put it back in, and it worked fine.

Sometimes God has to take us out of a situation, let the Holy Spirit breathe on us, and then put us back in so that we function properly.

Holy Spirit, breathe on us the breath of life. Restore our ability to function as God intends for us to function. Don't let us be cast aside as worthless, but make us once again usable in Your hands. In Jesus' name, Amen.

June 2

But when you give to the needy, do not let your left hand know what your right hand is doing, so that your giving may be in secret. Then your Father, who sees what is done in secret, will reward you.... But when you pray, go into your room, close the door and pray to your Father, who is unseen. Then your Father, who sees what is done in secret, will reward you.... But when you fast, put oil on your head and wash your face, so that it will not be obvious to men that you are fasting, but only to your Father, who is unseen; and your Father, who sees what is done in secret, will reward you.

—Matthew 6:3-4, 6, 17-18

ONE OF THE MOST REWARDING EXPERIENCES OF my life is when I graduated from college. I was one of the first ones to graduate from college in my family, after my mother and an uncle. My graduation was an answer to my grandmother's prayer, my mother's prayer, and my prayer. My whole family came down to Bishop College to watch me cross that stage and get my diploma. It was very rewarding to me to publicly receive that reward. But then it dawned on me that even though the reward came in public, all the hard work leading up to that day was done in private.

That's the way it is in the kingdom of God. There are some things done quietly and behind the scenes, but God rewards us publicly.

God, let us be content to do what You ask of us quietly and behind the scenes. We know that it is up to You to decide whether to reward us openly, but our work is to be done in secret—only for You. In Jesus' name, Amen.

June 3

"Give, and it will be given to you. A good measure, pressed down, shaken together and running over, will be poured into your lap. For with the measure you use, it will be measured to you."

—*Luke 6:38*

EVERY NOW AND THEN, WHEN I TAKE my kids to the movies, they always want to get something from the concession stand. It doesn't matter whether they've just eaten or not; they always want something. So we order popcorn. I notice that the counterperson will grab a box and scoop popcorn into it. Then, even though it looks already full to me, he or she stops and shakes it down, puts in some more, stops and shakes it down again to get out all the air pockets; and then puts in even more popcorn. When the box is finally handed to me, it is full and running over.

That's the way God does even to us: He shakes us and pushes us down until we're full and running over. It is only then that He sends us into the world to feed hungry souls, even as Jesus broke the bread and fish and distributed them to feed a hungry multitude. God isn't going to send us out empty or only half-full. He is going to make sure we have enough within us so that we can meet the needs of those to whom He sends us. As we give out, God continues the process, so that we can give generously and find that He continues to fill us generously.

God, help us to give generously from all that You have placed within us. As long as we keep giving out, You give back to us that much and more. In that way, we are continually overflowing. Let us not fear or reject that shaking process, because we know that is how we become of value in Your kingdom. Please let us never become empty or partially filled, worthy only to be tossed aside. Continue to fill and use us, we pray, O God. Amen.

June 4

Evening, and morning, and at noon, will I pray, and cry aloud: and he shall hear my voice.

—*Psalm 55:17 (KJV)*

SOME PEOPLE SAY THEY WANT TO GET in shape physically, but if they just go to the gym one time, lift weights one time, and exercise one time, nothing is going to happen. It takes regular exercise over a period of time before they will see a difference.

The same is true in prayer and giving. Both of those spiritual disciplines come with promises from God—promises of answers to prayer and promises that we will receive when we give. But we can't just pray once or just give to God once and expect to see a difference in our lives. We have to keep praying and keep giving, and just like when we exercise the body, eventually we'll see the results in our lives.

God, we are too often more willing to practice physical disciplines than spiritual ones. We are willing to get up early and go to a gym and work out till we're sweating and tired, but we don't want to spend that same amount of time in prayer and intercession. We will spend an inordinate amount of money buying what we want for ourselves, but then we want to give so little to care for Your kingdom. Yet we still expect results. God help us! Amen.

June 5

"And when you pray, do not be like the hypocrites, for they love to pray standing in the synagogues and on the street corners to be seen by men. I tell you the truth, they have received their reward in full."

—*Matthew 6:5*

THE KING JAMES VERSION OF THE BIBLE is still one of my favorite translations. The language is beautiful and poetic. I enjoy reading it and, because I grew up with it, I understand the language even though it is not how we speak today. The King James Version of the Bible was commissioned in the sixteenth century by the king of England, so it was written in the language of that day. It was not written in the languages that Jesus, His disciples, or any of the people in the Bible spoke; instead, it was written in the language of a British ruler in the sixteenth century.

What I don't understand is why some Christians in America today try to pray in sixteenth-century King James English when they aren't living in that time period. That is not God's native language. God understands Swahili. God knows every one of the Chinese dialects. God speaks Tagalog. God knows how to sign! There's no value in trying to speak with "thee's" and "thou's"; God isn't impressed with that. When we pray, we need to talk to God just as we talk with one another. That's what God will hear.

God, thank You for being a God who wants to communicate with us. Thank You for allowing the Bible to be translated into so many languages so that all around the world people can read Your Word and understand it. And thank You, God, that You know the language of our hearts. You hear the thoughts of our hearts before our words ever reach our tongues. Help us to just be ourselves when we talk with You so that our prayers may be heard. In Jesus' name, Amen.

June 6

Going a little farther, he fell with his face to the ground and prayed, "My Father, if it is possible, may this cup be taken from me. Yet not as I will, but as you will."

—*Matthew 26:39*

DR. JOHN D. MANGRUM, DEAN OF THE chapel at Bishop College when I was there, used to say when he prayed in the pulpit, "Father, make my will Your will so that when I'm doing my will, I'm automatically doing Your will." Dr. Mangrum understood that real prayer is not trying to get God to do what we want *Him* to do; instead, it is aligning our will with what *God* wants to do.

Nowhere do we see this principle lived out more fully than in the life of Jesus. Even He learned to submit His will to the Father. Even when it meant being asked to lay down His life in such a horrific way—not for something He did, but as a sacrifice for *our* sins—He said, "Yet, not as I will, but as You will."

Father, may the same Spirit of Christ that said yes to You and to the cross work within our spirits to say yes to Your will for our lives as well. In Jesus' name, Amen.

June 7

And even the very hairs of your head are all numbered.

—Matthew 10:30

WHEN MY WIFE CAME TO PICK ME up at the airport one day, I began combing my hair in the car. When I looked in the mirror to do that, I noticed that I had three or four strands of gray hair. I was trying to get rid of them, but Sharon said, "No, that gray hair makes you look distinguished." I responded, "That gray hair makes me look *old*!" So I was trying to pull out the gray hairs, but I realized that I was pulling out more black than gray. Then I looked at my comb and saw how many hairs were there. If God knows the number of hairs on my head, He's going to have to keep counting them continually.

Just think of how intimately acquainted God is with us that He would number all of the hairs on our heads. That illustrates for us the level of care and concern that He has for each one of us.

God, how could we ever question Your love and concern for us when You have even numbered the very hairs of our heads? Help us to understand why You told us that. Help us to understand that You want us to know that we are loved by One who knows us intimately. Forgive us for ever doubting that You care about us. In Christ's name, Amen.

June 8

You have been a refuge for the poor, a refuge for the needy in his distress, a shelter from the storm and a shade from the heat.

—*Isaiah 25:4*

IN OKLAHOMA CITY, WHERE TORNADOES FREQUENTLY HIT, a woman decided to invest in reinforcing her closet with steel so that when a tornado came, she and her family could hide in the closet and be safe. She did it just in time. A tornado soon hit her house, and the only thing that remained after the storm was the foundation of her house and the closet. After interviewing the woman and hearing her story, the reporter turned to the camera and said, "It's very expensive to have a closet reinforced, but it's a good investment. It's something you use every day, and then when the storm comes, it keeps you safe."

That's true of prayer as well. We pray every day. We communicate with our heavenly Father from day to day, telling Him what is on our hearts and minds and listening to what He wants to say to us. We delight in His presence and enjoy His company. But on those days when the skies darken, the winds rage around us, and the storms hit, we find that we are safe in His familiar presence.

Father, thank You keeping us safe in the storms. But thank You, too, that You are our God in the everyday routine of life. Both in good days and bad, Your presence makes all the difference. We love You. Amen.

June 9

*"Everything is permissible for me"—but not everything is beneficial.
"Everything is permissible for me"—but I will not be mastered by anything.*
—1 Corinthians 6:12

WHEN I FIRST GOT TO INDIANAPOLIS, THERE was a young woman in our congregation with diabetes. I prayed with her, visited her in the hospital, read scripture, laid hands on her, and anointed her with oil. I did all the things the Bible says to do when someone is sick. But the young woman died. Her doctor told me later, however, that all she needed to do to live was to change her eating habits. Her appetite killed her.

Adam and Eve sinned by eating. Esau traded his birthright for something to eat. The devil's first temptation to Jesus was in the area of food—tempting him to turn stones into bread. We have to avoid letting our appetites control us.

God, forgive us for not acknowledging that food—the wrong kind in the wrong amounts—can be just as harmful to us as the abuse of drugs or alcohol. Forgive us for being critical of others while we wallow in our own sin of gluttony. Help us, God, to break free while there is yet time. Help us to change our eating habits for Your glory and for our good. In Jesus' name, Amen.

June 10

Do you not know that your body is a temple of the Holy Spirit, who is in you, whom you have received from God? You are not your own; you were bought at a price. Therefore honor God with your body.

—1 Corinthians 6:19-20

ABOUT TEN YEARS AGO, MY DOCTOR TOLD me I had high blood pressure. That surprised me because I have been a pseudo-athlete most of my life, and I thought I was in good shape. He told me my blood pressure was so high that I would have to start taking medicine. But the medicine had side effects. It wasn't working for me. It was messing with my body in ways that I couldn't live with, and it wasn't healing me. I told my doctor that the medicine wasn't going to work and he said, "Well, you can change your diet and exercise." "You mean that if I change the way I eat and start exercising, my blood pressure will go down and I won't have to take medicine? Why didn't you tell me this before?" That's when I began running and watching what I eat. I overcame my high blood pressure by eating right and exercising. Now all of my body functions as it's supposed to.

Sometimes, we become our own worst enemies. We don't need a devil to try to kill or destroy us—we are doing it to ourselves. Change isn't easy, but when it comes to our bodies, it can be a life-and-death issue. Many of us would be irate if our church, "God's house," were not kept attractive and maintained well. Yet, we don't treat the temple of the Holy Spirit, our bodies, with the same level of care as we do a church building. There's something wrong with this picture.

God, we stand convicted in Your presence. We acknowledge that we have not cared as we should have for the temple of Your Spirit who lives within us. We've done what we pleased with our bodies, and our carelessness is evident in our health as well as our appearance. Forgive us, God, and help us to change the way we care for Your temple. In Jesus' name, Amen.

June 11

Now to him who is able to do immeasurably more than all we ask or imagine, according to his power that is at work within us, to him be glory in the church and in Christ Jesus throughout all generations, for ever and ever! Amen.

—Ephesians 3:20-21

IUPUI BASKETBALL COACH RON HUNTER TOLD ME about Samaritan's Feet, an organization that gathers thousands of pairs of shoes here in the States and takes them to countries where the people cannot afford to own even one pair of shoes. He went to the athletic director and the president of IUPUI and got permission to coach one game barefoot to try to raise money for this organization. He coached the game against Oakland with a suit on but his feet bare. His goal was to have forty thousand pairs of shoes donated, but he was a guest on a radio show that morning and got fifty thousand pairs of shoes donated before the game even started. By the end of the game, people had donated 110,000 pairs of shoes and an additional twenty thousand dollars in cash. His team also won the game.

When we have the willingness to do what God wants, God will work in our lives. His resources are far greater than our imagination, but if we do nothing, we limit what He can do.

Now to You who are able to do immeasurably more than all we ask or imagine, according to Your power that is at work within us, to You be glory in the church and in Christ Jesus throughout all generations, for ever and ever! Amen.

June 12

Remember the former things, those of long ago; I am God, and there is no other; I am God, and there is none like me. I make known the end from the beginning, from ancient times, what is still to come. I say: My purpose will stand, and I will do all that I please.

—*Isaiah 46:9-10*

WE CAN'T DETERMINE THE GREATNESS OF GOD by our current situation. For some of us, when our circumstances are going great, we believe God is great; when our circumstances are failing, we believe God is failing. We need to remember that our current situation is only a small piece of a very large puzzle. Right now, we can't see how that piece fits, but someday we will see it clearly and know that even during those trying times, God was still great.

We human beings are stuck in the *now*. If we look back to yesterday, that's recollection; if we look ahead to tomorrow, that's speculation. But God sees the past, present, and future all at the same time. He can look around corners. He sees the *when* and the *where*, the *then* and the *there*. He works in our *not yet*. By the time you get from your *right now* to God's *not yet*, your trouble is in the *no longer*.

God, we recognize that we are stuck in the now, but by faith we look to You for our tomorrows. We know that even when we can't see how all the pieces of our puzzling life can possibly fit together, You see the end from the beginning and You are carefully and purposefully arranging each piece. We choose this day to trust You and to declare our confidence in You. In Jesus' name, Amen.

June 13

And we know that all things work together for good to them that love God, to them who are the called according to his purpose.

—Romans 8:28 (KJV)

THE LATE DR. E. K. BAILEY, FOUNDER OF Concord Missionary Baptist Church in Dallas, said that this verse is inclusive, exclusive, and conclusive. It is *inclusive* in that it includes a certain group of people: "and *we* know"— *we* who believe Jesus died on the cross and have accepted salvation through His death and resurrection. It is *exclusive* in that it excludes those who keep rejecting Jesus; we can't stand on promises that don't belong to us—this is a conditional promise. And it is *conclusive* in that it doesn't say we know this "might" happen; we *know* that God is behind the scenes working things together for our good.

People argue about the perfect will of God and the permissive will of God. There is nothing that can happen in this world unless God arranges it or allows it. If God allows it, He is working something together for our good. God has purpose in all He does, even when something evil or bad happens to us. He can take what others do against us and use it *for* us. Job was a rich and righteous man who loved and obeyed God. God removed the hedge of protection that was around Job and allowed the enemy to do bad things to him, but the situation was never out of God's control. At the end of Job's life, he had twice as much as before.

God, we believe You, and we believe in Your promise that all things are working together for our good. We wait now for that to come to pass. In Jesus' name, Amen.

June 14

Praise be to the God and Father of our Lord Jesus Christ, the Father of compassion and the God of all comfort, who comforts us in all our troubles, so that we can comfort those in any trouble with the comfort we ourselves have received from God.

—2 Corinthians 1:3-4

WE HAD A YOUTH CONFERENCE AT OUR church one year, and it closed out with a dance that used contemporary gospel rap music. One of the gospel bands brought little lights to hand out to everyone there. One of the kids grabbed two lights and gave them to me, but I couldn't figure out how to turn them on. Everybody's light was shining but mine. I was still in the dark because I couldn't figure out how to get the light to come on. Another young person, seeing me in the dark, came over and showed me that the light had to be broken before it could be used.

How are we going to tell others that God is a Father to the fatherless, a Mother to the motherless, a Lawyer in a courtroom, or a Doctor in the sickroom unless we have experienced those situations for ourselves? God takes the situations of our lives that could devastate us and uses them to prepare us to help others. The situation breaks us, but God comforts us so that we can comfort others with that same comfort we have received from Him.

Lord, we want to be used of You to help bring comfort to others. We know that it is our hard times, our times of brokenness, that prepare us to minister to others. Help us then not to run from those times as though we believe You no longer love us. Instead, help us to come to You and allow You to comfort us so that we will then have comfort to pass along to others who are in troubling situations. We ask this in the name of the One who suffered for us, Amen.

June 15

He is the God who avenges me, who puts the nations under me, who sets me free from my enemies. You exalted me above my foes; from violent men you rescued me.

—2 Samuel 22:48-49

IN GENESIS, JOSEPH WAS GIVEN A COAT of many colors from his father. His envious brothers beat him, stole his coat, and sold him into slavery. He eventually ended up in prison. But from there, Joseph began to rise up even in the midst of his situation. He was eventually put into a powerful position as the second-in-command in Egypt, where he helped save the world from famine. It was then that even his brothers—the very men who had hurt him and sold him into slavery— came to him for help. God knows how to set us free from our enemies, avenge us, and even lift us up above our foes.

But Joseph recognized that had none of the bad things happened to him, none of the miraculous things would have ever happened either. He would never have been in the position to do such good things for others. Joseph could forgive his brothers, "his enemies," freely when he saw God's hand at work behind the scenes, allowing the evil in order to accomplish the good. Can we see God's hand behind the scenes of our own lives, and trust Him to rescue us, avenge us, and lift us up in His time and His way?

God, we thank You for Your faithfulness to us. Even when it looks as though our enemies are defeating us, You are only setting the scene for our miracle. Thank You that Your Word is true. Thank You that as we obey You and trust You, You will take care of us and deal with our enemies. Amen.

June 16

I know, O LORD, that your laws are righteous, and in faithfulness you have afflicted me. May your unfailing love be my comfort, according to your promise to your servant.

—*Psalm 119:75-76*

THE STORY IS TOLD ABOUT THE LITTLE boy who was playing with his boat out on the water. Somehow, the boat drifted away from the boy on the shore. It kept going farther and farther away from him, so he started picking up rocks and throwing them on the other side of the boat to get it to come back to him. The stones created ripples and waves that brought the boat back to him. Then he picked it up and took it with him.

When God is throwing troubles our way, He isn't trying to take us out: He's trying to draw us back to Himself. Too often, we don't pray when everything is going well. It is when we are in trouble that we turn to God. Sometimes God allows trouble to improve our prayer lives. My mentor, Dr. A. Louis Patterson, pastor of Mount Corinth Baptist Church of Houston, Texas, says that sometimes we have a pattern of playing through the calm and praying through the storm. Since we play through the calm, God turns our calm into storms just so we will stop playing and start praying.

God, we thank You for sending the ripples and waves that draw us back to You. Teach us not to drift away from You, and teach us to pray to You even in the sunshine. We don't want You to have to "afflict" us just to hear our voices. In Your holy name we pray, Amen.

June 17

"The LORD gave and the LORD has taken away; may the name of the LORD be praised."

—Job 1:21b

IN ORDER TO GET OUR KIDS TO grow up, we take away their bottles and give them sippy cups. We take away their cribs and give them beds. We take away the diapers and give them training pants. Even though they cry, we do these things because we know they need to grow up.

Sometimes God has to take away what we've grown comfortable with to give us what we really need. It is during those times that our level of maturity will become apparent. Can we trust God even when He makes our lives uncomfortable, or do we throw temper tantrums?

God, we're not even thinking today about the level of commitment that Job had to face. We're just thinking of the way that You at times take away those things that make us comfortable and complacent—the things that we have come to "expect" and take for granted. Help us, God, to know that You want us to grow up, to mature, and to become disciples rather than those who simply tag along to see the miracles and eat the free food. Help us to grow worthy of following You, Amen.

June 18

May the God of peace, who through the blood of the eternal covenant brought back from the dead our Lord Jesus, that great Shepherd of the sheep, equip you with everything good for doing his will, and may he work in us what is pleasing to him, through Jesus Christ, to whom be glory for ever and ever. Amen.

—*Hebrews 9:14*

PEOPLE WHO KNOW THAT I RUN THIRTY miles or so a week sometimes ask me what I do when winter comes. I tell them that I keep running. I can keep running in the cold because I cover myself differently. There are special hats, gloves, socks, shoes and other items of clothing that are designed especially to help runners be able to endure the cold of winter. So, in the winter, I make adjustments, not excuses.

It is because of the blood shed by Jesus that God is able to equip us with all that we need to do His will, to please Him, and to keep running the race set before us. We all face winter seasons in life, just as we find in nature. When we face a winter season—when the wind is cold and the atmosphere bleak and harsh—the blood of Jesus is still sufficient to equip and protect us. We make adjustments to keep running, not excuses for bowing out of the race.

God, thank You that You can keep us running the race set before us in all seasons. It doesn't matter whether it is raining, or cold, or if the hot sun is beating down upon us. We want to do Your will, and to please You, O God, so help us not to make excuses when life gets hard, but help us to make adjustments and keep on running. In the precious name of the One whose blood was shed for us, Amen.

June 19

"So do not fear, for I am with you; do not be dismayed, for I am your God. I will strengthen you and help you; I will uphold you with my righteous right hand."

—*Isaiah 41:10*

AT VANDERBILT HOSPITAL IN NASHVILLE, TENNESSEE, a baby named Samuel Armas was still in his mother's womb when the doctors learned he had spina bifida. A lot of people encouraged the mother to have an abortion, but she refused to do that. A doctor operated on the baby while still in the womb so that when he came out, he wouldn't have the problems he would have otherwise. The doctor went in to help the baby while he was still in a situation that was difficult, dark, and undeveloped so that he could be whole. A picture in the newspaper showed the baby reaching out and holding onto the finger of the doctor.

Dr. Jesus works on us while we're still in our difficult, dark, and undeveloped situations. When we sense the hand of God working in our midst, we should reach out and take it, knowing we can trust Him that when we are delivered, we are whole.

Jesus, we thank You that You do care for us even as the Great Physician. Thank You that nothing we are facing is beyond Your ability to heal. Thank You that You can bring us forth from our dark places fully whole and prepared to serve You. Amen.

June 20

A righteous man may have many troubles, but the LORD delivers him from them all.

—Psalm 34:19

THE VERSE TODAY COMES FROM A PSALM of David. Just look at the troubles King David faced. He was anointed by Samuel to be king, but he had to wait a long time before that came to pass. In fact, he first went to the palace as a staff musician, not as the king. He experienced working for a crazy employer. He had years of unemployment and homelessness. He was forced to live in a neighborhood he didn't want to live in. His home burned down. He saw his children end up in bondage. One of his sons raped one of his daughters. And he lost a son who was just seven days old. Yet, David sang, "But the Lord delivers him from them all."

Whatever our situations, God will deliver us out of all our afflictions. God doesn't always deliver us by *removing* us from the situation but by *staying* with us in the midst of the situation. His grace is sufficient.

God, let us watch and wait in patience and faith, knowing that You do deliver us from all of our troubles. In Christ's name, Amen.

June 21

Everyone who competes in the games goes into strict training. They do it to get a crown that will not last; but we do it to get a crown that will last forever.

—*1 Corinthians 9:25*

LEBRON JAMES, ONE OF THE GREATEST PLAYERS in the NBA, used to lead the league in scoring with thirty points a game, but he only took twenty shots during each game. Of the twenty shots, he was hoping to hit at least ten of them because if he could hit ten shots and two or three of them were three-pointers, he could pick up twenty-three points from the field. Then he would get another seven or eight points from the line. Look at the math. He was averaging thirty points a game, but he only shot twenty times and was hoping to hit ten of them. (If you can hit half of your shots in the NBA, you can be a multimillionaire.) But in order to hit those ten shots, James practiced by making a thousand shots a day. He made seven thousand shots a week so that he would be able to hit ten shots when he was needed. It was what James did on the ordinary days that enabled him to accomplish what he did on those major occasions.

Like James, if we want to be able to win victories on the extraordinary days when others are taking notice of us, we must be in strict training on the ordinary days when no one is looking. We can't expect to be strong in the faith if we never exercise our faith. We can't expect to get a promotion if we don't do an excellent job at the level we're at. We can't preach the Word if we never spend time in the Word. It is what we do on the ordinary days that prepares us for the moments of crisis or acclaim in our lives.

Father, help us to be faithful on the ordinary days. When we are simply doing what we have to do each day in our routine lives, You are preparing us for those critical moments yet to come. Help us not to wait until the "big game" before we learn how to gain victory, for then it would be too late. Let us use each daily opportunity to develop the skills of victory. Amen.

June 22

Then I told them of the hand of my God which was good upon me. . . . And they said, Let us rise up and build. So they strengthened their hands for this good work.

—Nehemiah 2:18

DR. FREDERICK D. HAYNES III, SENIOR PASTOR of Friendship-West Baptist Church in Dallas, has a book out entitled *Soul Fitness*. The last chapter is called "You Can Bounce Back." He says if you throw a plate down, it will break; if you throw down a bag of sand, it will stay down; but if you throw down a ball, it will bounce back. Pastor Haynes says the difference in whether something will break, stay down, or bounce back is determined by what it is made of.

Because we are Christians, we need to know what we are made of. God has made us with resilience so that we can bounce back. In fact, the harder you throw us down, the higher we come back up.

God, when Your hand is upon us, we can bounce back, we can rise up, and we can keep moving. You will never give us a command without giving us strength to fulfill it. Thank You for making us resilient by Your grace. Amen.

June 23

"The LORD who delivered me from the paw of the lion and the paw of the bear will deliver me from the hand of this Philistine."

—1 Samuel 17:37

DAVID DIDN'T HAVE A COMPUTER WITH DATA saved on the memory of his hard drive. But when he was writing, it seemed almost like he had some information on a file in his own internal hard drive. When he pulled up the file on deliverance, he was reminded of some things. He was reminded that there was a bear, but God delivered him; and there was a lion, but God delivered him. Those remembrances gave him faith to believe that even though there was a giant named Goliath who was terrifying the Israelites, God could deliver him from this giant as well.

Some of us need to click on our memory file and recall that there were some things that should have taken us out, too, but God delivered us. We've faced our own share of bears and lions, but just as God has delivered us from those, He will deliver us from the giants that come now to make us afraid.

God, let us not be like those men who shrank back in fear at the sound of the giant's voice, but let us rather be like David. Let us remember all that You have done for us in the past, and let those memories give us faith to deal with the giants that are trying to keep us from serving You even now. In Jesus' name, Amen.

June 24

Then the Lord said to him, "What is that in your hand?" "A staff," he replied. . . . "But take this staff in your hand so you can perform miraculous signs with it."

—*Exodus 4:2, 17*

WHEN THE LORD SENT MOSES OUT TO deliver the Israelites from the hands of the Egyptians, he told Moses to use the staff that was in his hand. When David faced the giant Goliath, he used his own slingshot to bring him down. King Saul offered him some armor, but it didn't fit David. David used what he had, started where he was, and did what he could. And that was enough.

We must do the same. We cannot use what we do not have; we cannot start where we are not; and we cannot do what we cannot do. But when we step out, using just what God has given us, God will give us victory even over giants.

God, too often we say, "If I only had. . ., I would. . .," "If I only had her voice, I would sing praises to God all day long," "If I only had his ability to preach, I'd be out there winning people to Christ," "If I only had her money, I'd go back to school," or "If I only had his father, I'd be a success in life." All the while, You are saying, "What is that in your hand?" You have given us all that we need to accomplish all that You want us to do. Help us to use what You've given us, and to know it is enough. Amen.

June 25

And they overcame him by the blood of the Lamb, and by the word of their testimony; and they loved not their lives unto the death.

—*Revelation 12:11 (KJV)*

A NINE-YEAR-OLD BOY NAMED JACOB WAS playing with his friends on thin ice over a body of water. The ice gave way, and the four boys fell into the water. Jacob made it to the side along with one of his friends, and someone pulled them out, but his brother and another friend didn't make it. When a reporter asked Jacob why he thought he and one friend made it out while the others didn't, he said he thought it was because the water was so cold. The puzzled reporter pointed out, "But the water was cold for you, too." Jacob responded, "Yes, it was really cold, but I had my coat on." He realized that he had made it because he was covered.

As a child of God, we are covered by the blood of Jesus; therefore, God can raise us out of what is trying to take us under. We can overcome by the blood of the Lamb.

Lord, it is not because we believe in ourselves that we have faith to overcome the threats in our lives. Rather, we believe we can overcome in our spiritual battles by the blood of the Lamb, the blood of Jesus. It is in His name we pray, Amen.

June 26

You hem me in—behind and before. . .

—Psalm 139:5

A MOTHER WAS BUSY CLEANING HOUSE BUT SAW her baby crawling towards the stairs, so she went over, picked him up, and turned him around so that he was going in her direction. The baby, grinning and smiling, then began crawling away toward the fireplace, so once again, the momma went over, picked him up, and turned him around. Again, he started smiling, laughing, and crawling away. This third time, the mother knew that the baby was yet again going somewhere he couldn't handle, so she picked him up and put him in a playpen for his own protection.

Sometimes we can get ourselves into predicaments that may not kill us but will keep us from being effective for God. If you find that God is restricting and restraining you, you should start praising Him instead of crying, because it means that God is keeping you from harm. He is keeping you from getting into a situation you can't handle. He knows you better than you know yourself. If He stops you from getting something you want, or from going someplace you want to be, it is because He knows you can't handle what you want, and His love is keeping you from getting it.

Father God, we get so frustrated when we want something so much and You keep us from getting it. It looks like it is well within our reach, but all of a sudden, we find ourselves headed in what appears to be the wrong direction. Help us to trust You in those moments, knowing that You love us and have our best interests at heart. Help us to know that someday, when we are more mature, we will understand that You weren't being mean to us—You were protecting us. Amen.

June 27

"But as for you, be strong and do not give up, for your work will be rewarded."

—2 Chronicles 15:7

A PASTOR FRIEND OF MINE WAS TALKING about the second fight between Roberto Duran and Sugar Ray Leonard. In their first fight, Sugar Ray Leonard found out why they called Roberto Duran "Hands of Stone"; he got whipped. In the rematch, the analysts said Leonard could not handle the strength and power of Duran's hands for twelve rounds. But Sugar Ray changed his strategy. He was dancing around Duran; he was jabbing and moving; then he'd come with an overhand right. Duran, even with his powerful hands, couldn't touch Leonard because Leonard was dancing and moving, and weaving and dodging. In the eighth round, the bell rang, but Roberto Duran wouldn't come out of his corner. He was so frustrated that he yelled out, "¡No mas! ¡No mas!" — "No more! No more!" He had been hurt, beaten down, taunted, and teased so much that he wouldn't answer the bell.

Life has beaten some of us down so hard that we are unwilling to answer the bell. But unless we stay in the fight, we can't win the victory. How sad it is for us to give up by sitting on the bench.

God, You know that we have been hurt in the battle. We feel beaten down, and our enemies are taunting us. We want to give up and just walk away. But we know that You have not made us quitters. You have not made us to be a people who give up when life gets rough. So, God, we are getting up again, but we know that it is only in Your strength that we can win, so we trust in You. In Christ's name we pray, Amen.

June 28

Even my close friend, whom I trusted, he who shared my bread, has lifted up his heel against me.

—*Psalm 41:9*

WHEN SUGAR RAY LEONARD FOUGHT, HE WOULD go to the corner at the end of each round and be met by his people who would refresh him, make sure he was all right, encourage him, give him water, and keep him going.

If *our* corner people—those in our families, those among our friends, those in the church—hit us with a stool and discourage us, it takes away our strength and willingness to answer the bell. Enemies are expected to dog us, lie about us, and talk crazy about us. But when folks who should be close to us hurt us, it's hard to answer the bell.

Lord Jesus, You know how much it hurts when our friends turn against us. You felt the pain when Judas betrayed You with a kiss. You felt the wound to Your heart when Peter disowned You three times. Your heart ached when all of the disciples deserted You. But that didn't keep You from going on to fulfill the mission the Father had given You. You stayed in the fight. And even though it appeared for a moment that You had been defeated, on the third day You claimed Your victory! Help us not to be discouraged by what those close to us do or fail to do. Help us to keep focused on the work our Father has given us to do and to trust Him for the ultimate victory. In Your name we pray, Amen.

June 29

…Then Peter got down out of the boat, walked on the water and came toward Jesus.

—*Matthew 14:29*

BISHOP DEREK TRIPLETT, PASTOR OF HOPE FELLOWSHIP Church in Daytona Beach, preached at a revival service at Eastern Star Church. He told about Peter getting out of the boat and walking on the water to Jesus. Peter was actually walking on the water until he began looking at the waves and then he began to sink. Bishop Triplett said, "The enemy will make us think that we cannot do what we are already doing."

We are not so different from Peter. God enables us to begin doing something, but then we start looking at all the obstacles and threats on every side. Then the voice of the one who wants to defeat us starts telling us we can't do that, so we stop and we begin to sink. Listen, God wants us to know that we can keep on doing what we're already doing.

God, we know that the enemy wants to tell us we can't be Christians. He tells us we've been too bad; we've committed too many sins. But we are already new creatures in Christ! The enemy wants to tell us that we can't gain victory over that sin that keeps pulling us back. But we've already had victory for the last hour, the last day, and the last week! The enemy wants to tell us that we can't follow Christ: it's too hard and we will fail. But we are already following Him—spending time with Him, reading His Word, and praising Him! Help us not to listen to the enemy's lies but rather know that the One who has started a good work in us can and will continue it. It is You we trust to keep us doing what we're already doing. Amen.

June 30

Whether you turn to the right or to the left, your ears will hear a voice behind you, saying, "This is the way; walk in it."

—*Isaiah 30:21*

MULTIPLE RESPONSIBILITIES AND CONCERNS MAKE IT HARD sometimes to know the will of God. I get invitations to preach all over the world. But every time I get on a plane to go somewhere else, I am reminded of my responsibilities here. I have a wife here, a family here, a church here, and a community here. I want to go *there* because God opened the door, but I know I also have responsibilities *here*. Conflicting concerns and responsibilities are overwhelming.

It isn't hard to know what to do when we are faced with good and evil. We know we should always choose good over evil. But what do we do when we are faced with two "good's"? It is in those moments that we cannot listen to the cacophony of voices calling for us to come in one direction or another. Instead, we must listen to that still, small voice, that voice we have learned to recognize as our Shepherd, and wait until we hear Him say, "This is the way, walk in it."

Loving Shepherd, we are grateful that You take it upon Yourself to make sure that we know which direction to go. When there are so many options for us, we need to hear Your voice telling us which way to go. Let us never be distracted by any of the other voices, no matter how sweet, convincing, or demanding they sound. Help us to respond only to Your voice. Amen.

July 1

But the land you are crossing the Jordan to take possession of is a land of mountains and valleys....

—*Deuteronomy 11:11*

SOMETIMES LIFE IS AN EMOTIONAL ROLLER COASTER. One minute we're going up, and then we're going down. Sometimes we're right side-up, then upside-down. As a pastor, I experience it every day. A couple comes up to me at church and announces they're having a baby, so I get excited and caught up in their joy. But then I round a corner, and someone else comes up and says, "Pastor, I don't know if you heard, but my mother died." I immediately come back down emotionally so I can be with this person where he is. Then, a couple tells me they are getting married, so I rejoice with them. Then, a mother tells me her son has just been jailed, so I come down again to pray with her.

Others are on that same roller coaster whether it's at work or elsewhere. Some folks are sitting in the hospital at the bedside of a loved one. One minute the doctor says it looks like he's turned a corner; then, suddenly, he relapses. Some folks even have a roller coaster right in their own home. One minute a couple is experiencing great love and joy; the next minute, anger reigns. Mountains and valleys are a part of life. Rather than let our emotions carry us away and torment us, we need to obey God's gentle command in Psalm 46:10: "Be still, and know that I am God...."

God, thank You for reminding us that no matter what the circumstance, who is involved, what the emotion within us, we can be still and know that You are God. You are God for this circumstance, this person, and this moment. Thank You that You are an ever-present help in trouble, and You are One who shares our joys as well. Thank You that You are God. Amen.

July 2

He will be the sure foundation for your times, a rich store of salvation and wisdom and knowledge; the fear of the LORD is the key to this treasure.
—*Isaiah 33:6*

LAST YEAR, WHEN I CALLED J. ALLEN to wish him a happy twentieth birthday, he gave me an illustration that happened when his mother went down to visit and celebrate his birthday with him. He said his mother had rented a Jeep Cherokee, and they went to church that day. When they came out, she tried to open the Jeep with the remote key entry, but it wouldn't open. Even though she was going through the right motions, nothing was happening. I asked, "Well, son, what was the problem?" He said, "Well, even though we were standing at the right vehicle, Momma was using the key from the Mustang that's at home. We were at the right door, but we had the wrong key."

Some doors will not be opened by education, money, contacts, or other keys we try to use. We need to make sure that when we're standing at the right door, we are using the Master Key.

Father, how much time we waste trying to gain access to something You want us to have, but we're using the wrong keys. We are using what "looks right" to us, but it isn't the key You have given us to use. Sometimes, the key could be prayer; other times, praise; other times, obedience; other times, patience. . . . But we know that if we seek You, You are the Master Key. You hold all things in Your hands and if we have You, we have the Key to all things. Amen.

In that day you will ask in my name. I am not saying that I will ask the Father on your behalf. No, the Father himself loves you because you have loved me and have believed that I came from God.

—John 16:26-27

THERE IS NO OTHER VOICE THAT GETS my attention like that of one of my sons calling me "Daddy." Some people call me Jeffrey, some Pastor, some Reverend, some Doctor, some even Bishop, but none of these get my attention like when one of my sons comes up to me and calls me "Daddy."

God always hears when one of His children comes to Him and calls him "Abba/Daddy." Some of us have grown up thinking that Jesus loves us; but the Father is distant, judgmental, always angry with us and looking for reasons to punish us. What a misconception that is! Jesus wanted us to know that "the Father himself loves you." We can pray directly to the Father because our Father loves to hear us come to Him and call Him "Daddy."

Father, thank You for loving us. Thank You for correcting the image we have of You. Some of us grew up with absent fathers, distant fathers, angry fathers, abusive fathers. So when we think of God as Father, we get that same image—only a million times worse. But God, You are a loving Father. You Yourself love us, so we come to You today sensing Your closeness to us and Your love for us. We delight to be in Your presence. Amen.

July 4

Have mercy on me, O God, according to your unfailing love; according to your great compassion blot out my transgressions. Wash away all my iniquity and cleanse me from my sin.

—Psalm 51:1-2

WHAT WOULD YOU THINK OF SOMEONE WHO washed his car before taking it to a car wash? That would be pretty weird, wouldn't it? You don't wash your car and then take it to the car wash. You take it just as it is.

So, too, when we come to God, we must come just as we are and let God take care of cleaning us up. No matter how hard we scrub our souls, we can never make ourselves clean. The only agent that can make us clean is the blood of Jesus Christ. The only One who can do the cleansing is God. Let's stop wasting time trying to do for ourselves what we can never do.

Just as we are, O God, we come to You. With all of our sins, faults, and failures, we come to You. Cleanse us, we pray, in the blood of Jesus. We give up trying to do it ourselves because we can't. We trust You now to make us clean in mind, body, soul, and spirit. We thank You for doing that. In Jesus' name, Amen.

July 5

As they approached Jerusalem and came to Bethphage on the Mount of Olives, Jesus sent two disciples, saying to them, "Go to the village ahead of you, and at once you will find a donkey tied there, with her colt by her. Untie them and bring them to me.

—*Matthew 21:1-2*

IT WAS NOT INCONSEQUENTIAL THAT JESUS CHOSE a donkey for his triumphal ride into Jerusalem. We have lost sight of what a donkey really is. A donkey is thought of as a stupid animal, a stubborn animal, a foolish animal. By choosing such an animal, Jesus is trying to show us that even though we may be stupid, stubborn, and foolish, if we will only come to Jesus, He will use us.

We don't have to be Black Beauty, Trigger, Secretariat, Silver, or even Mr. Ed! We don't have to be a Clydesdale; what we are is fine with God. We may have lived our lives as stupidly, stubbornly, and foolishly as an old donkey, but if we come to Jesus, He will use us in His service.

God, especially in the times in which we live, we are enamored with celebrities. We feel a sense of excitement when we hear that a famous actor, a rock star, or a champion athlete has turned his or her life over to Jesus because we think of how wonderfully You can use that individual. But You don't think as we think. You can take a simple donkey and make its role in the kingdom so special that it is noted in the Bible. God, let us know that there is a place for us to serve You. Let us see that it is about You and not about us. In Jesus' name, Amen.

Let us draw near to God with a sincere heart in full assurance of faith, having our hearts sprinkled to cleanse us from a guilty conscience and having our bodies washed with pure water.

—Hebrews 10:22

WE WERE DOING A FORTY-DAY FAST at our church, and I had been drinking nothing but water and pure juices. I was looking on one of the juice bottles and saw that it said, "Recycled Bottle." It was almost as if the bottle began testifying to me that it was a recycled bottle. So I said to the bottle, "Okay, go ahead and give me your testimony," The bottle said to me, "Jeffrey Johnson, just because I'm meeting your needs at this moment doesn't mean that I've always been just like this. No, at one point in time, somebody used me and then discarded me, treated me like trash, set me down, and walked away from me. But then someone else came along, saw me, and treated me like treasure. He picked me up and took me to a recycling center where they washed and purified me. They melted me down and reshaped my life. Then they filled me all over again, and here I am meeting your needs while you are trying to get closer to God."

That's what it's like for the life of a believer. What people see today isn't the way it has always been. Just because we look clean, filled, and refreshed today doesn't mean we've never been used, never been mistreated, never been treated like trash. But Jesus came along and found us. He reached down and picked us up. He brought us into the church, which is the recycling center. There, He cleaned us up, filled us up, and made us usable for His service.

God, some of us have been so mistreated and abused in this world that it is almost impossible for us to imagine a different life. But, God, today we dare to believe You. Today we bring what little bit of faith we have, and we place ourselves in Your hands. We trust You now to cleanse us, mold us, fill us, and use us in Your kingdom and for Your glory. In Jesus' name, Amen.

July 7

Not forsaking the assembling of ourselves together, as the manner of some is; but exhorting one another: and so much the more, as ye see the day approaching.

—Hebrews 10:25 (KJV)

AS IS TRUE OF MOST ADULTS IN our country, I own a car. It is my car. I can drive it anywhere I please. This car is a car whether I am driving it in Indiana or in Wisconsin. It is a car whether it is parked on a deserted road or moving in the midst of traffic on an L.A. freeway. It is a car whether it is bright, shiny, and clean or whether it is dusty and dirty from the roads it has traveled. It is a car whether it is on a mountain top or down in a valley.

Some people say, "I don't have to go to church to be a Christian." That's true, and it's also true that my car doesn't have to go to a gas station to be a car. But if it's going to run effectively and get me to my destination, every once in a while I have to pull in and get it refilled. The church is where we get what we need to be effective in this world.

God, help us not to think we can keep running and serving without going to church. It is in church, among Your people, that we can get a message that will speak to us. That is where we can simply worship You, where You can minister to us away from the hustle and bustle of life, and where You can fill us afresh with Your Holy Spirit so that we can go back into the fray with something fresh to offer. Help us not to neglect being among your people in church. In Christ's name we pray, Amen.

Jesus entered the temple area and drove out all who were buying and selling there. He overturned the tables of the money changers and the benches of those selling doves. "It is written," he said to them, "'My house will be called a house of prayer,' but you are making it a 'den of robbers.'

—*Matthew 21:12-13*

THERE WAS NOTHING WRONG WITH EXCHANGING MONEY. Jerusalem was home to the temple of God, so people from all over the known world came there for a holy pilgrimage. Places were set up in the temple where people could exchange their foreign money for local currency so that they could give an offering. There was nothing wrong with selling doves because these travelers had to buy doves to offer as a sacrifice. There was something wrong, however, when the sellers took advantage of the worshipers.

Jesus gets frustrated with the same thing that frustrates us. There's something wrong if only two or three people are benefiting from the sacrifices. There is something wrong when somebody preaches about prosperity, but he is the only one who is prospering. Jesus gets frustrated if a ministry is expensive but not extensive, if a fortune that comes from many pockets is funneled into one pocket. Jesus is tired of a church that has had a building program for twenty-five years, but the people giving have never seen a building. It's about integrity, honesty, and accountability.

God, help us each to know that we are responsible and accountable to You for what we do in the house of God. Let our integrity match Your expectations. Let us be so open and honest that any persons doubting us would themselves be embarrassed when the truth is revealed. Let us remember that what we do as Christians reflects upon You, and help us always to reflect You as we know You to be—holy, righteous, and true. In Jesus' name, Amen.

July 9

But thanks be to God, who always leads us in triumphal procession in Christ and through us spreads everywhere the fragrance of the knowledge of him.

—2 Corinthians 2:14

MY WIFE SHARON WAS TALKING ON THE PHONE WITH me while she was at a car wash. Suddenly, she stopped talking to me and started talking to someone else. I asked, "What's going on there?" She explained, "Well, I'm at a car wash, and they just brought this certificate over and told me that if I come back in thirty minutes, they'll wash my car for free. They apologized and said there's something wrong with the car wash, so they can't let anybody in right now." Recognizing how unusual this was, I was curious about what caused the delay. She said, "I can look inside the car wash and see that there is a car there that is off-track." I asked, "Sharon, are you trying to tell me that there is a line of dirty cars trying to get in, but they can't get in because somebody who is already in there is off-track?"

That's what's wrong with some of our churches. There are a lot of dirty people outside wanting to come in, but there are too many people already inside who are off-track. Too many of us on the inside are living defeated Christian lives. We must understand that we are part of the "triumphal procession" (the parade of victors) only when we are "in Christ"—looking to Him, depending on Him, and living for Him. When we are in Christ, we are not victims; we are victors!

God, thank You that You desire for us to live victorious Christian lives. You desire for us to live moment by moment in Christ. It is when we live in anything or anyone other than Christ that we find we are no longer victorious. Other things and other people cannot do for us what Christ can do. Help us to check ourselves in this moment and to renew our relationship in Him. We pray in His name, Amen.

July 10

He who conceals his sins does not prosper, but whoever confesses and renounces them finds mercy.

—Proverbs 28:13

I'VE SEEN ENOUGH MOVIES TO KNOW ABOUT the Miranda rights. In movies and on TV, when a police officer arrests someone, the officer must read the Miranda rights to the one under arrest: "You have the right to remain silent. If you give up the right to remain silent, anything you say can and will be used against you in a court of law. You have the right to an attorney. If you desire an attorney and cannot afford one, an attorney will be obtained for you before police questioning." People don't have to say anything because they have a right to remain silent, but everything they do say can and will be held against them in a court of law.

We don't live in a court of law; instead, we live in the kingdom of God. In that kingdom, the opposite is true. We do not have a right to remain silent, and what we *don't* say can and will be held against us. It is only by confessing our sins that we can find forgiveness for those sins.

God, thank You that we live in the kingdom of a God who is Love, and that You desire fellowship and a relationship with us. God, thank You for offering us mercy and grace in exchange for the confession of our sins. Thank You that You do not use our confessions to imprison us but to free us. In Jesus' name, Amen.

July 11

These commandments that I give you today are to be upon your hearts. Impress them on your children. Talk about them when you sit at home and when you walk along the road, when you lie down and when you get up.

—Deuteronomy 6:6-7

"NOW I LAY ME DOWN TO SLEEP. I PRAY THE LORD MY soul to keep. If I should die before I wake, I pray the Lord my soul to take." This is a prayer that my great-grandmother taught my grandmother when she was a child; years later, my grandmother taught it to my mother; my mother taught it to me; and I taught it to my children. It continues through the generations as a means of teaching our children the principles of prayer and the power of God. That prayer is so embedded within me that even now, it sometimes comes to mind and I realize I have been reciting it subconsciously.

Psalm 31:5—"Into your hands I commit my spirit; redeem me, O LORD, the God of truth"—was a scripture routinely memorized by the Jewish people. It has also been identified as a prayer that was commonly taught to children who would recite it at night, just as some of us recited "Now I lay me down to sleep." Those weren't then merely words that Jesus thought appropriate as He prepared to die. They were familiar words that came to Him as He faced the most difficult moment of His life, at the moment He needed them most. As parents, we need to teach our children those things that they will remember—those things that will stay with them throughout their lives and come to their remembrance when they need them.

God, You have put us in families so that we might share our knowledge of You from generation to generation. Let us be faithful to impress Your Word upon our children. Let us talk of You in our homes, as we walk along, when we lie down, and when we get up. Let Your Word ever be on our lips so that our children will learn of Your faithfulness. Amen.

July 12

Deliver me in thy righteousness, and cause me to escape: incline thine ear unto me, and save me.

—*Psalm 71:2 (KJV)*

SHARON TOLD ME SHE WAS WATCHING THE news one day and saw a story about a woman from South Carolina who survived a severe storm that went through her town. She had taken refuge inside her closet during the storm, but when the storm was over and she was ready to get out of her closet, she found that the door was locked. She remembered that the door could only be locked from the outside; it couldn't be locked or unlocked from the inside. So when the storm was over and she was ready to leave the closet, she couldn't get out. She began to kick and beat on the door to try to force her way out, but it wouldn't budge. She finally went to sleep and woke up, still in the closet. She banged again on the door and kicked it, feeling imprisoned now in this place that was once a shelter for her. The woman then said that she began to pray for God to help her: "God, there's got to be a way out of what I've gotten myself into." She said God told her, "I want you to stop trying to get out through the door; turn around and try to get out through the drywall." She began beating and kicking at the drywall. It began to give way, and after a while, she had a big enough space to crawl out of the closet. She learned that when she was stuck and couldn't find a way out, she could talk to Someone who could provide an escape for her.

God has a way of getting *us* out of locked closets, too. Even when we are imprisoned in a place of our own making, He can help us to find a way of escape. We just have to call upon God, as the woman did from the closet.

God, You know we are in a dark place right now—a place that once seemed safe and comfortable but now has become a prison to us. Deliver us, O God. Show us a way of escape. Free us, we pray. In the name of Jesus, Amen.

July 13

...be filled with the Spirit.

—*Ephesians 5:18*

A FEW YEARS AGO, IN OUR CHURCH'S JEWEL preschool, the coffeepot in the teachers' break room was repeatedly broken. We kept buying replacements every other week or so until we decided we needed to check it out to find out why that was happening. What we learned is that when someone got the last cup, she would put the empty coffeepot back on the heating element. If the coffeepot is filled, the heating apparatus keeps the coffee warm and makes it taste better; but if the pot is empty, it breaks.

We can learn a lesson from that coffeepot. If we are filled with the Holy Spirit, heated situations will only make us better. But if we're empty, the heat can cause us to break.

Lord, it seems that we often find ourselves in heated situations. In our homes, at our jobs, and even in our churches, we find the heat becoming extremely intense at times. Please fill us continually with Your Holy Spirit so that the heat will only make us better, never bitter or broken. In Jesus' name, we pray, Amen.

And the LORD God formed man of the dust of the ground, and breathed into his nostrils the breath of life; and man became a living soul.
—Genesis 2:7 (KJV)

WE HAD A TOUGH WINTER LAST YEAR. One day it rained really hard. By the next day, the wind chill had lowered the temperature below zero and the rain froze, turning streets and sidewalks into sheets of ice. A woman driving on the north side of Indianapolis had her four-year-old daughter in the back seat of her SUV. As they hit some ice, the SUV began to slip and slide. Then it flipped over, went into a retaining pond and began to sink. Two passersby, one of whom is a member of our church, stopped to help. They went into the frigid water and rescued the mother and child. The little girl, however, was not breathing. A nurse who had stopped to help began CPR on her. The child is alive and well today because that woman blew breath into her lifeless body.

If a human being can breathe into a lifeless person and bring her back to life, how much more can God breathe into our lifeless spirits and make us live? Some of us have had the experience of sliding into some circumstance in which we had no intention of being. But we needn't give up. If we have slipped, flipped, turned upside down, and are sinking fast in a situation that's over our head, the One named Jesus will come and breathe new life into our dead situation.

Lord, we find that we have lost control and have landed upside down and are drowning. Come rescue us and breathe new life into us that we might live again. In Christ's name, Amen.

July 15

God is our refuge and strength, an ever-present help in trouble.

—Psalm 46:1

THE HEBREW WORD FOR "GOD" IN THIS verse is "Elohim." The Hebrew people traditionally gave God a new name each time He brought them out of various experiences. These names expressed how God had helped them: El-Shaddai, the Lord God Almighty; Yahweh, the God with whom we enter into relationship; Jehovah, the Lord who makes and keeps promises. There are even compound names: Jehovah-Jireh, the Lord who provides; Jehovah-Rapha, the Lord who heals; Jehovah-Shalom, the Lord is peace; Jehovah-Shammah, the Lord who is there.

Our grandparents used to name God in that way: God is a doctor who's never lost a patient; God is a lawyer who's never lost a case; God is bread in a starving land; God is water in dry places. Based on what they were going through, they would give God a specific name. God can always be called the Great I Am. God is everything you need Him to be—even Elohim, who is the Creator God, the God who makes a way out of no way.

Our Precious Companion, we thank You that we can call You by so many names because You have done so many things for us. You are our Everything, and You are Faithful. We thank You for all that You are. In Jesus' name, Amen.

July 16

The LORD is my strength and my shield; my heart trusts in him, and I am helped. My heart leaps for joy and I will give thanks to him in song.

—Psalm 28:7

PEOPLE IN BIBLE DAYS UNDERSTOOD THE ANALOGY of a shield because the soldiers in those days had such huge shields that a soldier's whole body could fit behind one of them. Therefore, when the enemy attacked, the soldiers could hide behind their shields.

Since God is our shield, when the enemy attacks, we can simply hide behind our Shield and we will be safe. Shields are only effective, however, if we are close to them. When we are close to God, God is our safe Shield, our Protector.

God, thank You for being our Shield and not leaving us unprotected in the face of our enemies. Our hearts, too, leap for joy, and we give thanks to You in song. In Your holy name we pray, Amen.

July 17

In him was life, and that life was the light of men. The light shines in the darkness, but the darkness has not understood it.

—John 1:4-5

YEARS AGO, THERE WAS A BLACKOUT IN New York City. There were no lights in homes, in the countless entertainment facilities, on the streets, or in the skyscrapers. There was darkness throughout the city. Yet, the Statue of Liberty was still shining brightly. People were puzzled as they observed that phenomenon, and newscasters and others were trying to figure that out. It didn't take too long, however, for the researchers to find out that the Statue of Liberty gets her power from New Jersey. So, when everybody else was in darkness and had no power, she could keep shining.

We need to be careful where we get our power. Most sources are vulnerable, so their power is limited. If, however, we get our power from God, our light can shine even in the midst of the darkness.

Jesus, thank You that You are a Light for us, lighting our way to the Father. And You are the Source of our light so that we may shine brightly even in the darkness, no matter how dark it gets. Amen.

July 18

The LORD will march out like a mighty man, like a warrior he will stir up his zeal; with a shout he will raise the battle cry and will triumph over his enemies.

—*Isaiah 42:13*

THERE IS A STORY TOLD ABOUT A man who walked into a museum with a tour group, but he got so intrigued by one particular painting that he stayed back while the rest of his group went on. This man was a chess player, and the painting that attracted his attention was of a man playing a game of chess with the devil over his soul. He could tell the man in the picture was losing because he had a frown on his face, while the devil was smiling. He could also tell because the title of the painting was "Checkmate." That indicated to him that the game was over; the devil had won. The man stood there for hours. The museum was closing, and he was being asked to leave. But he protested, "There's something not right with this picture." They asked, "What do you mean?" He said, "I've been standing here for hours looking at this painting, and I can see that the king still has another move."

When it looks like it's over and the devil has the victory in your life, I dare you to look at your situation from another angle. You will see that God is able to make another move. You can still win the victory.

Our God, we thank You that You are King of kings and Lord of lords. You are never at a loss to know what to do. You are never bewildered. You are never perplexed. You know exactly the right move to make, and when You are ready, You will move on our behalf and win the victory. We are so grateful to You. We praise Your wonderful name. Amen.

July 19

I know your deeds. See, I have placed before you an open door that no one can shut. I know that you have little strength, yet you have kept my word and have not denied my name.

—*Revelation 3:8*

DOORS AT CERTAIN GROCERIES, SHOPPING CENTERS, AND elsewhere open automatically as we keep walking toward them. Somebody has gone ahead of us and designed a door that is going to open if we just keep walking.

God has some doors prepared to open for us if we just keep walking. It doesn't matter what has happened in the past concerning our finances or education, God is still in the door-opening business. He opens doors supernaturally, but we have to keep walking.

Thank You, God, that we aren't dependent upon our own strength to open doors, or our own wisdom to know which doors to open. God, we are so dependent upon You. We need Your strength and power to open the right doors for us. Thank You so much for Your faithfulness in doing just that. In Christ's name, Amen.

I am the door: by me if any man enter in, he shall be saved, and shall go in and out, and find pasture.

—*John 10:9 (KJV)*

WHEN NOAH BUILT THE ARK, GOD INSTRUCTED him to "put a door in the side of the ark...." (Genesis 6:16). He was told to build only one door because everybody who came into the ark had to come through that one door.

Jesus says, "I am the door." If any of us are going to be saved, get right with God, or make it through the storms of life, we have to come in by that same one door.

God, we hear so often today that there are many doors to You, but that is not what Your Word teaches. Help us not to be found outside the ark because we are looking around for another door through which to enter. Jesus, You died to open the way for us. We receive with thanksgiving what You have done for us, and we humbly but joyfully enter into the kingdom through You. In Your holy name, Amen.

Come, let us bow down in worship, let us kneel before the LORD our Maker.

—Psalm 95:6

THE BUFFALO BILLS WERE LEADING 24-19 AGAINST the New England Patriots in their 2009 season opener. With less than two minutes left to play, Leodis McKelvin took the kickoff and, as he was bringing it out of the end zone, he fumbled the ball. The Patriots went on to score a touchdown and won the game 25-24. What upset so many fans is that the Bills would have won the game if McKelvin had simply taken a knee.

We need to recognize that Jesus already won our victory on the cross. We can be part of a winning team if we just "take a knee"—kneel down and acknowledge Him and give Him the glory for our victory. If, however, our personal arrogance, inflated self-confidence, or uncontrolled passion prompts us to try to grab a win for ourselves, we will likely find that we "fumble" and bring a defeat upon ourselves and our team.

O, Lord, we thank You today that we already have our victory through You and what You did on the cross for us. Forgive us for trying to usurp credit for what You have done. Help us never to think that we no longer need to depend upon You—that we can take it from here on our own. We bow before You today in humble admission that apart from You we can do nothing. We wait for Your instructions and seek no glory for ourselves. Have Your own way within us, O Lord, we pray in Your precious and holy name, Amen.

July 22

A gift opens the way for the giver and ushers him into the presence of the great.

—Proverbs 18:16

IN THE EARLY 1900S, MADAM C. J. WALKER BUILT a magnificent estate in an exclusive community on the Hudson River in New York. How, in that day and age, did an African American woman, an orphaned daughter of former slaves, make a place for herself alongside Carnegie, Rockefeller, Gould, and Vanderbilt—some of the wealthiest white males in the country? She did it by using the gifts God had given her—gifts that made her the first African American millionaire and first self-made female millionaire in the country. Her advice to others was often to stop depending on someone else to give them an opportunity and to make their own opportunity, as she had.

God has placed within us gifts that will open doors for us if we use them. As the King James translation of Proverbs 18:16 says, "A man's gift maketh room for him…." God's gifts to us will make room for us. Some of us, however, would rather sound so spiritual, saying, "I'm waiting for God to open a door for me." All the while, God is waiting for us to use the gifts He has *already* given us to open those doors. We must discover, develop, and use our own gift or gifts. It doesn't matter whether we have one gift or a dozen; it is sufficient.

Our God, help us to quit waiting for some person to come along and create an opportunity for us. Help us to know that our miracle often comes in using what You have already given us. Help us to see our gifts as the keys that will unlock the doors You want us to enter. We often look outside for the supernatural, when You have already placed the supernatural within us. Thank You for Your gifts to us. Amen.

July 23

My dear children, I write this to you so that you will not sin. But if anybody does sin, we have one who speaks to the Father in our defense—Jesus Christ, the Righteous One.

—1 John 2:1

I GOT TO A HOTEL LATE ONE night, tired and just wanting to rest. But when I got to my room, I couldn't get in. I kept trying to use the key card I had been given, but it didn't work. Now, I know that if we keep doing what we've always done expecting to get different results, we're crazy. But even though I was at the point of insanity, I still kept trying because I didn't want to face the alternative. But no matter how I entered the card into the slot or how many times I tried, the door just did not open. So, even though I didn't want to, even though I was tired, frustrated, and wishing that the situation were different, I still had to go back down to the hotel desk. They sincerely apologized, recoded the card, and I was able to get in my room.

Some of us keep trying and trying to get into the right door, but we're using the wrong key. We try it one way and then another. Sometimes, we even just stand and pound on the door in frustration, but no matter what we try, it stays closed. In times like these, we have to humble ourselves, go back to God, and ask Him to recode us so that we can get through the door we need to enter.

God, You are the great Miracle Worker. But one of the greatest miracles You ever work is that of changing us, transforming us into the persons we need to be—the persons You created us to be. We confess that sometimes we insist on going through a particular door, and we insist that it open right now. We become frustrated with You when You don't respond to our demand and You don't seem to understand how important it is that we get through that door. But You are not about to let us go through that door as we are. We need to come humbly to You and let You make us into those persons who belong on the other side of that door. Please change us, O God. Renew a right spirit within us, we pray in the name of Jesus, Amen.

July 24

Dear friends, do not be surprised at the painful trial you are suffering, as though something strange were happening to you.

—*1 Peter 4:12*

IN THE MOVIE, *SAVING PRIVATE RYAN,* A mother was about to lose her last son who was fighting in the military during World War II. The U. S. Army sent a rescue mission out to bring her remaining son back alive. Early in the movie, we see military ships landing on the beaches of Normandy. When they land, the huge door of the ship opens, but some of the soldiers who rush out of the ship don't even make it to the beach. They weren't expecting the opposition that met them—the machine guns and the massive artillery fire. The soldiers were taken by surprise when the door opened.

Opportunity and opposition go hand-in-hand. If we do what is good, we're going to run into some bad. If we do what is positive, we'll run into some negative. Some of us will find doors of opportunity opening for us educationally, in our jobs, in business, and in relationships, but we must be ready for the opposition that will meet us on the other side of those doors.

God, let us not be taken unaware when the fight begins. Remind us that we are engaged in spiritual warfare and the enemy is not going to let us skip merrily through a door of opportunity without offering a fight. Help us to be prepared as we start back to school, get a new job, get a promotion, or enter a wonderful new relationship. Help us to be prepared for the opposition that the enemy will throw at us. Help us to walk through the door of opportunity ready to fight for what God has just given us. In Christ's name, Amen.

July 25

If I say, "Surely the darkness will hide me and the light become night around me," even the darkness will not be dark to you; the night will shine like the day, for darkness is as light to you.

—Psalm 139:11-12

AS JESUS HUNG ON THE CROSS, THE SKY DARKENED. During the time of day that should have been the brightest, it was the darkest. It was so dark in Jesus' life, He cried out: "My God, my God, why have you forsaken Me?" (Matthew 27:46). God had not forsaken Him, but He felt that God had left Him.

We sometimes experience that same contrast in our own lives. We have just gotten married, or just had a baby, or just been accepted in college, or just been promoted at work, and it should be the brightest time in our lives. But we are already having difficulties that make it dark for us. Whatever the situation, we must remember that God does His best work in the dark. God created light in the darkness; the children of Israel were set free in darkness; Jesus walked on the water in the night; it was midnight when Paul and Silas were freed from prison by an earthquake; and it became dark when Jesus died on the cross. We may feel forsaken during those dark moments, but we must watch to see what God is about to do.

God, You know it is hard for us when darkness comes into our lives; we don't know how to handle it—especially when it comes at a time when we least expect it, a time when our lives should be shining the brightest. God, we thank You that we know You are with us; You have not forsaken us. We trust You to guide us in the dark and work miracles for us even in the darkness. We await the dawning of a new day in our lives. In Jesus' name, Amen.

July 26

Consider him who endured such opposition from sinful men, so that you will not grow weary and lose heart.

—*Hebrews 12:3*

MY KIDS LIKE BASKETBALL, BUT, AS THEY were growing up, they always wanted to prove they were better than I was. So they asked me at what age I started dunking the ball. When I told them I did that when I was thirteen, they want to be sure they could do it at twelve. "What are the most points you ever scored in a game?" they asked. I once scored fifty points, so they wanted to score at least fifty-one points sometime. "Could you dunk backwards? Could you throw it off the backboard, catch it, and dunk it? Could you do a reverse slam?" "Yes," I told them, "I could do all that." So, my youngest son K. J. asked, "Well, Daddy, if you could do all that, if you weren't preaching, would you be in the NBA?" "No, I wouldn't be in the NBA," I replied. "Why not, Daddy, if you could do all that?" "Son, I could do it; I just couldn't do it when people were trying to stop me."

Do you know what sets aside the great players? It isn't just that they can do all the great moves, but it's that they can do them even when others are trying to stop them from getting to their goal. We must be able to face the opposition if we are to win the goal.

God, help us to learn how to do all that we need to do, not only on good days but on the bad days as well. Let us be effective in season and out of season. Help us to be victorious, not only in times of peace but also when we are facing opposition. Let us not grow weary and lose heart, but help us to keep going in spite of what the enemy throws at us. In the name of the One who gives us victory, Amen.

We do not want you to become lazy, but to imitate those who through faith and patience inherit what has been promised.

—*Hebrews 6:12*

JUST BECAUSE WE GET IN AN ELEVATOR, we don't automatically go up. If we don't push the button, we aren't going anywhere. And how about the times we've gotten on the wrong elevator? We stand there, letting ourselves go down because we're too embarrassed to let the others on the elevator know we were intending to go up but got on the wrong elevator. We need to be willing to say, "Wait a minute. Let me out. I'm going up, not down."

Sometimes our opposition is within ourselves. Some of us don't have the motivation or passion, so even if the door opens, we don't take advantage of the opportunity. We aren't willing to graduate from high school, go on to college, get our training, find a mentor, and do the things necessary to prepare us for the open doors. We won't be able to get anywhere then, no matter how many doors open. Even though we were supposed to go up, some of us will even stand by and let ourselves go down because we don't want to tell those around us we are heading in a different direction from them.

Father, give us fresh resolve to serve You and go in the way of our destiny. Help us to recognize our part in getting to where You want us to be. Help us to do those things that will enable us to succeed. Help us to stop silently following those who are going in a different direction; give us the courage to let them know we are headed up, not down. In Your name we pray, Amen.

By faith we understand that the universe was formed at God's command, so that what is seen was not made out of what was visible.

—Hebrews 11:3

I HAD TO UPGRADE MY EIGHT-YEAR-OLD CAR a couple years ago because I had over two hundred thousand miles on it. (I put 169 miles on my car every week just by driving back and forth to our church's three separate locations for Sunday services.) With my new car, I can just grab the door of my locked car, and it opens because I don't need a key. However, no matter how many other people grab my car door, it won't open for them. It only works only for me. But you don't need to be envious; there's nothing special about me. The only reason my car opens and starts just for me is that I always have the "key" with me. It isn't the type of key I have to hold in my hand and that is visible to others. It just has to be *with me* for the car door to open.

Some people get envious or jealous of others because they get a promotion on their job or they get a new job. What they don't understand is that God opened the door for that person. If we have Jesus, He doesn't even have to be visible to anybody else: if He is in us, doors will open.

God, help us to know that the invisible realm is as real and powerful as what we can see—usually even more so. Help us to rely on You to create and do things in our lives by using that which is invisible. Most of all, let us remember that it is Your unseen presence in our lives that makes all the difference. Amen.

July 29

But ye are not in the flesh, but in the Spirit, if so be that the Spirit of God dwell in you....

—*Romans 8:9 (KJV)*

MY WIFE AND I HAVE BEEN MARRIED for twenty-three years. We are so different from each other; we are proof that opposites do attract. One thing we have in common, however, is our love for the beach. We like the water, so we've been to beaches all over, including Paradise Island in the Bahamas, Disney's private beach, Pensacola's beach, Daytona Beach, Miami Beach, and my favorite—South Beach in Miami. But it suddenly dawned on me one day that of all the times we've been on the beach, Sharon has never gotten into the water. She just likes to see it. We've rented boats, and she has gotten *on* the water. We've rented suites at the beach, and she has been *over* the water. We've held hands and walked on the beach in the moonlight, so she's gotten *near* the water. She has gotten over the water, on the water, and near the water, but never *in* the water.

That's the way some of us are with the Spirit of God. We will come near to the Holy Spirit, we like being around where He is, and we like seeing how He works. But we won't get *in* the Spirit.

God, we thank You today that we can not only be near the Holy Spirit but we can be in Your Spirit. May we never be content only to watch You from outside, but let us always be in Your Spirit and have Your Holy Spirit dwell in us. In Christ's name, we pray, Amen.

July 30

He reached down from on high and took hold of me; he drew me out of deep waters.

—Psalm 18:16

WHEN WE WERE KIDS, WE DIDN'T GO to the YMCA or to a club for swimming lessons. Someone just took us to a body of water and threw us in the deep end. We had to make our way somehow. That may have been effective, but it wasn't the best way to learn to swim.

God doesn't do that. He never just drops us in the deep end. He helps us to progress a little at a time. We can trust God to help us develop over time. He knows what we're ready for and never expects us to handle that which is too deep for us.

God, thank You for Your patience with us. Thank You for the loving way You deal with us. Thank You for not giving us more than we can handle and for not leaving us alone as we learn to follow You and to obey Your voice. In Jesus' name, Amen.

July 31

So I tell you this, and insist on it in the Lord, that you must no longer live as the Gentiles do, in the futility of their thinking.

—Ephesians 4:17

J. ALLEN CALLED ME ONE DAY WITH an illustration for me. On the Discovery Channel, he saw a story about a doctor who had separated Siamese twins joined at the head. The doctor said the reason why so many of these twins don't make it after surgery, even if the operation itself is successful, is because they don't have a proper covering for their heads. The doctor talked about the covering they had to put over their heads; in fact, they wouldn't let anyone even *touch* the babies' heads because they needed time to heal. Later on, however, the doctors also realized that the babies couldn't walk because something was wrong in their brains: their arteries were twisted. Even though the twins had the proper covering, they were still twisted on the inside. As a result, they couldn't walk right.

That's what's wrong with so many of us. We've got the proper spiritual covering: we're under the blood of Jesus. Yet, we still have some twisted thinking in our heads that keeps us from walking right.

God, whose mind is pure and holy, help us to walk in Your ways and to think as You think. Keep us under Your covering, and operate on our minds so that our thoughts will not be twisted or futile but rather be in accordance with Your Word and Your ways. We pray this in Jesus' name, Amen.

August 1

And pray in the Spirit on all occasions with all kinds of prayers and requests. With this in mind, be alert and always keep on praying for all the saints.

—Ephesians 6:18

WHEN I WAS A YOUNGSTER GROWING UP, the deacons in our church would pray the same prayer during devotions every Sunday. That's when we knew it was time to go into the sanctuary. We could time ourselves based on where the deacon was in the prayer because he prayed exactly the same thing every time. The deacon prayed: "God, here I am, knee bent, and body bowed to Mother Earth."

The knee represented the prayer life. When the anointing of God gets knee deep—when we are praying in the Spirit—it's going to have an effect on our prayer life. We can't just walk in the Spirit; we also have to pray in the Spirit. There is power in prayer.

Father, let us always pray in the Spirit. Let us know that if we are merely saying our own words, asking for things that express our desires but not Yours and praying without our will bent to You, our prayers will be in vain. We need Your anointing, O God. We need Your Holy Spirit. Amen.

August 2

I call on the LORD in my distress, and he answers me.

—*Psalm 120:1*

ONE OF THE FEATURES IN MY CAR is an SOS button for emergencies. If I ever get stranded, involved in a wreck, or caught up in some crisis situation, I can just press that button. The SOS is connected with a satellite that tracks me wherever I am. It then sends a signal that alerts the monitoring center to send someone to help me.

When we became Christians, God placed an SOS alarm within us to help us. Whatever your problem, when you call on God, He will come to your rescue.

God, we thank You for Your faithfulness. Thank You that we can call upon You anytime we are in distress, in need, or in danger, and You hear our cries and respond. There is no other God like You, and we love You today. In Jesus' name, Amen.

August 3

But thou art holy, O thou that inhabitest the praises of Israel.
—Psalm 22:3 (KJV)

AS HARD AS IT IS TO BELIEVE, in most churches you will find that some people intentionally come to church late on a regular basis. They do this because they are trying to miss the time of praise and worship. They may not like the music, they may not like to sing, or they may even consider praise and worship just a warm-up act for the main attraction, which they believe to be the preaching. These folks want to come to hear the sermon and they want to say they have been in church, but they don't understand that God inhabits the praise of His saints.

What a blessing we miss when we fail to praise and worship God. We're not talking here about some sort of an emotional high but about God's own presence expressed in a special way. It is as though when He hears His people praising Him, He is drawn to be with them. He is there in all of His fullness. He takes up residence and dwells in the praises of His people. How can any follower of God not want to be where He is?

God, we acknowledge that even though we get to church early and are there from the first notes of the first song that is sung, we still sometimes do not fully recognize what we are doing when we participate in praising You. Sometimes, we just go through the motions. We sing the songs, we stand, we sit, and we may even kneel before You; yet our thoughts are far away from You. We are thinking about our problems, all that we have to do that day, other people who are around us—even of where we're going for dinner after the service. O God, forgive us. Our praise creates a dwelling place for You. Help us to put ourselves fully into that act of service to You every time we are given the privilege of praising You. In Christ's name we pray, Amen.

August 4

"As soon as you hear the sound of marching in the tops of the balsam trees, move out to battle, because that will mean God has gone out in front of you to strike the Philistine army."

—*1 Chronicles 14:15*

A FEW YEARS AGO, THE UNIVERSITY of Wisconsin Badgers football team was playing against Michigan. This was in the day that Michigan was a powerhouse. It was a home game for the Badgers, but Michigan was killing them. The game ended at 40-7; Wisconsin was defeated. During the entire time, however, the Badger fans continued to cheer, clap, and celebrate, even when they were losing. The sportscasters were even asking, "Did they see the same game we saw?" What they found out later was that the Milwaukee Brewers, the Major League Baseball team, was playing a playoff game in another venue at the same time, and many of the Badger fans came in with radios so they could hear that Brewers' game. They were *watching* the Badgers lose their game, but they were *listening* to the Brewers and cheering them on at the same time.

We can be—we need to be—so tuned into God that, even though we see what's going on and how bad a situation looks, we can still keep rejoicing and praising God because we know He has already won the victory. If we aren't on the same frequency with God, we may look around us and think He is losing because of what we see. Yet, if we hear His voice and listen to His Word, we will know that our God is victorious.

Lord, help us to hear You. In the midst of voices that are negative, threatening, and frightening, help us to hear You and to recognize the sound of victory. In Jesus' name, Amen.

August 5

In my anguish I cried to the LORD, and he answered by setting me free.
—Psalm 118:5

A TEN-YEAR-OLD BOY IN MEXICO CITY WAS enjoying his Christmas break so much that when it was time to go back to school, he determined he wasn't going to go. Knowing that his parents would make him go, however, he tried to avoid the inevitable by gluing his hand to his bed. His mother couldn't get him unstuck. She called for help, however, and paramedics came and got him free.

Too many of us are stuck to ungodly relationships, to places we shouldn't be visiting, and to habits that are harmful to us. We may have let ourselves get stuck there initially because we were trying to avoid something. But now, we realize how foolish we were because no matter what else we want to do, we can't because we're stuck. At times like this, we need to remember that we can call on the Lord who will come and set us free.

Thank You, Lord, for answering the cries of our hearts and setting us free from all that keeps us bound. Amen.

August 6

When he had finished speaking, he said to Simon, "Put out into deep water, and let down the nets for a catch."

—*Luke 5:4*

SIMON AND THE OTHER FISHERMEN HAD BEEN fishing all night but had caught nothing. Jesus told Simon that he needed to go out into the deep water in order to make the catch. They had been trying all night to catch fish. Maybe they had been trying to find the fish in the shallow waters. Maybe they had been in the deep water but had grown tired of being out there. Now they were at least able to rest comfortably on the shore. But, because Jesus had told Simon to go into the deep water, he did so, and he and his partners caught so many fish that even two boats couldn't hold them all.

We need to get deep into the things of God. We need to connect with others who are in the deep waters, too. When we're in shallow water, we can't do the things we can do when we are deep into God. We will miss so much and fail so miserably if we remain safe and shallow.

God, give us the courage to go out into the deep. Let us know that we cannot do the same things in shallow water as we can do in deep water. Remind us that the abundance of blessing from our labor comes when we are in the deep. We may feel safer when we are in the shallow water. It may be easier to get around in the shallow water. We may think that we have more control in the shallow water. But we will never know the abundant harvest that comes from trusting and obeying God, and launching out into the deep. Make us deep-water Christians, we pray, in Jesus' name, Amen.

August 7

. . .for God's gifts and his call are irrevocable.

—*Romans 11:29*

NO ONE CAN RIDE IN MY CAR unauthorized. If, for example, my car were stolen, I can call a number from anywhere, give my code word, and my car will immediately be shut down. That's my car. I bought it, and no one else can have it. Even if others can see it, they can't have it. Even if others get to ride in it, they still can't have it. Even if others were to use dishonest means to try to take it, they still can't have it. It is my car.

In the spiritual realm, we don't have to worry about someone taking what God intends for us. If they aren't authorized to have it, their efforts will be shut down. They can't have what God has meant for us. Even if they use deceitful or manipulative means to try to take what God intends for us, He will just shut that thing down immediately. What God has for us is for us.

God, help us to stop being afraid that someone else may be getting what belongs to us. Some of us want to be married, so when someone else announces his or her engagement, it crosses our minds that maybe that was the person meant for us. Some of us want to have a baby, but that hasn't happened yet. So when another couple becomes pregnant, we feel sad, as though that baby was supposed to have been ours. When You provide financially for someone around us, we feel that the money should have come to us because we have been praying about a financial need. God, help us to know that Your supply is limitless. You can give to the whole wide world and still not give away our gifts. What You intend for us is for us. In Jesus' name, Amen.

August 8

Do not be misled: "Bad company corrupts good character."
—*1 Corinthians 15:33*

IN 2008, DANICA PATRICK BECAME THE FIRST woman to win an IndyCar series race. Some of the men in the racing world had said she needed to drop out of racing and become a model because they felt that she wasn't taking racing seriously. That night in Japan, she proved them wrong. She said after the race that her win depended upon fuel strategy, and she gave credit to her pit crew for calling it accurately for her. They were able to manage the fuel so that she could win the race. There were some other top drivers in that race, but she got the victory because of her pit crew. This crew replaces, repairs, refuels, and refreshes the car quickly so the driver can get back into the race.

Some of us don't get the victory because we don't have the right pit crew in our lives. Some of us surround ourselves with people who don't honor God in their lives, yet somehow we expect to be victorious in our Christian lives because of the input they give us. Some of us surround ourselves with negative thinkers. No matter what we do or what God does in our lives, they have something negative to say about it. Some of us surround ourselves with people who are gossipers and slanderers, and we don't realize that they deplete our "fuel" and leave us trying to run on empty. Some of us need to get new pit crews.

God, help us to realize how important the people are with whom we hang out. We can't always choose our family, our coworkers, or the acquaintances in our lives, but we can choose our friends; we can choose those with whom we spend our personal time. Help us to spend our time with people who can repair our attitudes, refuel our spirits, and refresh us in ways that allow us to continue to run victoriously. In Jesus' name, we pray, Amen.

August 9

Then Paul stood in the midst of Mars' hill, and said, Ye men of Athens, I perceive that in all things ye are too superstitious.

—Acts 17:22 (KJV)

THERE WAS A SUPERSTITION AMONG THE HEBREWS in the first century that caused people to believe that if they could just touch the clothes of a rabbi, they would be healed. We are still superstitious. Some people read their horoscope but not their Bible. Some people try to align their lives with the stars instead of with Jesus. Some people have a Bible in their hand but a rabbit's foot in their pocket.

Somebody asked me the other day, "What's your sign?" Jesus said in John 13:35, "By this all men will know that you are my disciples, if you love one another." The sign of disciples of Christ is that they love one another. That is the sign we should aim for as Christians. Do people see that sign in us? Do they know we are Christians by our love? Is love our sign?

Lord, we want others to know we are Your disciples. Help others to see the sign of love in our lives. Since "God is love," there is no better sign by which others can know we are Your followers. Let that sign be visible in all we say and do. In Jesus' name, Amen.

August 10

...God changed Saul's heart, and all these signs were fulfilled that day.
—*1 Samuel 10:9*

MY SON JORDAN HAD A SPECIAL EVENT he was going to, and his mother and I wanted to take pictures of him in a tux. Jalon has the best camera in the house, but he wasn't home, so I asked Jordan to call him and ask where his camera was. We located it, and I adjusted the settings on it properly. I turned it on, focused it, and pushed the right button, but I didn't get a picture. A message came up saying, "Card locked." I tried to push every button on the camera, but nothing worked. I called Jalon, and he told me to take the card out, flip the switch, and then put it back in. I followed his instructions, and the camera worked fine.

Sometimes, we will find that our lives are in a locked position. Everything looks right. We are doing all the things we've always done. We are praying just as we've always prayed. But nothing is happening. Our prayers just aren't being answered. We aren't seeing the power of God working through us. Everything just seems "locked." When that happens, we need to ask God to take out our hearts and change them—"flip the switch," if you will—and put them back in so that we can continue to function as He intends for us to function as Christians. A camera that only looks like a camera but doesn't function as a camera is worthless.

Father, we know that if we simply look like Christians but are not functioning as Christians, we are worthless. We are like salt that has lost its savor. Please come and unlock that which is keeping us from serving You—that which is keeping us from being all that You created us to be. Change our hearts this day so that we might be used of You in this world. We ask this in Jesus' name, Amen.

August 11

Then he reached out his hand and took the knife to slay his son. But the angel of the LORD called out to him from heaven,… "Do not lay a hand on the boy," he said.

—*Genesis 22:10-12*

ONE OF THE THINGS THAT MAKES PEYTON Manning such a great quarterback is his ability to read defenses. The Colts get in a huddle, and he calls the next play. But then when he sees how the other team's defense is set up at the line of scrimmage, he changes the play at the last minute. He hollers down the line that he is changing the play and tells his teammates what the new play is. He even uses hand signals so that those men who are too far away to hear his voice can still get his instructions.

God wants us to be willing to listen and watch for His signs when He decides to change the play in our lives in order to help us accomplish His goals. We may assume, on the basis of what we can see, that we should say or do a certain thing. But God has a far better view of the situation than we do, and He knows how to interpret all that He sees. It is better for us to simply listen to His voice and obey Him than to decide for ourselves what we should do in a given situation.

God, help us to remember that You are God and we are not. Help us to listen to Your voice and to trust Your judgment in each situation. Let us know, too, that what You told us to do last time may be different from what we are to do this time, even though the situations seem similar. Help us to be ever attentive to what You are saying in the moment. In Christ's name, Amen.

August 12

The people walking in darkness have seen a great light; on those living in the land of the shadow of death a light has dawned

—Isaiah 9:2

I HAVE A CONFESSION TO MAKE. DURING the 2008 NBA playoffs, I was able to go to one of the Atlanta Hawks basketball games, but secretly I was there to see the Boston Celtics. I got tickets from then Hawks executive vice president and general manager Billy Knight, who used to be a member of Eastern Star Church, but I actually wanted to see the Boston Celtics. The Celtics had the best record in the NBA and experienced the biggest turnaround in NBA history. The Hawks were then the worst team in the conference finals and had already lost the first two games of the series at Boston. So, even though I went to the game looking like a Hawks fan dressed in red and black, I actually expected to see them lose badly. But there, on their home floor with all of their fans cheering them on, they stomped Boston. Yet, when they went to Boston, their enemy's territory where there was nobody cheering them on, they lost. Back in Atlanta, their fans spurred them on, and they won again. They could win in Atlanta, but they lost in Boston. If the Hawks were going to sustain their position of victory, they would have to learn how to fight in enemy territory.

We may have a good job with good benefits, but we're thinking about quitting because somebody there doesn't like us. We're complaining that we are the only Christians in our particular workplaces. But God wants us to be the light in the darkness, learning to be victorious even in the midst of our enemies.

Lord, it would be so much easier to let our lights shine in the midst of a bunch of other lights. It's hard to feel like a tiny candle in the midst of a very dark place. Yet, we know that You have sent us out to be a light in the darkness—to reflect You to those who do not know that You are the Light of the world. Let us shine faithfully even in the darkness. Let us know that You can give us victory even in the midst of our enemies. In Jesus' name, Amen.

August 13

The ravens brought him bread and meat in the morning and bread and meat in the evening, and he drank from the brook

—*1 Kings 17:6*

RAVENS ARE KNOWN SCAVENGERS. THEY TAKE; they don't give. Yet God used ravens to feed Elijah. God had told Elijah where He wanted him to go and had said to him, "You will drink from the brook, and I have ordered the ravens to feed you there" (1 Kings 17:4). That might have been a bit disconcerting to Elijah to think of having to depend upon ravens for his food, but Elijah's faith was not in the ravens. His faith was in the God who said He would provide food for him.

God can use the least likely things to turn our situations around. Who are we to tell God what or whom He can and cannot use to supply our needs? We need to learn to keep our faith in God and allow Him to determine how He will provide for us.

Father, You know that too often we want to tell You how to take care of us. We ask You to provide something for us, and then we spend a lot of our prayer time telling You just how we want You to do that. Forgive us, God. Help us to keep our trust in You and realize that You have ways of amazing us as You provide for our needs. We do trust You, God, and we wait now to see what messenger You will use to bring our provision. In Your name we trust, Amen.

August 14

When a man's ways are pleasing to the LORD, he makes even his enemies live at peace with him.

—*Proverbs 16:7*

IN A SOFTBALL TOURNAMENT WITH CENTRAL WASHINGTON University, Western Oregon senior Sara Tucholsky hit a home run over the fence with two players on base. This was the first time she had ever done this in all of her years of high school and college play. All she had to do then was run around the bases and her team would score three runs. But on her way to first base, Sara tore a ligament in her knee, collapsed, and had to crawl to first base. The umpire ruled that a pinch runner could run for her, but she would be credited only with a single, and her team would get only two runs. Sara was in pain and couldn't move; her team couldn't help her. But, unbelievably, Central Washington's first basewoman Mallory Holtman asked if there were any rules against the opposing team coming to her aid. The umpire said no, so she and shortstop Liz Wallace picked Sara up and carried her around the bases to home plate. With those three points, Western Oregon won the game.

God can make even our enemies come to our aid. The boss who doesn't like us can become the means of our getting a promotion. The teacher who is so critical of us can help us pass the course. The relative who hasn't been speaking to us can give us just what we need. God is not limited in whom He uses to meet our needs.

Our Almighty God, we want to acknowledge today that we sometimes limit You by our faith, or lack thereof. We determine in our own minds whom You can and cannot use, when in fact You are able even to make our enemies be at peace with us. Help us not to limit You. Help us to keep our hearts and minds open to the fact that our God can do whatever He pleases with whomever He pleases. Help us to keep our focus on pleasing You. Amen.

August 15

"Bring the whole tithe into the storehouse, that there may be food in my house. Test me in this," says the Lord Almighty, "and see if I will not throw open the floodgates of heaven and pour out so much blessing that you will not have room enough for it."

—*Malachi 3:10*

WHEN I WAS A KID, MY MOMMA used to make homemade rolls. She would sift the flour, beat the eggs, and knead the dough. She would roll the dough, cut out the rolls, and preheat the oven. Then, after she had sifted, beaten, kneaded, rolled, and cut that dough, she would put it into the oven. When she put the dough in that hot environment, it was flat. But after a while, the dough began to rise because Mother had put something in that bread so that when it got in a heated situation, it didn't remain flat but began to rise.

No matter how you raise your children, at some point in time they are going to be sifted and beaten by life. They are going to go into a heated situation. But if you put the right ingredients into them in advance, that heated environment will only make them rise.

Father, teach us to be wise parents whether it be to our natural children or our children in the faith. Help us not to leave out any ingredient that will be of value to them in the future. Let us not instill only those things that will help them to survive in pleasant conditions, but let us be faithful to instill within them that which will allow them to rise when they get into heated situations. In Jesus' name, we pray, Amen.

August 16

A father to the fatherless…is God in his holy dwelling.

—Psalm 68:5

WHEN I BECAME PASTOR OF EASTERN STAR Church, one of the issues of concern was blessing babies. I take that very seriously, so every fourth Sunday we lay hands on newborn babies and bless them the way that Hannah blessed her son Samuel. But when I first came to this church twenty years ago, some people were concerned because I would bless the babies of single parents—children born out of wedlock. (They called them "illegitimate" children back then.) They thought I was sending a mixed message to the teenagers because I would preach about sexual purity, virginity, and waiting until marriage to have sex; but when it was time to bless babies, I blessed some who were the product of two people having sex outside of marriage. Some people in the congregation thought that was wrong.

But here's what I believed then and I still believe it: 1) If any baby needs a blessing, it's the one who is likely going to grow up without a father in the home; and 2) There are no illegitimate children; the babies didn't do anything that was wrong or immoral. There are no illegitimate babies, only irresponsible parents.

O God, You Yourself become a Father to the fatherless. If we reject "fatherless" children, we are rejecting children who belong to You, children whom You have adopted as Your own. Let us never be so heartless as to dismiss any child as being of lesser value than any other child. Let us remember that we are all Your children, and You have a plan and purpose for every single one of us regardless of what our parents did or did not do. Thank You, God, for loving us all. Amen.

August 17

A wife of noble character who can find?

—*Proverbs 31:10*

AFTER ASKING WHO CAN FIND A WIFE of noble character, Proverbs 31:10 starts describing this virtuous woman, this woman of noble character. One day I told a preacher friend of mine that I was going to preach on the virtuous woman of Proverbs 31, and mentioned this tenth verse that asks, "Who can find such a woman?" He said, "The reason we have trouble finding a woman of virtue is because many of us aren't looking for a woman of virtue." He continued, "It's hard to find a woman of virtue if we're looking for one in strip clubs because women of virtue aren't stripping at the club."

Women of character will be found where they are building up their character. This should offer some good advice for individuals in at least three types of situations: 1) If a man is looking for a woman of good character, he needs to be looking in places where women go in order to develop their character; 2) If a woman wants to become a woman of virtue, she needs to be going to places that will develop her character; and 3) If a woman wants to find a man who wants a woman of character, she needs to be in the places where he will go looking for her.

God, let us never settle for being less than what You want us to be, and let us never settle for having less than You want us to have. You did not include this description of a virtuous woman in Your Word just as filler. It is important for women to aspire to be women of virtue, and for men to desire to marry such women. Let us not settle for less than Your best. Amen.

August 18

...She is worth far more than rubies.

—Proverbs 31:10

PROVERBS 31:10 SAYS THE VALUE OF A virtuous woman is more than rubies; it's more than jewelry. Her virtue is what makes her who she is. Her value is not tied into jewelry and what she puts on: her value is tied into who she is. I'm focusing on this because there are some people whose self-esteem is so messed up that they think if they have jewelry, clothes, a house, a car and all the material things, that will make them persons of value. Conversely, they think that if they don't have these things, they are not of any value.

The Word of God is trying to show us that our value is not tied into what we have but into who we really are. We are not human *havers*; we are human *beings*. It is in our virtue, in our being, that we find our value. By understanding that our value is in God, we are then ready to be in a relationship with Him, with our world, and with another person. The material can never substitute for the spiritual; and it is the spiritual, not the material, that needs to be our focus. If we gain material things, we have only more stuff. None of that makes us better or more attractive individuals. But when we gain spiritually—when we add virtues of compassion, kindness, humility, gentleness, patience, tolerance, forgiveness, and love—we become individuals pleasing in God's sight and of great value to Him and to others.

Father, too often we feel so bad about the way we look, or the family situation from which we've come, or our current status in life, that we feel bad about ourselves. We think if we can accumulate some material things, they will somehow make up for what we believe is lacking within us. Help us to understand that is not true. Help us to quit wasting time on things that will never satisfy us and never get us that for which we are truly longing. Amen.

August 19

For you created my inmost being; you knit me together in my mother's womb.
I praise you because I am fearfully and wonderfully made; your works are
wonderful, I know that full well.

—Psalm 139:13-14

WHEN BISHOP JOSEPH WALKER, PASTOR OF MT. Zion Baptist Church in Nashville, was in our church, he pulled out a genuine hundred-dollar bill. He said then that he could take that hundred-dollar bill, ball it up, spit on it, throw it down, kick it, and walk away from it. But if he walked away from it, somebody else would come along and pick up that same hundred-dollar bill, straighten it out, wipe it off, put it in his or her pocket, and walk off rejoicing over having found something of such great value. Why? Because the value of that hundred-dollar bill is not based on how it is treated: the value is in itself.

We need to determine our value based on what God thinks about us, not what other people think. God tells us that He made us and that we are fearfully and wonderfully made. When a woman recognizes she is a person of value, she will be treated in that way. Brothers tend to treat women the same way that the women think of themselves. If a woman has self-respect, men approach her in one way; however, if they think she sees herself as worthless, they will approach her in another way. A woman who thinks poorly of herself will often sabotage a relationship with a good man because she thinks she doesn't deserve him. She will settle for a dog because she thinks that's all she's worth. But a woman who knows her value, even if she is treated badly, will not see herself through that person's eyes. Instead, she will turn to God to see how He is looking at her and then recognize that her price is far above rubies.

God, help us all, men and women, to recognize our value in You.
You made us, and You made us well. Help us never to devalue
Your creation, even when that creation is us. Let us see ourselves
through Your eyes, not through the eyes of others. In Your name
we pray, Amen.

August 20

". . .everyone who is called by my name, whom I created for my glory, whom I formed and made."

—*Isaiah 43:7*

ONCE, MY WIFE AND I WERE AT a church where a young preacher was preaching. As I listened, his voice and demeanor seemed strangely familiar. I turned to my wife and asked her, "Is he trying to be *me*?" We smiled over his efforts, and wondered what he would have been like if he had just been himself.

We are all born valuable originals, but most of us die as cheap copies because we don't understand our value. We tend to think we're too short, too tall, too light, too dark, or too whatever, so we try to be like someone else. We end up dying as a cheap copy rather than the valuable original God made us.

God, how sad for us if we were to die without ever becoming the original masterpiece You created us to be. Let us work individually at being the best we can be and recognize we will never be the best someone else can be. Remind us that You created us for Your glory. Amen.

August 21

Deliver my life from the sword, my precious life from the power of the dogs.
—*Psalm 22:20*

I'M A BIG FAN OF STEPHEN KING, who writes a lot of crazy, scary movies. A few years ago, he was walking down the street in his own neighborhood and was hit by a car. The accident was so bad that he broke several bones in his body and had to have reconstructive surgery. It took time for him to heal, but he is doing fine now. The investigation into the accident found that the woman who ran over King was distracted by a dog. Now, Stephen King is a multimillionaire and a man of influence. He produces movies, writes books, and has empowered a lot of people. Here is a man who has risen to the top of his profession, but there was a woman so distracted by a dog that she ran him over. Two days after this news item broke, there was a follow-up story that indicated the dog was in the car with the woman. I had previously thought that she was trying to avoid the dog, but she was trying to control the dog she already had.

You cannot control a wild dog. Some men have such animalistic attitudes and beastly behavior that they are hard to distinguish from dogs. How sad if a woman gets so involved with such an animal that she runs over a good man while she is contending with the dog.

God, we pray today that women will seek men who are worthy of them and that men will seek women who are worthy of them. Let us distinguish the dogs from humans and not be content to have a relationship with someone who is not living as one who was created in Your image. In Your holy name we pray, Amen

August 22

...as being heirs together of the grace of life...

—*1 Peter 3:7 (KJV)*

DANICA PATRICK MADE A PIT STOP DURING a practice for an Indianapolis 500 race and accidentally hit one of the pit crew. In the pit area, the people there refresh the driver, repair the car, change the tires, and make sure the driver can continue the race.

I wonder if some of us think how careless it was of Danica Patrick to hit one of her pit crew, yet sometime today we will run over the person in our own home who is a gift from God to us. This person is there to refresh us, to repair the damage done by the world, to meet our needs, and to help us continue on in this race of life. But some individuals run their spouses over every chance they get. Whether they are talking about their spouse to their children, to other relatives, to friends—or are even talking directly to their spouse—they disrespect and demean them. How many times will a person allow himself or herself to be run over before deciding to get out of the pit area?

O God, let us not take Your gifts for granted, and most especially the husband or wife whom You have given us. Let us love and honor that one and recognize how blessed we are to have that person present in our lives. Let us husbands love our wives as Christ loves the church, and let us wives respect our husbands even as the church respects Christ. Amen.

August 23

Jesus said to them, "My Father is always at his work to this very day, and I, too, am working."

—John 5:17

SOME WOMEN GREW UP READING FAIRY TALES and thinking that they would come true. They imagine a handsome prince riding in on a great stallion, rescuing them from a life of drudgery and letting them live forever in a palace surrounded by servants who are there to meet their every whim. These women don't know what to think, then, when they can't find a man who is willing to take care of them in the manner to which they had hoped to become accustomed. There are also some men who, even without the fairy tales, grow up expecting someone—a parent, a spouse, or the government—to take care of them. They become angry when someone suggests to them that they need to find a job.

Work is not a curse; it is a blessing. Bill Gates is worth over sixty billion, but both he and his wife Melinda still work. Adam and Eve worked, even before the Fall. God Himself works! We have to quit teaching our little girls to look for a man who will take care of them so they'll never have to work again. We have to instill within our boys a sense of responsibility so that they will accept work as a natural part of life. Work is a blessing.

God, somewhere along the line we have become confused about the role of work in our lives. Help us to see working as one of the ways that we are to be like Jesus. He saw You working, so He worked. We, too, must work. We must work for the kingdom of God. We must work to put bread on our tables. We must work to have something to share with others. We must work to put to use all of the gifts and abilities which You have given us to use. Let us be able to say as Jesus said, "My Father is always at his work to this very day, and I, too, am working." In His name, Amen.

August 24

Therefore they say unto God, Depart from us; for we desire not the knowledge of thy ways.

—Job 21:14 (KJV)

WE'VE HEARD ABOUT THE ATHEIST WHO WENT TO the woods to get his spirituality from nature, not from God. One day, he was in the woods, and a big grizzly bear came out of nowhere. The man ran, but fell, and the bear caught up with him. The big ol' grizzly bear started reaching out his paws toward the man. The atheist suddenly broke out in a prayer. God froze everything. God had never heard from this man before, so He was intrigued and wanted to hear what he had to say. The atheist said, "God, I need for You to do one of two things: I need for You to do a miracle and get me out of this situation, or I need for You to make this bear a Christian so that he won't kill me." God chose the latter request; He made the bear into a Christian. Then God unfroze the scene, and the bear continued to reach out and grab the man. But suddenly, the bear thought, "Wait a minute; I'm a Christian." So he stopped, put his paws together, and said, "I thank You, God, for what I am about to eat." Then he enjoyed God's provision.

The little story is funny, but the reality isn't. Many in our world choose not to believe in God. There are more organized groups of atheists now than ever before. They will not be coming into our churches, but God loves them and sends us to them. We need, therefore, to be sure that our lives are showing forth Christ so that they will meet Him in their workplace, at the gym, in the supermarket, in every walk of life.

Heavenly Father, we know You love those who love You and You love those who don't even acknowledge You. Help those of us who love You to let our lights shine so that those who don't even acknowledge You will see the light in us and ask where it's coming from. In Jesus' name, Amen.

August 25

Then Nebuchadnezzar the king was astonished, and rose up in haste, and spake, and said unto his counsellors, Did not we cast three men bound into the midst of the fire? They answered and said unto the king, True, O king. He answered and said, Lo, I see four men loose, walking in the midst of the fire, and they have no hurt; and the form of the fourth is like the Son of God.

—Daniel 3:24-25 (KJV)

SAMUEL ARMAS, WHOM YOU READ ABOUT EARLIER, was twenty-one weeks old—still in his mother's womb, still being developed—when he was diagnosed with spina bifida. Because this condition results in brain damage and spinal problems, many women decide to abort their pregnancies upon receiving this news. But because Samuel's mother didn't believe in abortion, the doctors in Nashville decided to do fetal surgery—to operate on the baby while he was still in his mother's womb. The doctors said in essence, "We aren't going to wait for you to come out to us; we're going to come to you and help you in your need."

God doesn't have to pull us out of our situations in order to help us. God will step into our situations and work for us while we are still in that very place. God didn't keep Daniel from the lions' den; He sent an angel into the den with Daniel to shut the mouths of the lions so they couldn't hurt him. God didn't keep Shadrach, Meshach, and Abednego out of the fiery furnace, but a fourth man "like the Son of God" was seen in the furnace with them. God will get in your situation with you.

Lord, help us not to be afraid of the lions' dens and furnaces in which we sometimes find ourselves. In those moments, help us to look around, expecting to see You. We know that we will not be disappointed. Thank You for getting into our situations with us and keeping us from harm. Amen.

August 26

I LOVE CARTOONS, ESPECIALLY THE JUSTICE LEAGUE, featuring Batman, Hawkgirl, and Superman. But they've got some new people in there now, and there have been some changes over the years. The Green Lantern used to be white; now he's black. And evidently, they fired the Wonder Twins—whatever happened to them? Do you remember them? They looked like just normal people, and actually they were normal if they were apart. But if all hell broke loose and there was an attack against the Justice League, while everybody else was running in all directions, the Wonder Twins would find each other. Then they would touch and agree, and Wonder Twin powers would activate so that what they couldn't do by themselves, they could now accomplish.

When all hell is breaking loose in our lives, we need to find a brother or sister in Christ with whom we can pray in agreement. The power of Christ will then be activated, and we will find that we can do then what we couldn't have done on our own.

Our Lord, we thank You for the Spirit of unity who draws us together even in our crisis situations. Thank You for the power in numbers. It doesn't take a crowd, but even two of Your people in agreement can see the forces of heaven come to bear on a situation. Deliver us from our independent spirits that think we never need help from anyone. Help us to realize that Your plan is for Your people to come together—in good times and in trials. Amen.

August 27

You will be his witness to all men of what you have seen and heard.
—Acts 22:15

A LOT OF TIMES WHEN I'M OUT witnessing and sharing my faith, people will ask me something such as, "Okay, Preacher, then where did Cain get his wife from?" Here I'm telling them about how they can be saved—how they can turn their lives over to Jesus, be forgiven from their sins, and experience new life in Christ—and they want to know where Cain's wife came from. What does that have to do with anything? My answer is, "I don't know because I wasn't there. I don't even know where you got your wife from." But I can tell people what I've seen, heard, and experienced.

When we try to witness for the Lord, there will always be people who want to change the subject, get us sidetracked, and move us from talking about a God who cares about us to some piece of trivia that has no bearing on them or their spiritual lives. At those times, we need to keep our focus on what we have seen, heard, and experienced. That is all to which we can bear witness.

God, we thank You for the privilege of introducing You to others and sharing with them what Jesus has done in our lives. Help us in those moments to keep our focus on Jesus, and to know He is our only message. Amen.

August 28

As you do not know the path of the wind, or how the body is formed in a mother's womb, so you cannot understand the work of God, the Maker of all things.

—*Ecclesiastes 11:5*

I DON'T UNDERSTAND HOW ELECTRICITY WORKS. Because of wires running through walls and ceilings, I can flip a switch and the light comes on. I don't understand it. But you don't see me sitting in the dark. No one comes to my house, sees me sitting in the pitch dark, and says, "Pastor, are you okay?" and I respond, "Yes, I'm fine." "Then why are you sitting in the pitch dark?" "Because I don't understand electricity." No, even though I don't understand it, I still flip the switch. I don't understand when a man and woman come together and a man releases millions of seeds, how just one seed is able to find that woman's egg and somehow they connect. Then, a baby is developed over nine months and—boom!—there's another human being in the world. I don't understand it. I can talk about it, but I don't understand it. Yet even though I don't understand it, I've still got four sons.

You can believe even when you don't understand. You can believe and act on that belief, even when you don't understand why something happens as it does. When you don't understand what God is doing, keep on believing in Him, acting upon Your trust in Him, and doing what He's told you to do. You may never understand why or how things worked out as they did, but you will eventually see the results of your faith.

Father, we know we can never understand how You work in our world and in our lives. What we do know, however, is that when we have faith in You, we see things come to pass. We know that when we trust You, You always prove trustworthy. We know that when we obey Your Word, Your Word proves true. We know that when we pray to You, You respond. We don't understand, but what we know is good enough for us on this side of heaven. In Your holy name we pray, Amen.

August 29

Blessed are they who maintain justice, who constantly do what is right.
—Psalm 106:3

WHILE I WAS A STUDENT AT BISHOP College, Dr. Manuel Scott Sr., one of the best preachers who ever lived, was a local pastor. He had pastored for about thirty years in Los Angeles, California, and then moved to Dallas and pastored successfully at the St. John's Baptist Church of Dallas. A group of us students used to follow him around the city to learn from him. We would go to his church to hear him preach, and when he would preach somewhere else, we would go there too. One day, we finally cornered this great preacher and began to ask him about the secret of his success—how he became so successful in his ministry, his preaching, and his life. We waited with great anticipation for the profound and mysterious response to the secrets of his success. But listen to what he said, which I've never forgotten: "If you want to be successful in life, find out what's right and do it."

Dr. Scott's secret was that simple. Just find out what's right and do it. This works not only in our ministry but also in our families, in our companies, in our finances, in any walk of life in which we want to be successful. Just find out what's right and do it.

God, we try to make things so hard when You have made them so simple. Help us in every area of our lives to find out what's right and do it. Amen.

August 30

Endure hardship with us like a good soldier of Christ Jesus.
—2 Timothy 2:3

A FEW YEARS AGO I WAS PREACHING IN A REVIVAL and in my free time one day, I decided to go to the mall and look for some running shoes. A clerk about seventeen or eighteen years old was at the counter. I started witnessing, and asked her what she was going to do with her life. She told me she was going into the military, and then related what a recruiter had told the students at her school—about the educational opportunities, the promotions, the benefits, and the ability to retire in twenty years. This conversation was during the pre-Iraq days, but even then I asked her, "Did your recruiter tell you that you might have to fight in a war?" She said naïvely, "No, he didn't say anything about that."

The reason why so many people want to quit following Christ in this twenty-first century is because we recruit them for the army of the Lord by telling them that God will give them a big house, a car, lots of money, and even a husband or wife if they want one. But we never tell them that they are going to experience conflict. So a few weeks after becoming Christians, they want to quit. They were expecting just the benefits of being a Christian. We failed to tell them that they were entering spiritual warfare, and would have to put on the armor of God and endure hardships even while they were receiving the benefits.

God, we confess that in our efforts to win others to You, some of us have not been totally honest. We have given people a fairy-tale version of Christianity in which the "happily ever after" comes in this life, not as a reward in heaven. People receive Christ for the wrong reasons, and then we wonder why they don't continue following Him. Forgive us, God, for misrepresenting You. Help us to preach the same gospel Jesus preached and nothing less. In Jesus' name, Amen.

August 31

I urge you, brothers, to watch out for those who cause divisions and put obstacles in your way that are contrary to the teaching you have learned. Keep away from them.

—Romans 16:17

MY SON JORDAN WAS ONCE OVER AT his friend's house, using his friend's computer to pull up his e-mail and check some of his messages. But while he was using the computer, the screen froze and he couldn't get his messages. I asked, "Well, son, what did you do? Did you quit?" "No, I didn't quit," he replied. "I called my friend over since it was his computer and asked him if he could help me get the screen to unfreeze." He tried some things, but still the screen was frozen. Yet, even then, Jordan didn't quit. He told me, "We finally figured out that the screen was frozen because of a bunch of pop-ups." There were messages he needed to receive, but he couldn't access them because there were so many advertisements popping up between him and his messages that they even froze the screen. "So how did you get the screen to unfreeze?" "I just began to click on the pop-ups," he replied. "When I got rid of all of them, the screen unfroze so I could get my messages."

When we're trying to live right for God, we're going to have all of these pop-ups come between us and God so that we are unable to access messages from Him. Haters, bad attitudes, mean dispositions, enemies, backstabbers, ungodly relationships: pop-ups! We can't ignore them because they won't go away. We have to deal with them one at a time, get rid of each of them, and then we can move forward.

Every day, God, there are so many pop-ups that interfere with our desire to hear Your voice. We need so much to receive messages from You, but constantly there are obstacles put in our way. Show us how to deal with each one that confronts us so that we may be able to freely receive from You what You want to say to us. Help us not to think we can avoid such obstacles, but let us instead learn how to deal with them as quickly and thoroughly as possible. Amen.

September 1

The Reubenites, the Gadites and the half-tribe of Manasseh had 44,760 men ready for military service—able-bodied men who could handle shield and sword, who could use a bow, and who were trained for battle.

—1 Chronicles 5:18

GREAT ATHLETES ALWAYS TRAIN MORE THAN THEY compete. Mike Tyson was one of the greatest heavyweight champions. Before becoming famous, he just came out in his boxing shorts and shoes, and proceeded to knock out his opponent in the first or second round. In one fight, however, he was facing the great Michael Spinks. I was at a friend's house to watch that match. We were eager to see somebody finally give Mike Tyson some competition. Just before the fight started, I ran into the kitchen to get a beverage. When I came back, the fight was over! Tyson had knocked out Michael Spinks in ninety-one seconds. However, although Tyson defeated his opponent in ninety-one seconds, he didn't train for ninety-one seconds! He trained for years—hours and hours, every day for years. Had he not trained for years, those ninety-one seconds could have been very different. Great athletes train more than they compete.

When I stand up to preach, it's only for about thirty-five minutes. But it takes me fifteen hours to prepare for those thirty-five minutes. I spend fifteen hours in preparation when my church is not looking so that I'll get it right when they are looking. Let's stop worrying about the times people are watching us. It's when they're not watching us that matters most.

God, many of us try to perform our Christian lives instead of living them. When the spotlight is on us, we do whatever we think we are supposed to do; but when there is no light, we do whatever we want to do. Help us to be "trained for battle." Motivate us to spend our time in preparation so that when the moment comes to represent You, we do so as ones who are prepared, not as those who are pretending. In Jesus' name, Amen.

September 2

When he takes the throne of his kingdom, he is to write for himself on a scroll a copy of this law, taken from that of the priests, who are Levites. It is to be with him, and he is to read it all the days of his life so that he may learn to revere the LORD his God and follow carefully all the words of this law and these decrees and not consider himself better than his brothers and turn from the law to the right or to the left....

—Deuteronomy 17:18-20

THE LAW OF GOD WORKS JUST LIKE THE LAW OF GRAVITY: it works the same for everybody. It doesn't care if we're struggling with a limited income, or wealthy and of great influence. We can't say, "Well, I'm an exception; the law of gravity doesn't work for me." Yes, it does! We can't say, "I understand the law of gravity is in place for those who need it. But I have special circumstances, so I'm exempt from that law." No, you're not!

Just as the law of gravity is the same for everyone, so is the Law of God. When the Bible tells us we are supposed to give God our tithes and offerings, we can't beg off because we're in a financial crunch right now. When the Bible tells us to honor one another above ourselves, we can't say that doesn't mean us because we really deserve the most honor. When the Bible tells us to seek first the kingdom of God and His righteousness, we can't defer that until sometime later on because we're really just too busy right now. Actually, we can ignore God's laws, just as we can ignore the law of gravity. But we all know what's going to happen when we jump off the roof.

Father, help us to remember that Your commands and instructions are written for our good. Our ignorance of them does not annul them, nor does our choice to disobey them make them invalid. Help us not to fool ourselves by thinking that we somehow are exempt. Let us rid ourselves of excuses and simply be obedient to You. Amen.

September 3

For I envied the arrogant when I saw the prosperity of the wicked…. Surely in vain have I kept my heart pure; in vain have I washed my hands in innocence…. When I tried to understand all this, it was oppressive to me till I entered the sanctuary of God; then I understood their final destiny. Surely you place them on slippery ground; you cast them down to ruin. How suddenly are they destroyed…

—*Psalm 73:3, 13, 16-19*

MAJOR LEAGUE BASEBALL PLAYER MARK MCGWIRE HIT sixty-two home runs in one season, breaking the record at that time. He was given a 1962 sweet red Corvette convertible. But now, years later, Mark McGwire is not in the Baseball Hall of Fame. Why? He didn't follow the rules. Floyd Landis rode his bicycle in the Tour de France one year. He crossed the finish line first, but he didn't get the prize. Why? He didn't follow the rules. Pete Rose played for the Cincinnati Reds, amassing over four thousand hits— a record then in Major League Baseball. He helped Cincinnati win the World Series, got the MVP award, and was nationally known. But Pete Rose isn't in the Baseball Hall of Fame. Why? He didn't follow the rules. Ben Johnson ran against Carl Lewis in the 1988 Olympics and won. But he didn't get to keep the gold medal. Why? He didn't follow the rules.

It may seem that there are people who are not keeping the rules of life—honesty, integrity, justice, etc.—and yet are winning. But rest assured that at the end of time when we can look back on all that has happened, we'll realize that the only ones with lasting rewards are the ones who followed God's rules.

God, help us not to worry and fret over those who seem to be blessed at the expense of others. There are those who seem to lie, cheat, and steal their way to wealth and prestige. Yet we know that Your eyes are always open, and while it may appear that they are getting away with something, You will have the final say. In the end, Your Word will prove true. Let us live accordingly, we pray in Jesus' name, Amen.

September 4

Let the wise listen and add to their learning, and let the discerning get guidance.

—*Proverbs 1:5*

I RAN ACROSS A HEADLINE IN *USA Today* that said, "When Nothing You Do Seems to Work." Because I know so many people who are living frustrated lives, I began to read the article. But it wasn't about life: it was about technology. We live in this high-tech society; and sometimes, no matter how high-tech we are, some of the things we do don't seem to work. Most people in our society have cell phones, computers, entertainment centers, iPods, and so much technology. Even for someone really low-tech like me, it's still easy to set up all this equipment because it's all color-coordinated. Even I know how to put the red plug into the red hole, the blue in the blue, and the white in the white. But what if we do all those things to get our computers, printers, and monitors all set up; yet, no matter what we do, they just won't work. The *USA Today* article offered some pointers that are applicable for life as well as for technology.

If what you are doing isn't working, stop and start over. Don't keep doing the same wrong thing, thinking that somehow it's going to work on the thirtieth try, even though it hasn't worked the first twenty-nine times. Also, remember that just as your computer came with an owner's manual, we have been given the Bible that we can read to learn what to do in life. Finally, don't be afraid to call for help. We can always call on God in times of trouble, and He will answer us and help us.

Lord, you know how frustrating this life can get sometimes. Even when we are trying to do all the right things, there are times when nothing we do seems to work. Help us, God, in those moments to stop, consult Your Word, and talk things over with You. We know that You will be faithful to get our lives running again in working order. We thank You for providing solutions for us. Amen.

September 5

I will repay you for the years the locusts have eaten.... and you will praise the name of the LORD your God, who has worked wonders for you....
—Joel 2:25-26

ONE OF MY FAVORITE SONGS IS "FAITHFUL Is Our God," composed by Hezekiah Walker. It encourages us that we will reap our harvest and take back what the devil stole from us. Then, the song closes with the confidence that we will recover it *all*. That is wonderful encouragement.

But think about it: we cannot take *back* something we never had. Some of us are singing about something that isn't relevant for us. We cannot even *have* a harvest if we have not planted any seed. Some of us need to stop singing that song until we plow the field, plant some seed, get rid of the weeds, wait for the crops to grow, and reap our harvest. *Then*, if the devil comes and tries to take it away from us, we can stand up against his wiles and get the victory. Even if he manages somehow to take something from us, we have the assurance that we can get it back. But to reclaim what *is* ours, it has to first *be* ours. Hard work precedes the harvest.

We come to You today, God, with praise and thanksgiving for the fact that You do reclaim for us what the Devil has stolen away. Whether it is financial stability, a positive family situation, success in our jobs, a healthy body, or whatever, we are grateful that the enemy does not have the last word. Yet, God, we confess that recently we haven't brought forth anything that the enemy has thought worth taking from us. Help us, God, to be willing to put forth the effort to reap the harvest in the first place. We ask this in Jesus' name, Amen.

September 6

God brought them out of Egypt; they have the strength of a wild ox.
—Numbers 23:22

ON MAY 1, WE READ ABOUT A DISORIENTED LOGGERHEAD sea turtle. An interesting fact about those animals is that the mother turtles come on shore to lay their eggs in holes over a foot deep that they dig in the sand with their flippers. After a period of incubation, the baby turtles hatch from their eggs and have to laboriously make their way to the surface of the sand and out into the ocean. They aren't well adapted to walking on the sand, so it's a slow and difficult ordeal for them. Experts, however, warn people not to try to "help" the turtles by carrying them into the ocean. The little, immature animals need to make that slow path for themselves because it builds their muscles and gives them the strength they will need for their long journey once they reach the ocean. If someone "helps" them and makes the struggle shorter, the turtles stand less chance of surviving and making it to their destination.

The Bible speaks much about waiting for the Lord. Psalm 27:14 says, "Wait for the LORD; be strong and take heart and wait for the LORD." Lamentations 3:26 admonishes, "It is good to wait quietly for the salvation of the LORD." Yet, as soon as we get into a situation that requires us to put forth effort or go through any struggle, we expect God to immediately rescue us. We get tired of trudging through our circumstances and we want to be freed from all the "sand" that makes our way so difficult. But all the while, the Lord is allowing us to continue on the difficult path because He knows it is building our strength for what lies ahead.

Father, You know how quickly we tire of struggles and obstacles. We constantly cry out for deliverance. Yet today, we learn that it is love that prompts You to let us continue for a while in some of our trials. The difficulties aren't intended to harm us, but to help us. Thank You, God. Amen.

September 7

And I will ask the Father, and he will give you another Counselor to be with you forever—the Spirit of truth. The world cannot accept him, because it neither sees him nor knows him. But you know him, for he lives with you and will be in you.

—John 14:16-18

AN ARTIFICIAL RETINA WAS INVENTED A FEW years ago for people who have become blind from a degenerative eye disease. The retina is about the size of a pinhead—so small it can't even be seen with the naked eye. Yet it contains thirty-five hundred solar cells that transmit impulses to the brain, helping the people see what they could not see before. But for the solar cells to work, they must be in proper relationship with the sun.

Second Corinthians 4:4 says, "The god of this age has blinded the minds of unbelievers, so that they cannot see the light of the gospel of the glory of Christ, who is the image of God." The Holy Spirit is the "Spirit of truth" who reveals to us the truth of Jesus Christ and empowers us to see and know Him. When the Holy Spirit comes into us, His presence is not visible. Yet, even though others can't see Him, He enables us to see as we could not see before. But in order for the Holy Spirit to continue doing His work within us, we have to stay in proper relationship with the Son.

God, we recognize that we see differently from the way the world sees. We thank You that Your Holy Spirit enlightens our eyes and enables us to see clearly. Thank You for taking away our blindness so that we might see and know Jesus. Amen.

September 8

But you are a chosen people, a royal priesthood, a holy nation, a people belonging to God, that you may declare the praises of him who called you out of darkness into his wonderful light.

—1 Peter 2:9

WHEN I WAS FIRST CALLED TO PASTOR Eastern Star Church, it was a bigger responsibility than the church I pastored in Terre Haute. The size of that congregation was about one hundred, but at the time Eastern Star Church had about two hundred and fifty to three hundred people in attendance on Sunday mornings. With this larger church, I also acquired a bigger house and an upgrade on my car. When that happened, there were some folks who said, "Jeffrey Johnson sure thinks he's something." They were right. But what they didn't realize was that I thought I was something when I didn't have a house or a car—when I was struggling and had nothing. I thought even then that I was a child of the King.

We need to learn that our value doesn't come from what we have but from who we are. According to God's Word, we are chosen, royal, and holy; and we belong to God. That should be the image we have of ourselves, and it is on this basis of what God says about us that we derive our sense of worth.

Father, thank You that we are of great value, but not as the world measures our worth. We are of value not because of what we have but because of who we are—because of who You have made us to be. Our value, then, is not dependent upon our changing circumstances but upon Your unchanging character. We love You today, God, and we pray that we will learn also to love ourselves. In Jesus' name, Amen.

September 9

Having a form of godliness but denying its power. Have nothing to do with them.

—2 Timothy 3:5

A LOT OF PEOPLE STILL LIKE TO get suntans even though it's dangerous because of the risk of skin cancer. Apparently they've heard the old adage that says, "The darker the berry, the sweeter the juice." Anyhow, the skin responds to the time it spends in the sun. But rather than waiting for that to happen naturally, some folks want a tan faster, so they go to a tanning salon that will spray on a tan instantly. The problem with that, though, is that it doesn't last long because it isn't real. It's even called a "fake bake" because it is done without involving the sun.

Some people today are taken in by ministries that operate without the Son. These folks want immediate spirituality, immediate gratification of their needs, and an immediate facade of holiness. So, rather than seeking what's real, they opt for the religious equivalent of a "fake bake." They settle for a Christianity without Christ. When we see anyone offering a ministry, a miracle, or material goods without the Son, we know it's not real.

God, may we never be fooled by those offering a fake relationship with You. Help us to guard against wanting something so quick and easy that we are willing to accept the false and the phony. Thank You, God, that our relationship with You is the real thing. We could be satisfied with no less. Amen.

September 10

...God, who richly provides us with everything for our enjoyment.
—1 Timothy 6:17

I LEARNED A LONG TIME AGO THAT THE BEST WAY TO GET my wife something she really likes for our anniversary is simply to ask her what she wants. One year, the only thing Sharon wanted was to see The Lion King, which was being performed at the Cadillac Theater in Chicago. I thought that was an easy request to grant since Chicago is only thirty minutes away by air. I have a friend who owns a restaurant there, and another friend works at a four-star hotel, so I knew it would be a great night. But then I learned that The Lion King was sold out through the end of the year! Our anniversary was in May. I called friends in Chicago, but no one could help me. I was frustrated and didn't know what to do. But Pastor James Jackson, on staff then at Eastern Star Church, heard about my predicament, and asked, "Pastor, don't you know that the guy who plays King Mufasa is a member of our church?" "King Mufasa is a member of Eastern Star Church?" I asked incredulously. "Yes, he is," he replied. "How do I contact him?" "Here, I've got his number on my cell phone." He handed me his phone, and I talked directly to King Mufasa himself and told him what I needed. He assured me, "Pastor, the tickets will be waiting for you at the window." So, after talking to the king, I was able to go to Chicago and pick up tickets without even having to wait in line. And we didn't sit in the back either; we were right up front in the VIP section.

When we can't get to the place we need to be in our lives, we must remember we have a relationship with King Jesus. He can provide us with what we need, even doing exceedingly abundantly above all that we ask or think.

God, You are amazing to us. You are so lavish in the way You show us Your love. Your provision far surpasses our prayers. Thank You, God, for caring for us in such a special way. Amen.

September 11

May our Lord Jesus Christ himself and God our Father, who loved us and by his grace gave us eternal encouragement and good hope, encourage your hearts and strengthen you in every good deed and word.

—2 Thessalonians 2:16-17

IN *USA TODAY*, A WRITER HAD INTERVIEWED A minister who lamented that there are no fathers in the Bible who are good role models of manhood and fatherhood. He offered a couple negative examples. But, the Bible is filled with good fathers who are wonderful role models. Elkanah sent his son Samuel to Eli to be dedicated to the Lord and raised in the house of God. It was Samuel who anointed David to be the king over Israel. Jesse had two daughters and seven sons, one of whom became a man after God's own heart. In the New Testament, there was a father whose son was self-destructive, trying to throw himself at times into fire or water. When Jesus' disciples couldn't help him, this father was so determined to save his son that he didn't stop until he got him to Jesus. Jairus sought Jesus when something became terribly wrong with his twelve-year-old daughter. He locked himself and his wife in the room with Jesus and his little girl until Jesus healed his daughter. These are all fathers who made a positive difference in the lives of their children.

Yet if those fathers fail to impress us, there is still our heavenly Father. We know Him by the way He dealt with His sons and daughters throughout the Bible. From His Word and our experience, we know He loves us, is intimately involved in our lives, and provides for all of our needs. It is He "who loved us and by his grace gave us eternal encouragement and good hope."

Father God, thank You for the role models of good fathers, good men, in the Bible. Help us to read about them and take to heart what they did so that we can learn from their examples. In Jesus' name, Amen.

September 12

His name was Nabal and his wife's name was Abigail. She was an intelligent and beautiful woman, but her husband, a Calebite, was surly and mean in his dealings....When David heard that Nabal was dead, he said, "Praise be to the LORD, who has upheld my cause against Nabal for treating me with contempt. He has kept his servant from doing wrong and has brought Nabal's wrongdoing down on his own head." Then David sent word to Abigail, asking her to become his wife.

—*1 Samuel 25:3, 39*

WHEN MY SISTER TONETTE WAS A TEENAGER, LIKE A lot of teens, she got into a friendship with a boy who hurt her feelings. Tonette was really sad and upset, and our mother was trying to comfort her. She pulled her aside and said, "Tonette, boys are like buses. If you miss one, just stay right there. It might take a minute, but another one is coming."

This is good advice, and the same principle holds true, too, for men who have been hurt by women. If we have been involved with someone who didn't treat us right, that wasn't the only person in the world. Sometimes, when the pain of a relationship goes deep enough, we close up emotionally, determined never to be hurt again. But we shouldn't believe that because one person has treated us badly, there are no more good people out there. There are still men and women after God's own heart in this world. If we are seeking a godly mate, we must entrust our future to God, give Him time, and allow Him to bring that person into our lives.

God, you know how painful relationships can be for us because we are all imperfect people, living in an imperfect world. But we thank You that relationships can also be beautiful and fulfilling when two people come together who love You first and foremost. Make us into persons who love and seek You, and may those who are praying for a spouse give You time to work. In Jesus' name, Amen.

September 13

And he took bread, gave thanks and broke it, and gave it to them, saying,
"This is my body given for you; do this in remembrance of me."
—*Luke 9:22:19*

NBA BASKETBALL PLAYER GRANT HILL EXCELS IN his profession, making the All Star team and winning all sorts of accolades. He is also a Christian, who loves his wife and children. Furthermore, he is a multimillionaire who shares his blessings by investing millions back into the community. But he went through a long ordeal—breaking his ankle twice, battling an infection that almost killed him, and going through painful rehab. After he came back into the league, his wife Tamia Hill told an interviewer how proud she was of her husband. She said he worked hard work, kept faith in God, and overcame his broken body through his unbroken spirit. She shared that one blustery winter day when they stopped for gas, her husband had a cast from his ankle all the way up his leg, so he sat inside their warm car while she stood in the cold pumping gas. Passersby could see her husband's athletic build, but not his brokenness. One man said to her, "Sister, I don't normally get into other people's business, but you can do a whole lot better than that!" She smiled because she knows the man he is. She understood that just because he went through a period of brokenness, it didn't make him any less a man. She didn't judge him by his brokenness but rather by the totality of who he is.

When we go through periods of brokenness, it doesn't mean God cannot restore us. And if we know someone who is broken, it doesn't mean that he or she will always be broken. In fact, God often breaks those whom He intends to use so that they can minister to more people. What a blessing we'll miss if we desert ourselves or someone else during a period of brokenness.

God, let us realize that brokenness is part of the Christian life.
Even as Jesus was broken for us, we also experience brokenness so
that we can minister to others. Let us never give up on ourselves
or on anyone else during a time of brokenness. In Jesus' name, we
pray, Amen.

September 14

"I have set you an example that you should do as I have done for you."
—John 13:15

WHEN I WAS IN JUNIOR HIGH SCHOOL, I was going in the wrong direction. I was acting so crazy that both my behavior and my grades reflected it. But that fall, as a freshman in high school, I went from getting bad grades to straight A's. Two things happened that summer that turned my life around: I gave my life to Christ, and my mother married Alonzo Coleman. He became the male role model in my life. He raised me as his own son even though we have no biological connection. I had never seen what a real man looked like. But then, every day I would see a man get up at 5:30 in the morning so that he could head off to work at six. Every day I saw a man reading scripture and praying to God. Every week, I saw a man heading to church to worship God and get involved in ministry. His example placed in my head an image of what real men are like.

We need role models today to show young boys and girls how to live. This is especially important for kids growing up in single-parent homes. Let's keep our eyes and ears open to see if there are children with whom God would want to use us as role models. Let's see if we can become an example to someone else of this God we serve.

God, you could have taken us to heaven the moment we became Christians, but You chose instead to leave us here as examples of Christ to the world. Let us be faithful. Let our hearts especially reach out to those who have no positive role models. Let our lives make a difference, we pray. Amen.

September 15

He got up and rebuked the wind and the raging waters; the storm subsided, and all was calm. "Where is your faith?" he asked his disciples.
—Luke 8:24b-25a

IN FISHERS, INDIANA, TWO GUYS WENT BOATING. A storm came and flipped their boat upside down. So there they were, cast out into the water by the storm, and trying to make it out alive. They took a rope from the boat and tied themselves to a tree on the nearby shore. Then they took out their cell phones and called the authorities, who came and pulled them out to safety. When the storm came and their boat flipped, they didn't try to make it on their own. Instead, they tied themselves to a tree and called someone who could help them.

We've been through so many storms that sometimes we feel like giving up. But if we just tie ourselves to the cross and call on God, He will come and save us.

Lord Jesus, You know the storm we are in at this very moment. We call upon You now to help us. You will find us at the foot of Your cross. Amen.

September 16

Then the LORD said to Moses, "Stretch out your hand toward the sky so that the darkness will spread over Egypt—darkness that can be felt." So Moses stretched out his hand toward the sky, and total darkness covered all Egypt for three days. No one could see anyone else or leave his place for three days. Yet all the Israelites had light in the places where they lived.
—Exodus 10:21-23

GOD INTENDED TO TAKE THE CHILDREN OF ISRAEL from Egypt into the Promised Land. But He also knew they would spend forty years in the wilderness, with no streetlights, headlights, flashlights, floodlights, or fluorescent lights. It was going to be very dark in the wilderness. So God sent the Israelites three days of darkness while they were still in bondage in order to prepare them for the forty years of darkness they would face later. The darkness didn't come only because Pharaoh refused to let the Israelites leave Egypt, but the plague to the Egyptians was a training experience for the Israelites.

Darkness is part of our preparation, too, because sometimes we have to deal with dark days. It was in the darkness that the children of Israel learned that they could keep going by faith even when they couldn't see the way for themselves. Israel also learned that God would provide a light for them even while those around them sat in darkness. The Israelites learned not to let the darkness stop them. If we're going to stop every time it gets dark—every twelve hours—it's going to take us twice as long to get to our destination.

God, you have shown us that You can keep us going even in the darkness. Help us to look for the light that You send and to keep moving even when we cannot see into the distance. In Your holy name we pray, Amen.

September 17

For your love is ever before me, and I walk continually in your truth.
—Psalm 26:3

IF WE ARE WALKING DOWN THE STREET and people start throwing stones at us, we don't stop walking because that would put us directly within throwing distance. If we keep walking, we'll eventually get out of their reach. Just keep on walking and we'll get away from our enemies.

It's time that we learn to keep moving. In Psalm 23:4, we read, "Even though I walk through the valley of the shadow of death. . ." So how do we get through the valley? We do it by continuing to walk. If we stop, we will not make it through the valley. If we stop, we will be vulnerable to our enemies. If we stop, we will become discouraged and lose hope. But if we just keep walking, and following the One who is guiding us, we will get to the table prepared before us and to a cup that's overflowing.

Father, thank You that our destination is secure in You. Thank You that You know where we're going and how to get us there. Help us to keep walking in the direction You lead us. In Jesus' name, Amen.

September 18

Woe to those who go down to Egypt for help, who rely on horses, who trust in the multitude of their chariots and in the great strength of their horsemen, but do not look to the Holy One of Israel, or seek help from the LORD.

—*Isaiah 31:1*

I WAS IN TERRE HAUTE TO PREACH a homegoing service. As I sat there in the sanctuary at St. Paul's Baptist Church, where I pastored before coming to Eastern Star Church, I was reminded of the last sermon I preached there. I thanked the congregation for taking a chance on that young pastor just starting out in the ministry. I thanked them for praying for me. But I also thanked the ones who dug ditches, hoping that I would fall in; those who stabbed me in the back; and those who tried to kill my ministry. I thanked them because, in spite of what they were trying to do, they kept me praying and fasting, so they helped me to grow and develop in my ministry and my walk with God.

When we are attacked, we must rely upon the Lord to vindicate us. If we try to battle with flesh against flesh, we will lose. But if we trust in the Lord and seek help from Him, He will come to our aid, deliver us, and make us victorious over our enemies.

God, help us never to return to our old way of life to try to find help in dealing with our enemies. Help us as Christians to know that carnal weapons cannot fight spiritual battles. Let each attack of the enemy only draw us closer to You, we pray in Jesus' name. Amen.

September 19

For you know that it was not with perishable things such as silver or gold that you were redeemed from the empty way of life handed down to you from your forefathers, but with the precious blood of Christ, a lamb without blemish or defect.

—1 Peter 1:18-19

THERE ARE SO MANY STORIES SURROUNDING THE 9/11 attack on the World Trade Center. The late Pastor Adrian Rogers told of a woman who was not from New York but was working with some people at the World Trade Center at that time. As she left her hotel and was driving to the World Trade Center that morning, her nose started to bleed, and some of the blood got on her blouse. She decided she couldn't go to work with blood all over her, so she turned around and went back to her hotel to change. At the hotel, a TV was on, and she saw the first plane crash into one of the towers at the World Trade Center. She said to herself at that time, "I would have been in that building and I would have been destroyed, had it not been for the fact that I was covered with all of that blood."

What turned that woman around was the blood. What made her change was the blood. We, too, know that we would have been in a hellish situation and would have been destroyed, had it not been for the blood of Jesus turning us around and saving us.

Thank you, God, for the blood of Jesus that has saved us and has transformed our lives. You have both delivered us from certain destruction and delivered us to a full and meaningful life that is worth the living. With all our hearts, we thank You. Amen.

September 20

For since the creation of the world God's invisible qualities—his eternal power and divine nature—have been clearly seen, being understood from what has been made, so that men are without excuse.

—Romans 1:20

THIS IS A BASIC ILLUSTRATION OF APOLOGETICS commonly discussed in seminary: Let's say you are walking down an isolated beach. It's just you, the sand, the ocean, and the sky. You look down and find a watch that is ticking and letting you know the correct time. When you pick up the watch, you look around but don't see anybody. Yet, even though you don't see anyone, you certainly don't think that the watch just suddenly sprang into being on its own. The very fact that there is a watch indicates to you that somewhere there is a watch*maker*.

When we look around at the sun, sky, trees, rivers, mountains, and all of creation, we also come to the conclusion that there is Somebody who created all of this—God. The invisible qualities of God are seen through His very creation. When we look up at the sky, or see the view from the top of a mountain, or sit on a rocky cliff and look out upon the ocean, we see God's power expressed in the creation of this vast universe. When we consider the rotation of the planets and the precision of their orbits, when we think of the measurement of time through day and night and through the seasons, and when we look at the intricacies of an individual atom through the lens of a microscope, we recognize the order and detail of the nature of God.

God, thank You that we can see Your invisible qualities through that which You have made visible to us. Thank You that You have used Your creation to let us know You exist. Thank You, God, for revealing Yourself to us. We stand amazed in Your presence. Amen.

September 21

Be imitators of God, therefore, as dearly loved children.

—*Ephesians 5:1*

SO OFTEN, WHEN MY SONS WERE YOUNGER and we hung out together, someone would see us and say, "Man, he looks just like you," or "Preacher, that boy looks just like you." When people said those things, it always made me puff out my chest and feel really proud. That's one of the greatest compliments you can give to a father—telling him that his children look just like him. The worst thing you can say to a daddy is that his children don't look anything like him. If I produce a child, there ought to be something about him or her that reminds other folks of who *I* am. What I've discovered about my children is that as the older and more mature they get, the more they look just like me.

We are created in the image of God. Those of us who are Christians have been adopted by God to be His own children. Therefore, the more we mature in the faith, the more we ought to reflect the image of our Father.

God, what a shame it would be for both You and us if others looked at us and could see no resemblance between us and our Father. Help us, O God, to increasingly look more and more like You—in our thoughts, our emotions, and our actions. We pray in Jesus' name, Amen.

September 22

"If a fire breaks out and spreads into thornbushes so that it burns shocks of grain or standing grain or the whole field, the one who started the fire must make restitution."

—Exodus 22:6

WHEN I TOOK MY SECOND SON JORDAN TO TENNESSEE STATE for his freshman orientation, we stopped in Nashville to get gas. Inside the station, I overheard a young woman tell the attendant, "Listen, I already paid for my gas, but I came back in to tell you that I spilled gas all over the ground. My fuel gauge is broken; so when I went to pump the gas, I didn't know how much I already had in there, and I made a mess trying to put in too much. I wanted to tell you because I don't want it to blow up in someone else's face." This person was being considerate of those coming along after her. She was trying to prevent anyone from getting hurt by the mess she made.

Many of us go through life making a mess of things, not knowing that we've got broken fuel indicators. Because we aren't filled with the Holy Spirit, we keep trying to get our indicators to register full by seeking more clothes, cars, tools, sports, games, drugs, sex, food, attention, power—almost anything to try to fill that void. Our futile attempts result in big messes and far too often, someone getting hurt.

God, fill us with Your Holy Spirit and help us to stop trying to find a substitute for You. We are coming to You as the young woman went to the gas station attendant. We are sorry for the mess we made. Please take care of it so that no one else gets hurt by what we've done. And, God, if some of our messes have already blown up in someone else's face, help us to go to that person, ask forgiveness, and seek to make amends. Give us Your grace, we pray in Jesus' name. Amen.

September 23

The cords of death entangled me; the torrents of destruction overwhelmed me. The cords of the grave coiled around me; the snares of death confronted me. In my distress I called to the LORD; I cried to my God for help....He parted the heavens and came down....The valleys of the sea were exposed and the foundations of the earth laid bare....He reached down from on high and took hold of me; he drew me out of deep waters. He rescued me from my powerful enemy, from my foes, who were too strong for me.

—Psalm 18:4-6, 9, 15-17

IN 2005, A RUSSIAN SUBMARINE IN MOSCOW got entangled in some fishing nets, and began to sink. It fell six hundred feet down and was disabled. No man could go that low to try to save them. The authorities couldn't even send another submarine down to cut them out of the nets because they had sunk so low that no man could cut them free. So the British government sent over an unmanned vessel that was able to go down to those depths. It cut the submarine free and saved every life onboard in spite of how low it had fallen.

It doesn't matter how low we have fallen. Even though there is no man or woman who can save us, Jesus came from heaven to earth to rescue us and set us free. All we have to do is call upon Him, and He will hear and save us.

Jesus, thank You that no matter how low we fall, You are able to come to where we are and save us. Thank You that no matter how strong the cords are that bind us, You are able to free us. Thank You that no matter how powerful the enemy is, You are able to redeem and deliver us. We praise You, Lord Jesus, for who You are and for Your great salvation to us. Thank You for cutting the cords that bind us and setting us free! Amen.

September 24

This righteousness from God comes through faith in Jesus Christ to all who believe. There is no difference, for all have sinned and fall short of the glory of God, and are justified freely by his grace through the redemption that came by Christ Jesus.

—*Romans 3:22-24*

THE MEN WITH WHOM I RUN ALMOST daily are college football fans. I had to start getting more interested in NCAA football so I could join in their conversations more when we run. I remember once watching the then ninth-ranked Tennessee Volunteers play the unranked UCLA Bruins. That particular year, UCLA was rebuilding the team after getting a new coach and a new quarterback, so they were not expected to win. In the first half of the game, UCLA's new quarterback Kevin Craft threw four interceptions, allowing Tennessee to end the first half with a score of 14-7. But during the second half, Craft threw completed passes, leading his team to victory in overtime. After the game, the media asked UCLA's new head coach Rick Neuheisel what he said to Craft during halftime that brought about this turnaround. Coach Neuheisel said he told him that when he was a quarterback in college, he threw four interceptions during his first game, but he came back to win the game.

I've had at least four turnovers in my life, and I would guess that you probably have experienced at least that many moral turnovers in your life as well. But we have learned that God can give us victory in spite of our earlier setbacks. It's what we do with our lives right now that counts. We know that we all have sinned and come short of the glory of God. But it's what we do now, not what we did in our yesterdays, that determines whether we will have victory.

God, we are grateful that when we fall, You don't put us out of the game. You remind us instead that everyone has fallen at some point, and that our victory does not depend on us anyhow, but on our faith in Jesus. Thank You for second chances, and third, and fourth, and. . . . We love you today, God. Amen.

September 25

For they rebelled against the Spirit of God, and rash words came from Moses' lips.

—Psalm 106:33

WHILE HER FATHER WAS DRIVING, A LITTLE girl stood up in the backseat and started jumping up and down. Her father told her to sit down, but she continued jumping. Her father told her that if she didn't sit down, he would stop the car and take care of her, and she wouldn't like it. The little girl sat down. But a few minutes later she said, "Daddy, inside I'm still standing up."

Some of us come to church and look like we're doing the right thing on the outside. But inside we're mean, unrepentant, and defiant with God.

Lord, forgive us for being so childish and for having rebellious spirits. Teach us to obey You fully and with a right spirit. We ask this in the precious name of Jesus. Amen.

September 26

"Blessed is she who has believed that what the Lord has said to her will be accomplished!"

—*Luke 1:45*

MEL GIBSON SAID THAT HE PRODUCED THE film The Passion of the Christ because God told him to do it. He said that he had given his life to God and felt that God wanted the world to understand how much Jesus suffered for us. He approached one producer after another to get his movie financed, but they refused, so he used twenty-five million dollars of his own money to pay the costs. That film has now earned Mel Gibson almost one billion dollars.

The other producers thought God would fail to produce anything of value, so they invested nothing and got nothing. Mel Gibson dared to trust God, and he was rewarded with millions of dollars. How big is our God? Can we leap out in faith to do what God says to do, or is our God too small to safeguard us? Is our God worthy of our trust—or not?

Too often, God, we play it safe. We believe only what we can see, and we trust You only for what we can accomplish ourselves. Forgive us for saying we believe, yet failing to act on that belief. Forgive us for disobeying You when You told us to do something but we didn't do it because we were afraid. We were afraid that You wouldn't come through for us. God, help us to believe and to do what You tell us. In Jesus' name we pray, Amen.

September 27

Calling his disciples to him, Jesus said, "I tell you the truth, this poor widow has put more into the treasury than all the others. They all gave out of their wealth; but she, out of her poverty, put in everything—all she had to live on."

—Mark 12:43-44

MY GRANDMOTHER BOWLS NEARLY EVERY WEEK. AT eighty-seven, she is a good bowler, with good approach, form, and follow-through. Just last year, when my uncle was in town, our whole family went bowling. My grandmother scored 181 points and beat all of us! Sometime later, we were all at my mother's house "bowling" on an electronic game called a Wii. When my grandmother tried to bowl on this simulated game, she didn't do well because she couldn't grasp the idea of letting up on the "hold" button. She kept the button depressed so long that the ball went back up in the air and then fell with a thump onto the lane. At the bowling alley, she had perfect form and follow-through with the ball, but she couldn't gain the victory in this game because she wouldn't let go.

The widow in the scripture for today let go of all that she had in order to give to God. I wonder if she paused at all before letting go of her two coins. It may not have been great faith that prompted her action—she may not have expected God to repay her. She may have decided that, no matter what happened, she loved God enough that she would give Him everything she had. She expressed her love to God by letting go.

God, teach us to let go. We cling to so much stuff that we can almost imagine arriving someday at heaven's gate carrying boxes, bags, and baskets of things that we don't want to let go of; we want to take our junk with us even into heaven. O God, teach us the joy of letting go. In Christ's name, Amen.

September 28

The LORD blessed the latter part of Job's life more than the first.
—Job 42:12

IN JOHN 2, JESUS WENT TO A wedding feast at Cana in Galilee. At the wedding feast, the wine ran out, which was a great embarrassment for the family hosting the feast. Jesus' mother told Him about the situation, and she told the servants to do whatever Jesus said. He told them to fill up the water pots, and He turned that water into wine. They took a cup of the wine to the master of the banquet. He said, "You're doing something I've never heard of before. Normally, folks bring the good wine out first, and then once we get drunk and it doesn't make any difference to us, they bring out the lesser quality wine. But you've turned this thing around. You have saved the best till last."

That's how Jesus always works: He always saves His best for last. It's important that we keep that in mind. We must never give up, no matter how bad our circumstances seem to get. We must keep trusting and obeying the Lord because God always saves His best for last.

God, let our hearts be encouraged today. There are times when things have gotten so bad that we have felt like giving up. But You have reminded us today that You save Your best till last. So we wait now in confidence, trusting You that the best is yet to come. Amen.

September 29

He read in their hearing all the words of the Book of the Covenant, which had been found in the temple of the Lord. The king stood by his pillar and renewed the covenant in the presence of the Lord—to follow the Lord and keep his commands, regulations and decrees with all his heart and all his soul, and to obey the words of the covenant written in this book.

—2 Chronicles 34:30-31

IN 2008, THE INDIANAPOLIS COLTS' WIDE receiver Anthony Gonzalez was getting better and better every week. Even the media began noticing the change in him, and the sportscasters wondered what had happened to account for his improvement. Gonzalez told them, "I don't worry about how many catches I get, how many yards I pick up, or how many times I score. What I work on is my technique. If I do it right, the consequences will take care of themselves." Quarterback Peyton Manning was also asked why Gonzalez was seeing so much improvement. He replied that Gonzalez studies the plays, the games, and the defense. He studies in order that he knows how to read the defense, so he can react to the defense and adjust his own actions accordingly. He studies, reads, reacts, and adjusts.

Like Gonzalez, we need to focus on how we are living our Christian lives—not on the consequences. We don't become more Christlike by trying to look like Jesus. We become more like Christ by studying the Word of God, reading it, responding to it, and adjusting our lives to it. And like Gonzalez, who didn't try to adjust his game based on what the media said, we need to stop listening to people who try to discourage us. The Word of God can change us from the inside out. Let's concentrate on what God says to us as we live and grow in His Word.

Help us, God, to spend time reading and studying Your Word and then responding to life based on the adjustments Your Word has us to make. Help us to know that we can only follow You wholly when we know what You want of us. Thank You for providing us with the Bible, so that we need never be in doubt of how You want us to live. Amen.

September 30

"The LORD himself goes before you and will be with you; he will never leave you nor forsake you. Do not be afraid; do not be discouraged."

—Deuteronomy 31:8

BILL RUSSELL IS A RETIRED NBA PLAYER and Hall-of-Famer who used to play for the Boston Celtics. When he was a junior in high school, he went out for the junior varsity basketball team at his school; but even at six-foot-seven, he got cut. The junior varsity coach told him he wasn't good enough. He was really depressed. The next day, he was walking in the hallway and ran into the coach of the varsity team. The coach noticed his size and told him he wanted him to try out for the varsity team. Russell told the coach he wasn't good enough. He told him he wasn't even good enough for the junior varsity team, and explained that he had tried out for that team and got cut just the night before. The varsity coach said to him, "I don't coach junior varsity." Bill Russell decided to try out for the team. Not only did he make the team, win a state championship, get a scholarship to go to the University of San Francisco, and become a first-round draft choice in the NBA, but he still holds the record for having the most championship rings in the NBA. He later became the first Black coach in the NBA. Do you know why he had such success? He didn't listen to one man who told him he wasn't good enough. He moved on and moved up.

How many of us get bogged down in fear and depression because someone tells us we aren't good enough at something? When one person tells you that you're not good enough, move on and move up! It isn't what a man or woman says that counts, but what God says. We must listen to what He says. If He is sending us forth, we can go with confidence because He will not only go with us, but He will also go ahead of us to prepare the way.

God, we bring our feelings of fear and depression before You today. You know that they came upon us when we listened to what someone else said about us. We should have been listening instead to You. Forgive us. Free us from these negative emotions. Let us go forth now, knowing that You are with us, and seeing ourselves as You see us. In Jesus' name, Amen.

October 1

When your words came, I ate them; they were my joy and my heart's delight, for I bear your name, O LORD God Almighty.

—Jeremiah 15:16

BISHOP DEREK TRIPLETT HAS A DAUGHTER IN college who is beautiful and smart, and young men are calling to date her. Some of them are even envisioning a relationship with her, perhaps one that could become permanent. Bishop Triplett says that before he gives his daughter to a man to marry, he's going to check out the man's name. Right now, her name is Triplett. With that name, she can get credit, buy a house, or get a car. With that name, she gets honor and respect. Before she changes her name, her father is going to make sure that the new name she takes on will not lessen her value.

We should all remember that we bear the name of our Father; we are called by His name. In our Father, we have a positive identity. Because of His name, we have doors opened for us, financial stability, and the promise of good things yet to come. Let us stop living as beggars in this world and recognize that we are children of the King.

God, we don't always remember who we are or whose we are. We fail to remember whose name we bear and to think about what it means to be called by the name of our Father. Thank You, God, for the privilege of being called by Your name. Help us to walk worthy of the One whose name we bear. Amen.

October 2

Are not five sparrows sold for two pennies? Yet not one of them is forgotten by God. Indeed, the very hairs of your head are all numbered. Don't be afraid; you are worth more than many sparrows.

—Luke 12:6-7

A FATHER AND SON WERE SWIMMING ALONG THE SHORE when a riptide carried them out into the ocean. Helplessly, and without life jackets, they quickly moved farther and farther away from the land. The twelve-year-old autistic son loved to swim and exhibited no fear as he and his father treaded the shark-infested waters for hours. He never conversed, but had memorized phrases from Disney movies; so the two shouted lines to each other as they hoped for a rescue. But as darkness set in, stingrays stung them, and the father realized they wouldn't be found in the dark. In the stillness of the night, the father called out from Toy Story, "To infinity!" and the son called back, "And beyond!" But after a while, they drifted apart. The father could no longer hear his son's voice, and gave up hope of ever seeing him alive again.

The man felt like giving up himself, but he determined to stay alive for his daughter—not wanting her to lose her brother and her father on the same day. He found comfort during the night knowing that he was in God's hands. The next morning, rescuers resumed their search. Chances of finding them were nil. But a man on a fishing boat happened to see a flash of light as the sun shone on a religious medallion worn around the father's neck. He was rescued and taken aboard a Coast Guard ship. He waited below deck, hoping his son's body would be recovered but not wanting to witness it. Awhile later, he was called on deck. The crew pointed to a helicopter and told him his son was on that chopper—alive and well.

God, we are overwhelmed when we think of Your love for us. It is infinite and yet so intimate and personal. When we think that You would care for two human beings lost in an immense ocean, how can we doubt Your care for us wherever we are, whatever our circumstances? Thank You, God, for your infinite love. Amen.

October 3

For the message of the cross is foolishness to those who are perishing, but to us who are being saved it is the power of God.

—*1 Corinthians 1:18*

MY FAMILY AND I WENT TO THE Circle City Classic Parade. One of the sororities in the parade was celebrating its founding in 1922. Following behind their float were four little girls with helium balloons illustrating the "1-9-2-2." Unfortunately, the balloons had been filled with the helium the day before, so by the time of the parade, they weren't staying up in the air. The girls kept trying to push them back up into the air, but they kept falling limp. Someone sitting in front of us overheard us talking about the sad shape of the balloons and commented, "They should have used sticks."

Some of us are like those little girls. We are trying to keep our lives afloat and trying to keep holding ourselves up, but we can't do it. We need instead to rely on the wooden stick, the cross, to hold us up. There is power in the message of the cross of Christ that only those who are saved can know.

Lord, thank You today for the power that is in the message of the cross. To the world, it seems foolish that a Man who claimed to be innocent would die for someone who was guilty. Yet, that is exactly what You did, Lord Jesus. You knew no sin, yet You died to redeem us from our sin and the penalty of our sin. There is power in that message—a power that strengthens and holds us up, both now and through all eternity. Thank You for enduring the cross for our sakes. Amen.

October 4

Though you have made me see troubles, many and bitter, you will restore my life again; from the depths of the earth you will again bring me up.
—Psalm 71:20

ONE OF MY SONS HAD BOUGHT SOME new pencils. As he sharpened them, I thought about the lesson pencils teach us. When you buy a new pencil, it looks good but it can't do anything. It looks good, but it's not very practical. It looks good, but it can't accomplish any work. So my son took the pencil, stuck it in the pencil sharpener, and the sharpener began grinding away at the pencil: "Rrrrrr." He took it out, looked at it, blew on it, saw that it still wasn't usable, and stuck it back in: "Rrrrrr." Then he took the pencil out a second time, looked at it, blew on it, saw it still wasn't quite ready, and put it back in. He kept doing that until the new pencil was finally sharpened enough to be used.

When we gave our lives to Christ, we became new Christians, but we couldn't do anything at the time. So God put us in the grinder of adversity, took us out, and looked at us. He looked to see how we were forming, blew upon us with the Holy Spirit, and put us back in the midst of the challenge. He continues to do that until He can use us. Just as my son did with the pencil, He keeps grinding us until we get the point. At times, God lets us go through periods of tribulation to help us understand His mysteries—the hidden truths that He wants us to know. There is always purpose in our pain.

God, You know that we don't like to think about times of trials and troubles as coming from You. It's far less complicated to think that all good times come from You and all bad times come from the devil. But what we fail to see is that what we consider "bad times" are sometimes simply Your preparation times. Just like the refiner's fire purifies the silver, and just like the potter shapes and reshapes the clay and fires it in a kiln to make it into something of value and use, You let the fires of adversity make us usable in Your hands. We want to fulfill the purposes for which You created us, O God, so help us to trust You while we are still being prepared. In Jesus' name, Amen.

October 5

When your words came, I ate them; they were my joy and my heart's delight, for I bear your name, O Lord God Almighty.

—*Jeremiah 15:16*

I USED TO GET SINUS INFECTIONS ALL the time, but I haven't had one now for about fifteen years. The infection not only affected my sinuses but also my eyes, my head, my mouth, and my throat. It just knocked me out for days. Therefore, I would go to the doctor and he would give me a prescription for amoxicillin. I would take that prescription to the pharmacist who would give me what the doctor prescribed. But the medicine still didn't help me until I took it, until I got it inside my belly. Even then, the pharmacist warned me that I needed to take all of it. He said I would start feeling better when I began the medicine, but it wouldn't really get rid of the infection unless I took all of it.

God is the Great Physician and His Word can bring healing and joy. As a preacher shares with us from the Word of God, we may get a "prescription" for a particular issue we're dealing with that is trying to destroy us. But simply hearing those words aren't going to make us well. Those words aren't going to help us until we ingest them; they have to get inside of us before they can bring forth the healing. We also have to take in all of it; we can't accept what we feel like taking and then stop when the Word becomes harder to swallow or bitter to our taste. The Word of God is like medicine: It won't help us if we just keep it in the bottle. It doesn't work until we internalize it.

God, we come to You in this moment because we are sick. Our minds, our bodies, and our spirits need a healing touch from You. We thank You that Your Word brings life as we take it into ourselves. We do receive Your Word this day. Let it bring us life, health, and joy, we pray, in the name of Jesus. Amen.

October 6

The LORD reigns, he is robed in majesty; the Lord is robed in majesty and is armed with strength. The world is firmly established; it cannot be moved.

—Psalm 93:1

A SUNDAY SCHOOL TEACHER GAVE A LITTLE BOY A PICTURE of a globe to illustrate that "God so loved the world." On their way home, the boy's father asked him what he learned that day, but he wouldn't answer. He was in a bad mood. He refused to answer, and even tore the picture into lots of little pieces. When they got home, the father took those pieces, gave them to the boy, sent him to his room, and told him not to come out until he had put the picture back together. The boy tried to tape the pieces together, but eventually went to his father, saying, "Daddy, I can't get the picture together. I can tell you what the teacher said, but I can't figure out the picture." His father said, "You tore it up, so you can fix it. Go back in there and don't come out until you put that world together again." Soon, the boy returned, happy and smiling, with the world taped together correctly. "Here it is, Daddy," he said. "This is what the teacher taught us: that God so loves the world. . ." "But how did you do that so quickly?" his father asked. "I couldn't get the world together, but I remembered there was a picture of Jesus on the other side," his son replied. "So I put the picture of Jesus together, and when I did, the world came together too."

We have been trying unsuccessfully to put our broken world back together, but we have become frustrated after realizing our efforts are futile. Rather than focusing on restoring our world, we need to focus on restoring our relationship with Jesus. If our relationship with Jesus is whole, the pieces of our world will fall back into place as well.

Jesus, we acknowledge that our personal worlds are broken because our relationship with You is broken. Restore our relationship with You. We focus our attention upon You. We trust that as our broken relationship is rebuilt, our worlds will be mended as well. Thank You, Lord. Amen.

October 7

"Blessed is the man whom God corrects; so do not despise the discipline of the Almighty. For he wounds, but he also binds up; he injures, but his hands also heal."

—*Job 5:17-18*

ONE OF THE FIRST FUNERALS I PREACHED at Eastern Star Church was for a sixteen-year-old girl who had been stabbed. She had died from a two-inch cut. At that same time, another person in our church was cut eight inches in an open-heart surgery and lived. In fact, that person is still worshiping with us in our church today. The reason one died and the other lived is because one was cut to kill while the other was cut to heal.

The cut of a surgeon is so precise that, even though he or she may seem to hurt us, the incision is necessary for our healing. If God performs surgery to remove a spiritual cancer from us or address some malfunction within us, His wounds will only serve to make us well. God's wounds, while painful in the moment, always bring life and health.

We trust You, God. We know that things are not always as they appear. We know that when You wound us, You also bind us up. You never cut something from our lives that we need; You never operate on us unnecessarily. Your hand is always guided by the heart of a loving Father. Amen.

October 8

"How many loaves do you have?" Jesus asked. "Seven," they replied, "and a few small fish." He told the crowd to sit down on the ground. Then he took the seven loaves and the fish, and when he had given thanks, he broke them and gave them to the disciples, and they in turn to the people. They all ate and were satisfied. Afterward the disciples picked up seven basketfuls of broken pieces that were left over.

—*Matthew 15:34-37*

WHEN I WAS A CHILD, WE HAD TO DO CHORES. INSTEAD of taking turns every day, we each did dishes for a whole week—and if we didn't do them right, we got another whole week of dishes! Momma liked to cook big meals so that she could have leftovers and not have to cook everything from scratch every evening. To make those big meals, she used lots of pots, pans, and dishes. Even worse, my brothers and sister used a clean plate every time they went back for seconds. Sometimes, by the time the meal was over, the kitchen was a real mess. I was trying hard one evening to figure out a way to get out of doing dishes, and I thought I had found the perfect excuse. I noticed there wasn't much dishwashing liquid in the bottle. Relieved, I took the almost empty bottle to Momma, and explained that I simply wouldn't be able to do the dishes that evening. Spoiling my plan, she said, "Oh, there's plenty left in there." She took the almost empty bottle into the kitchen, ran some water into the bottle, shook it up, and said, "There! That's more than enough."

When we come to the end of our resources and think we don't have enough, we need to put what we have in the hands of Someone who knows how to multiply it.

Lord, You have shown us repeatedly in your Word and in our lives that You are able to multiply the little we have so that it becomes sufficient. What You provide is always enough. We bring to You what we have right now. In our hands, it isn't enough, but we entrust it to Your hands, knowing it will be sufficient. Amen.

October 9

I lift up my eyes to the hills—where does my help come from? My help comes from the LORD, the Maker of heaven and earth

—*Psalm 121:1-2*

IN BIBLICAL TIMES, THE ISRAELITES USED TO make pilgrimages to Jerusalem to worship. Some of them went once a year, some on occasion, and some made it only once in a lifetime. But because the travelers came in such a steady flow, they were an easy mark for thieves and robbers as they passed along the road to Jerusalem. The attacks were so common, in fact, that there were sentries posted in the hills to watch for attackers and assist those who were being assaulted. Therefore, when disaster overtook any of the Jewish people traveling this road, they would naturally look up to the hills to watch for the sentries coming to their aid.

We do not look for help from men in the hills but rather from the Lord. Just as the psalmist recognized that his help came from the Lord, we know that is true for us as well.

Maker of heaven and earth, we look unto You this day for our help. You know exactly what is happening in our lives and exactly the type of help we need. We know that there is no human being who can come to our aid in this matter, so we don't look to the hills and watch in vain. We look to You. We know that, as the One who created the heavens and earth, You are powerful enough to handle our situation. We eagerly wait for Your help. Thank You for Your loving faithfulness. In Christ's name, Amen.

October 10

And having disarmed the powers and authorities, he made a public spectacle of them, triumphing over them by the cross.

—*Colossians 2:15*

A FIFTY-SIX-YEAR-OLD MAN GOT MAD AT his attorney for not representing him properly during his trial. He became so irate that he went home, got a gun, and came back determined to kill the one who represented him. But even though the man had a gun, found the attorney, and shot at him at close range, he did not kill him. The only reason was because the attorney hid behind a tree and kept the tree between himself and his attacker.

We need to keep the tree of Calvary between us and the ones who attack us. We are no greater than our Lord. If He was attacked when He was here on earth, even by people whom He had helped, we should expect no better treatment. But we cannot withstand such attacks alone. We must remember that there is triumph in the cross of Christ.

God, help us to remember the power that is in the cross of Christ. When we are attacked and have no apparent protection from our attackers, hide us behind the cross. How amazing that the very instrument of death has become an instrument of victory for us. Praise be to Your name, O God! Amen.

October 11

The Spirit searches all things, even the deep things of God. For who among men knows the thoughts of man except the man's spirit within him? In the same way no one knows the thoughts of God except the Spirit of God.
—1 Corinthians 2:10b-11

BEFORE HIS DEATH, REV. E. V. HILL WAS PASTOR OF Mount Zion Missionary Baptist Church in Los Angeles and a strong leader during the Civil Rights Movement. He used to share that when he was growing up, he was raised by his grandmother in a two-room log cabin. His grandmother was not educated, but she made sure that he went to school. In the afternoons, after he got home, she often had him read to her from the Bible since she couldn't read. But she would stop him every now and then to tell him what the scripture meant. He had the education, but she had the revelation. He could read what the words said, but she could explain what they meant.

It doesn't matter how much education a person has, if he or she does not also have revelation, the things of God will remain a mystery. We need both education and revelation. Revelation without an education can leave us vulnerable; education without revelation can leave us unsatisfied. Thankfully, God wants to reveal His Word to us and to help us understand what He is saying. In John 14:26, Jesus told His disciples, "But the Counselor, the Holy Spirit, whom the Father will send in my name, will teach you all things and will remind you of everything I have said to you."

Holy Spirit, thank You for coming to teach us and to remind us of the words of Jesus. Thank You for helping us understand the things of God. We know that our education can only help us understand the words on the page. We need for You to help us understand the Person who wrote the book. Teach us and guide us, we ask You, in the matchless name of Jesus. Amen.

October 12

Be still before the Lord and wait patiently for him; do not fret when men succeed in their ways....

—*Psalm 37:7*

FOR A WHILE, WHENEVER I WENT TO the doctor, I always chose to schedule an appointment time that would be the doctor's first one of the day so that I wouldn't have to wait. But often when I got there, I discovered that twenty-five other people were given the same appointment! So I waited and waited. I read two newspapers, an issue of *Sports Illustrated*, and I was still waiting. The doctor's assistant came out and called one name after another, and I often got upset because she wasn't calling my name. But then I learned how to deal with the delay. Instead of begrudging someone else because her or his name was called, I took heart in knowing that the doctor was still seeing patients. That meant the doctor was still there, and it was getting closer and closer to my turn.

When we see God doing good things for our neighbors, we need to take heart because it means that God is still working and our turn is coming closer. Let's not waste our time being fretful and envious, but let's show our faith that His timing is perfect by waiting patiently for Him.

Father, we confess our tendency to become envious when someone else gets something for which we have been praying and waiting. Please forgive us. Help us to know that what another person gets in no way hinders what You have prepared for us. Help us to wait even more expectantly as we see You at work in the lives of others. In Jesus' name, we pray. Amen.

October 13

Here I am! I stand at the door and knock. If anyone hears my voice and opens the door, I will come in and eat with him, and he with me.

—Revelation 3:20

IF WE TELL OUR CHILDREN TO CLEAN THEIR ROOM AND they don't respond right away, we will often ask them, "Did you hear me?" That's because we expect a response from them if they hear us.

God expects a response from us when we hear Him as well. If we hear Him knocking at a door in our lives, we must not only hear Him, but also open that door and let Him in. We often think of this verse in terms of receiving Christ into our hearts. But there are other doors in our lives where we can hear the voice of God. He speaks to us at the door of our relationships, of our time, of our finances. Do we open those doors and invite Him in to fellowship with us there, or do we ignore that voice so that we can continue to do what we want?

Our consciences prick us today, Lord, because we know there have been times that we have heard Your voice, but we have done nothing. Like a rebellious child, or a child who simply doesn't want to be bothered, we have ignored Your voice. Only now, do we fully recognize our sin and realize how terrible it was that we felt we could ignore the King of the universe. We are so sorry, Father, and we ask You today to grant us grace and mercy that we might hear Your voice yet again. Without being able to hear You, we cannot survive in this world. Forgive us for thinking that we can listen when we feel like it and pretend not to hear You at other times. God, let us be quick to hear Your voice at the doors of our hearts, and to open those doors to You so that You can have lordship over every area of our lives. In Jesus' name, we pray, Amen.

October 14

"And why do you worry about clothes? See how the lilies of the field grow. They do not labor or spin. Yet I tell you that not even Solomon in all his splendor was dressed like one of these. If that is how God clothes the grass of the field, which is here today and tomorrow is thrown into the fire, will he not much more clothe you, O you of little faith? So do not worry, saying, 'What shall we eat?' or 'What shall we drink?' or 'What shall we wear?' For the pagans run after all these things, and your heavenly Father knows that you need them."

—Matthew 6:28-32

THE ADHERENTS OF THE RELIGION CALLED DEISM believe that God is the Creator of the heavens, earth, sun, moon, stars, us, and everything else. But they believe that after God created the world and everything in it, He put the laws of science and nature in effect and has just sat back since then and watched all that's going on.

But we can read one after another of the stories in the Bible and see how God got involved. Even in our own lives, God doesn't just sit back and watch, but He gets involved and acts on our behalf. Yes, God is the Creator of all things, but He also "dresses" the lilies of the field in their beauty and knows all of our needs before we even express them to Him.

Heavenly Father, thank You for the way that You love us. You are not like a pagan idol who sits mute and motionless, but You are intimately involved with humankind and with all of creation. We are fearfully and wonderfully made, the psalmist tells us. That didn't happen by some mere cosmic fluke, but by the hand of an almighty and all-loving God. We thank You, God, not just for what You do for us, but for who You are, and the way You express Yourself to us. We love You. Amen.

October 15

The LORD is my shepherd, I shall not be in want. He makes me lie down in green pastures, he leads me beside quiet waters, he restores my soul.
—*Psalm 23:1-3a*

I WATCHED THE UNIVERSITY OF TEXAS PLAYING against Texas Tech. Everyone expected number-one rated Texas to win, but Texas Tech was beating them. In the last quarter, however, Texas tied them and then scored one point for the lead. With one minute and twenty-nine seconds to go, Texas Tech—the team that had played 499 games and never won a single game against a number one team—didn't give up. They advanced the ball, ran, threw passes, and called a timeout. With only one second to go, their quarterback threw a pass to a wide receiver on a down-and-out. He caught the ball, spun around, and ran for a touchdown. The Texas Tech fans were elated. The major reasons they won is because they used their timeouts to slow down the game, and they got instructions from their coach.

Some of us need to use those same tactics in our Christian lives. We need timeouts to slow down our game, and we need to get instructions from our Coach. Most of us live at top speed, rushing around, multitasking, and juggling a bunch of balls in the air. Doing more of the same, only faster, doesn't help us defeat an enemy; it depletes our resources. We need timeouts from our frenzied pace. We need to lie down in green pastures, to be led beside still waters, to let God restore our souls, and to get instructions from Him. We may think we can win without timeouts, but we won't have the stamina, inner strength, or wisdom to gain the victory.

Father, it's hard to get off this merry-go-round. We constantly add more and more to our to-do lists until we ourselves are "done," unable to do anymore. Yet the demands upon our time continue to shout at us. We're losing here, and we need Your help. We call a timeout right now, and we rest in Your presence. Speak to us. Help us not only to finish this race, but to do so victoriously. In Jesus' name, Amen.

October 16

"The LORD who delivered me from the paw of the lion and the paw of the bear will deliver me from the hand of this Philistine."

—*1 Samuel 17:37*

EVEN THOUGH I NEVER PLAYED FOOTBALL, I was somewhat of an athlete. One thing I learned in sports is that when coaches call timeouts, they aren't designing new plays for the players to run. During a timeout, the coach is merely reminding the players of the plays they already know.

When we call a timeout to get alone with God, He isn't going to give us any new plays. God is going to remind us of what we already know. He will tell us things such as: "And we know that all things work together for good," "I can do all things through Christ," or "No weapon formed against you will prosper."

God, we need to hear Your voice, and we need to hear again those words that You gave us in the past. There was a time when we knew, for instance, that "no weapon formed against you will prosper." But in the heat of the battle, we have a hard time realizing that. It looks like the weapons of our foe are mighty, and we feel that we are overpowered. But when You remind us in Your own words that "no weapon formed against you will prosper," we believe it. We receive it. We act upon it. Rather than lying down in defeat or running away in fear, we stand in the name of Jesus and continue to fight against our enemy. Thank You, God, for Your Word that is ever true. Amen.

October 17

God is our refuge and strength, an ever-present help in trouble.
—Psalm 46:1

ONE THING I LIKE ABOUT THE NBA is the twenty-second timeout. Of course, they still have the full timeouts, but they also have the twenty-second breaks when a team just needs a quick timeout to regroup.

Sometimes we need a twenty-second timeout. We don't have time to kneel down or find a quiet place to pray, but we are facing a situation that requires a response from us right now. We need right now to answer an invitation, respond to a critical question, say something meaningful to someone who is hurting, act on the basis of integrity rather than self-interest, or make an urgent decision. We can't take a full timeout by getting away with our Bibles and spending quiet time talking over this situation with God. But we *can* take a twenty-second timeout to call upon God silently in our hearts, and He will help us to do the right thing in that moment.

Thank You, God, that You are an ever-present help in trouble. You are a God who is always with us in the "now," in that moment we need You. Thank You for being ever-present. Thank You that we can call upon You at any moment, day or night, and find that You are always there, always listening, always ready to help us. We praise You, O God. Amen.

October 18

He lifted me out of the slimy pit, out of the mud and mire; he set my feet on a rock and gave me a firm place to stand.

—*Psalm 40:2*

IN THE MILWAUKEE ZOO, ZERO THE POLAR bear was playing with a toy and fell into a pit, an empty moat. His handlers expected him to take the stairs and climb right out, but even after eighteen days, he didn't. So, to help the bear out of his predicament, zoo officials shot him with tranquilizer darts to anesthetize him. Then they had to go down into the pit with Zero in order to get him into a crate so that a crane could then lift him up out of that pit.

God did that for us. He sent Jesus down into the pit with us. By coming down to where we were, He was able to lift us up to the place of freedom and safety that we enjoy today. And God made sure that He set our feet on a firm place to stand—on the Rock, Christ Jesus.

God, thank You for loving us enough that You sent Your own Son down into the pit with us. Through Him, You brought us out and set us on the solid Rock. Thank You, God, for rescuing us. Thank You for our firm foundation. Amen.

October 19

He put a new song in my mouth, a hymn of praise to our God. Many will see and fear and put their trust in the LORD.

—Psalm 40:3

HAVE YOU EVER NOTICED THAT IN THE midst of all the wonderful gospel songs produced today, others just fall flat? They have no real message or substance. This is especially noticeable when compared with the old hymns that reach to the depths of the soul. I used to wonder why a songwriter would even write an empty song. Then I read Psalm 40:3, and realized that God Himself put a new song in David's mouth. Had David not had an experience with God, he would not have received a new song. The quality of our song matches the experience we've had with God.

God has new songs for us to sing, but we only receive a new song when we experience something new with God. Many of us are still singing the same old song we sang thirty years ago—the one we received when we accepted Christ as Savior. But God gives us a new song when we recognize His faithfulness, when He gives us victory in a spiritual battle, when we experience the depths of God's love and mercy…. Let's not go to the grave knowing only one song; God has many new songs to give us as we journey here with Him. And in Heaven, He will give us yet another—a song of victory!

Thank You, God, for all the wonderful new songs You give us as we grow in our relationship with You. And none of us has the same repertoire! Just as our individual experiences with You are unique, so, too, do our songs vary. But what harmony they make as we all sing the songs You have put in our mouths. You, God, are the Choir Conductor who melds all of our songs into one great concert that even the angels in Heaven cannot sing. Thank You, for giving each of us something to sing about. In Your precious name we pray, Amen.

October 20

Since, then, you have been raised with Christ, set your hearts on things above, where Christ is seated at the right hand of God. Set your minds on things above, not on earthly things. For you died, and your life is now hidden with Christ in God.

—Colossians 3:1-3

MY SON JORDAN, A STUDENT AT TENNESSEE State, called during the 2008 presidential election to tell me he was going to vote. He said the school was taking the students in buses to go to the polls so that they would not miss that opportunity. He said he was voting for Barack Obama for president of the United States. I said, "Son, you're eighteen years old. You don't quite understand the historical implications of your vote. This is your first chance to vote for president, and you are getting to vote for a Black man who has a legitimate chance of becoming president of the United States. I'm forty-six years old, and this is the first time I've had the opportunity to vote for a Black man for president. It took your grandmother eighty-seven years, but she went in during the early voting and voted for Barack Obama."

Whatever we're going through, we've just got to wait on God. He may not come when we want Him to, but He's always right on time.

God, we honor You today for who You are. We thank You that You are the God who rescues His people and the God who answers when we call upon You. Your timing is definitely not our timing, but we know that Your ways are perfect. We thank You for always coming at just the right time, and even today, we wait upon You. Amen.

October 21

For what I do is not the good I want to do; no, the evil I do not want to do—this I keep on doing. Now if I do what I do not want to do, it is no longer I who do it, but it is sin living in me that does it. So I find this law at work: When I want to do good, evil is right there with me. For in my inner being I delight in God's law; but I see another law at work in the members of my body, waging war against the law of my mind and making me a prisoner of the law of sin at work within my members. What a wretched man I am! Who will rescue me from this body of death? Thanks be to God—through Jesus Christ our Lord!

—Romans 7:19-25

EVIL IS "LIVE" SPELLED BACKWARDS.

A lot of us are living life backwards. God wants us to l-i-v-e, but we are content to be e-v-i-l. We need to get sick of living life backwards, of living an evil life. We need to get to the point that Paul did when he cried out, "What a wretched man I am!" It was then he learned that the same Jesus who rescued him from death unto life could rescue him from the "body of death" as well. Our bodies don't have to be instruments of evil and death. Through Christ—walking in His ways, being filled with His Spirit, and letting His mind be in us—we can overcome evil and live our lives as God intends for those of us who are called by His name.

God, we know so well how Paul felt when the battle raged within him between good and evil, between the good things he wanted to do and the evil things he actually did. We see that same battle within ourselves, O God, and we call upon You to help us. Deliver us from these bodies of death— these bodies that used to serve and be controlled by the god of this world. Let our very bodies be transformed into the likeness of Jesus when He was here on this earth, so that our mouths speak His words, our minds think His thoughts, our feet go where He would go, and our hands do what He would do. Thanks be to God that we do not have to live life backwards! In the name of Jesus Christ our Lord, Amen.

October 22

The eye cannot say to the hand, "I don't need you!" And the head cannot say to the feet, "I don't need you!" On the contrary, those parts of the body that seem to be weaker are indispensable.

—1 Corinthians 12:21-22

ALMOST ALL GREAT HEROES, REAL AND fictional, had a helper. Moses had Joshua, Esther had Mordecai, Michael Jordan had Scottie Pippin, Shaquille O'Neal had Kobe Bryant, Batman had Robin, the Green Hornet had Kato, Spiderman had Mary Jane, and Superman had Lois Lane. Even the Lone Ranger didn't work alone; he had Tonto. To seek help when it is needed is a sign of wisdom, not weakness.

No matter how strong we are, or how holy we are, there are times when we're going to need others to help us along. Members of the body of Christ must work together. Not only do we need to work together, but that is the way God planned it. Christ is honored when we, as individual members of His body, each fulfill the function for which we were intended—and when we each allow every other member to fulfill the functions they were given by the Holy Spirit.

God, help us to quit trying to be the body of Christ all by ourselves. Help us to know that we cannot do everything because it was never Your intention that any one individual do it all in the kingdom. Teach us to honor the other members of Your body by allowing them to fulfill the work that You have empowered them to do. In Jesus' name, Amen.

October 23

. . . "Let the beloved of the LORD rest secure in him, for he shields him all day long, and the one the LORD loves rests between his shoulders."
—*Deuteronomy 33:12*

WHEN I FIRST BECAME THE PASTOR OF Eastern Star Church over twenty years ago, four or five people came bursting into my office one day without an appointment. One of them pointed a finger in my face and said, "Now, we're the ones responsible for you being here." They then proceeded to tell me their personal expectations of me. They informed me that if I disappointed them, they would put me out. I responded, "Excuse me? I'm so glad you told me that you are the ones responsible for my being here, because I was of the understanding that the Holy Spirit placed me here."

When God places us where we are, we don't have to worry about other people. Our security is not in what they do or don't do. Our security is not in our circumstances. Our security is not in our position. Our security is not in holding on tight to what we have. Our security is in the Lord. We can rest between His shoulders because He shields us all day long.

Lord God, we thank You that we can rest securely in You. We don't have to fight, manipulate, or charm someone to try to gain position. If You don't put us in a particular place by Your grace, Your favor, and Your power, we don't belong there. Help us to rest in You and to trust You with our lives. In Jesus' name, we pray, Amen.

October 24

Do nothing out of selfish ambition or vain conceit, but in humility consider others better than yourselves. Each of you should look not only to your own interests, but also to the interests of others.

—Philippians 2:3-4

THERE ARE TIMES THAT WE HAVE TO choose victory over glory. In 2007, the Philadelphia Eagles were trying to pull off a win against the Dallas Cowboys. They were ahead by four points, but they had to run out the clock in order to ensure the victory. Brian Westbrook broke away from the Dallas defense and ran twenty-four yards on his way to score a touchdown. But at the one-yard line, he fell on his knees and covered the ball. He could easily have scored his touchdown and padded his statistics in the record books; instead, he fell on his knees and sacrificed personal glory for the sake of his team's victory.

Those of us in the kingdom could take a lesson from Brian Westbrook. It's not about us. First Corinthians 10:31 says, "So…whatever you do, do it all for the of God." If we do all for the glory of God and for the good of our fellow teammates, we will be living as befitting those in the kingdom of God.

God, let us live our lives even as Jesus did. He did nothing to glorify Himself, but always to glorify You. He did nothing to save Himself, but laid down His very life to save others. He did nothing to win the praises of others, but was satisfied always with Your praise. He did nothing to win a momentary victory for Himself by coming down from the cross, but won an eternal victory for You and for us by sacrificing Himself. Thank You, God, for both the reality of what He did and for the example He set for us. In His holy name, we pray, Amen.

October 25

The angel answered, "The Holy Spirit will come upon you, and the power of the Most High will overshadow you. So the holy one to be born will be called the Son of God.

—Colossians 3:1-3

I'M READING IN THE PAPER THESE DAYS that unemployment in the U.S. is at its highest level ever. Job losses have hit a new high. Housing foreclosures, depression, war, abortion, divorce—all of these things are at an all-time high.

But in Luke 1:35, God is referred to as the "Most High." That means that no matter how high all of the negative situations in our lives and in our world may get, God is still higher. All of these things are still under His feet. Let's live in the awareness of "the power of the Most High."

Lord God Almighty, we acknowledge Your power in our lives and in this world. We thank You that even when a multitude of bad things pile up in our lives, we will not be overcome by them because the God whom we serve is still higher than all those things! We thank You even now for the victory that You, O Most High, are working in our lives. We praise You. Amen.

October 26

"Have you not put a hedge around him and his household and everything he has? You have blessed the work of his hands, so that his flocks and herds are spread throughout the land."

—Job 1:10

I RUN AN AVERAGE OF 110 MILES each month. When I first began running, I was only doing two to three miles at a time. Because I didn't want to have to drive somewhere just to run a couple miles, I chose to run in my own neighborhood. But what I quickly found out is that nearly everyone in my neighborhood owns a dog. No matter how friendly a dog may be, when the animal sees someone running past its yard, it can become quite intimidating, to say the least. As I continued to venture out, however, I soon realized that my neighbors with dogs also had electric fences. These barriers were invisible, but when the dogs tried to cross them, they received a little shock that would force them back into their yards. There were parameters where the dogs could not cross. Now, all I could see were the dogs. I couldn't see the parameters, so they looked quite threatening. But the dogs really couldn't hurt me because they couldn't go beyond the space they were allowed.

We have enemies in our lives who would do us harm if they could, but God has put up invisible parameters to keep them from getting to us. This "hedge" not only keeps the enemies out, but it also keeps us in by helping us to know our boundaries. We can say then that God's hedge of protection protects us from our enemies, as well as from ourselves.

O, God, how grateful we are to You for the invisible fence, the hedge of protection, You have put around us. Thank You that it extends far enough to give us plenty of freedom, yet it is not so far that we end up in dangerous territory. Thank You, God, for protecting us from the enemies without and the enemies within. Thank You for keeping the dogs away. Amen.

October 27

"He will be great and will be called the Son of the Most High. The Lord God will give him the throne of his father David, and he will reign over the house of Jacob forever; his kingdom will never end."

—Luke 1:32-33

LUKE 1:33 TELLS US THAT JESUS WILL reign over "the house of Jacob forever." *Jacob* means supplanter, trickster, manipulator, deceiver. The verse *could* have said that Jesus will reign over the house of *Israel*, because God changed Jacob's name when He changed his heart. At that point, Jacob became Israel—one who contends with God, wrestles with God, and prevails with God. He had gone from being one who tried to get whatever he wanted by his own means to one who related intimately with God. This verse tells us, however, that Jesus will reign over the house of *Jacob*.

This gives us great hope. If Jesus can reign over one who is a manipulator and deceiver, He can reign today even over one whose life is dysfunctional—one who is trying to make it on his or her own. The good news is that Jesus is not limited either in love or in power. Jesus can still make an Israel out of a Jacob.

Jesus, with all our hearts we thank You that You love us enough and You have power enough to change our hearts and even our names. We are no longer the persons we used to be because You have come. Now You reign over our lives, and we are no longer the same. We magnify Your name, Lord, for Your goodness, and Your mercy, and Your love to us. Amen.

October 28

"I will show you what he is like who comes to me and hears my words and puts them into practice. He is like a man building a house, who dug down deep and laid the foundation on rock. When a flood came, the torrent struck that house but could not shake it, because it was well built. But the one who hears my words and does not put them into practice is like a man who built a house on the ground without a foundation. The moment the torrent struck that house, it collapsed and its destruction was complete."

—Luke 6:47-49

YEARS AGO, WHILE I WAS IN ST. LOUIS to preach, the pastor showed me around the city. He took me to a subdivision with homes that were once beautiful and stately, an area in which upwardly mobile African Americans aspired to live. But all I saw then were sunken streets, cracked sidewalks, caved-in roofs, and leaning houses.

This area stood as a sad reminder of its former days of glory. The pastor explained that this subdivision was built after World War II over a garbage dump. The developers merely packed down the garbage and poured dirt over it. As the rain, snow, freezing and thawing came year after year, the foundation shifted and eroded. So these homes built on garbage could not stand. What are we building on today?

God, You have offered us instructions for building a house that will endure. Whether we are talking about our marriage and family relationships or our lives in general, You want these structures to endure. We see all around us people who have built on "garbage," and their structures have collapsed. Now, instead of their visions realized, we see only sad reminders of what their lives and families used to be. God, help us to build our foundations on nothing less than the Rock, Christ Jesus. Let us hear Your words and put them into practice so that our foundations will stand secure. In Your holy name we ask, Amen.

October 29

"You will be with child and give birth to a son, and you are to give him the name Jesus. He will be great and will be called the Son of the Most High. The Lord God will give him the throne of his father David, and he will reign over the house of Jacob forever; his kingdom will never end." ... "The Holy Spirit will come upon you, and the power of the Most High will overshadow you. So the holy one to be born will be called the Son of God."
—Luke 1:31-33, 35

AS WE READ THE VERSES FOR TODAY, we recognize that they contain a prophecy. The angel Gabriel was telling Mary what was *going to* happen. He told her: "You *will be* with child; you *will* give birth; you *will* have a son; you *will* call Him Jesus; He *will* be great; He *will* be called the Son of the Most High; God *will* give Him the throne; He *will* reign; His kingdom *will* never end; the Holy Spirit *will* overshadow you; the Holy One *will* be born." That prophecy was spoken in the first century.

But this is the twenty-first century, and that prophecy has been fulfilled. The baby *was* born; He *was* called Jesus; He *does* reign; He *is* great. Jesus, in all His power and authority, *is* within us. Let's reflect today on what that means. God's Word is true. He *does* what He says He will do. When we read the "*I will*'s" in the Bible, we can be sure that someday we will say, "*And He did*." God's promises are the reality that is yet to be.

God, thank You that when You speak a word, it is as good as done. Thank You especially that You kept Your word about Jesus. Thank You that He came, that He is the Son of the Most High, and that He reigns. Hallelujah! Amen.

October 30

Therefore, strengthen your feeble arms and weak knees.

—*Hebrews 12:12*

I MENTIONED BEFORE THAT I DO A lot of jogging to stay in shape. I started doing it to become healthier, but now I'm addicted. I really enjoy running. One day I read that weightlifting could make my running more effective, so I tried going to the weight room. I used light weights and did about a million reps because I thought that would increase the benefits of my running. But in the weight room, I saw men with huge biceps and triceps, while I didn't see any change at all in my muscles. The reason I didn't see any changes in me is because I didn't do what those men did to get those muscles. They got their muscles by consistently and frequently picking up something heavy. I, on the other hand, have uniceps instead of biceps or triceps because I wasn't willing to pick up anything heavy.

Some of us are spiritual weaklings because we don't want to pick up anything heavy. We don't want to endure anything. We don't want to go through anything. But if we want to be strong, we have to put forth effort. The more weight we pick up, the stronger we get. The weights will eventually begin to feel lighter, but they don't get lighter—we get stronger.

Lord, help us to train well so that we can be strong. Help us to stop being spiritual couch potatoes—lounging around, doing nothing, and growing unhealthier by the day. Help us to change our ways and face our trials and struggles with courage and determination, so that we will grow strong and be able to be used of You. In Jesus' name, Amen.

October 31

Sarah became pregnant and bore a son to Abraham in his old age, at the very time God had promised him.

—Genesis 21:2

WHEN GOD PLACES A BABY IN A woman, He has to develop it before He brings it forth out of her. That development takes time. She cannot rush her pregnancy. She has to wait until she is due. If a baby is born prematurely, it has to be placed in an incubator, put on life support, in order to sustain its life.

The process of birthing something new takes time. God may be telling us to get married, to have a baby, to start a business, to enter a particular ministry. . .but is it the right time? Is this our due date? If we produce something prematurely, we will have to use artificial means to try to keep it alive because it came too early: it wasn't due yet. Let's give God time to work.

Lord God, we thank You that You are still making Your people productive. Thank You that You are still bringing forth something new from within us—a new relationship, a new ministry, or a new life. But help us to give You time to develop it before we rush into it. We don't want to have to try to sustain something so wonderful on life support just because we felt we had to have it now. Help us to watch and wait for Your timing. We ask this in Jesus' name, Amen.

November 1

Be self-controlled and alert. Your enemy the devil prowls around like a roaring lion looking for someone to devour.

—*1 Peter 5:8*

I ACCEPTED JESUS CHRIST AS MY SAVIOR when I was thirteen years old. By the time I was fifteen, I began to really get into reading and studying the scriptures. One thing I wanted to know was the devil's M. O., his *modus operandi*. I knew that if I weren't careful, he could trip me up in my walk with God, so I wanted to know how to recognize his ways and learn how to defeat him. After studying for a time, I finally felt that I got a fix on him. I thought, "Okay, this is how the devil works." But at that time, I didn't know he had seven heads. I didn't know he could come at me in six other ways besides the way that I recognized him.

Revelation 12:3 says, "Then another sign appeared in heaven: an enormous red dragon with seven heads and ten horns and seven crowns on his heads." The other day, I heard a Super Saint say, "I've got my foot on the devil's neck." "That's fine," I thought, "but you've only got two feet and the devil's got seven heads." One day he looks like marijuana, the next day he looks like Jack Daniel's; one day he looks like our enemy, the next day he looks like our friend; one day he looks like our spouse, the next day he looks like our boss; one day he looks like poverty, the next day he looks like great wealth; one day he looks like a threat, the next day he looks like a promise. The enemy comes in many guises. We have to stay close to God in order to recognize the enemy when he comes.

God, help us to recognize how sly and deceitful the devil is. Let us never think that we have him identified once and for all because he can come at us in ways we do not recognize. He even came after Jesus as bread one time, as power another, and as pride yet a third time. Help us to know that he is always on the prowl. Help us to stay alert and close to You and not go our own ways, so that he will not have an opportunity to devour us. In Jesus' name, we pray, Amen.

November 2

For as he thinketh in his heart, so is he....

—Proverbs 23:7 (KJV)

UPON GRADUATION FROM TENNESSEE STATE UNIVERSITY, OPRAH Winfrey sought jobs at various radio and television stations. One producer told her, "You don't have what it takes to make it in this field." If Oprah Winfrey, fresh out of college and trying to break into television and radio, had listened to him, she would never have birthed the baby that was in her. There would be no Oprah Winfrey Show, no O, the Oprah Magazine, no Harpo Productions, and none of the countless philanthropic efforts she has initiated.

If we want to become all that we were meant to be, we have to see ourselves as God sees us. We live in a society where every flaw is magnified, and nearly everyone is a self-appointed judge of others. If we allow others to hold us back from doing that for which we were created, we will never know the joy of being ourselves and watching God work through us. If we are always imitating others, we will lose our unique identities. We need to look at ourselves through God's eyes and love ourselves as God loves us.

Father, You think more highly of us than most of us think of ourselves. When we look in the mirror, all we see are the flaws and imperfections—those outwardly visible and those hidden within. So, if someone says something negative about us, we internalize that criticism and think, "Yes, that is who I am." But, God, You see us as Your talented and lovable children, made in Your image, standing in the righteousness of Jesus. Thank You for seeing beauty in us. Help us to have a healthy image of who we are so that we can embrace the life You want for us, rather than cowering in fear or discouragement. In the precious name of Jesus, Amen.

November 3

And I'll say to myself, "You have plenty of good things laid up for many years. Take life easy; eat, drink and be merry."

—Luke 12:19

MINNESOTA VIKING ADRIAN PETERSON IS ONE OF the best running backs in the NFL and leads the league in rushing. But even though he is a great player and a real threat to his opponents, when he is on the sidelines with his helmet off, the opposition isn't trying to tackle him. No one is trying to bring him down. But when he puts on the helmet and gets into the game, eleven men work together to bring him down. Others, in even higher places, are strategizing and sending down plays to tell those eleven men how to stop him.

As long as we are on the sidelines, our opponents are not going to trouble us. We are no threat, and we have no chance of contributing to the victory of our team. But when we put on our helmets, our breastplates, our swords, and the rest of our uniform, and we join in the battle on the field, we find that our enemy has a new attitude toward us. The enemy takes a new approach to dealing with us. We need folks who refuse to take life easy, folks who are willing to get into the game, folks who can produce even when others are trying to stop them.

God, we are sorry for trying to live a life of ease. We are sorry for being content to simply eat, drink, and be merry while our brothers and sisters are fighting for Your cause. We are sorry for choosing to live lives of comfort, avoiding that which was inconvenient or unpleasant, even though it meant that victories were being lost. We join You now, God, on the front lines of the battle. Equip us, train us, and inspire us to be faithful. In Christ's name, Amen.

November 4

But the LORD replied, "Have you any right to be angry?"

—*Jonah 4:4*

DR. FREDERICK D. HAYNES III TELLS ABOUT a seventy-three-year-old woman jumped and beaten by two men as she came out of North Park Mall. The men duct-taped her mouth, eyes, and hands, and stole her car—with her locked in the trunk! After driving from Dallas to Oklahoma City, they threw her into a ditch to die. Then it began to rain. I understood that these guys had a free will and chose to do evil. "But, God," I protested, "You could at least have kept it from raining on her and making her situation worse!" But then I heard that the woman explained how the rain loosened the tape so she could get free. God sent the rain to free her!

Some Super Saints mindlessly tell everyone that they are blessed and highly favored. They never question God or why things happen as they do. But that isn't my experience, nor the experience of most authentic Christians. Most of us who have known the Lord intimately have had at least one experience that caused us to question God's timing, decision, or thinking. That's not lacking faith or questioning God's character. It simply wondering why the reality is so different from what we know of God. When we question God, He may or may not respond. But even if He is silent, we know He always operates from a heart of love.

Lord, we don't always understand You or see things from Your perspective, but we have full confidence in You. Even if we get angry or upset with You, You are still the same. You don't change Your plans to accommodate our selfish desires or explain everything to calm our insecurities. You simply assure us that You are doing what is best, and You calm our fears with Your presence. Thank You, God, that our inadequacies do not affect Your adequacy in all things. We love You today, just for who You are. Amen.

November 5

So we fix our eyes not on what is seen, but on what is unseen. For what is seen is temporary, but what is unseen is eternal.

—Colossians 3:1-3

DR. TONY EVANS USES A WONDERFUL ILLUSTRATION from the movie *The Matrix*. The fictional character Thomas "Tom" Anderson, aka "Neo," is living a ho-hum life—doing humdrum work in a humdrum office, going home to a humdrum apartment, hanging out with his humdrum friends, and feeling that there's something wrong with the world. He meets another character named Morpheus, who tells him that there is an unseen reality that is entirely different from the monotonous, frustrating existence he experiences every day. He offers Neo the choice of taking either the blue pill or the red pill: the blue pill would allow him to go back to life as he knows it, but the red pill would allow him to see a world that is beyond the world he knows. Neo chooses the red pill, and his eyes are opened.

Jesus offers us an unseen reality, a kingdom that is not of this world. While it is a world that cannot be seen with our eyes, it can be experienced with our spirits. We can experience His kingdom by receiving Him. Unlike the world that was opened up to Neo—which was designed by special effects and the imagination of human beings—this kingdom is real, created by the same God who made the heavens and the earth. One day we will see it with our eyes, but thank God, we don't have to wait until then. For now, we can experience it with our spirits.

God, we acknowledge that Your kingdom is real. Thank You that we can be part of Your kingdom even now. We live there by Your Spirit. Let us become ever more aware of the reality of Your kingdom. We pray this in the name of the King of this kingdom, Amen.

November 6

Jesus said, "Let the little children come to me, and do not hinder them, for the kingdom of heaven belongs to such as these."

—*Matthew 19:14*

I HAVE BEEN PASTORING FOR OVER TWENTY years, and I am still criticized for the emphasis I put on children. Some people are upset because we sometimes baptize children who are five or six years old—or any age at which they have received Jesus into their hearts. We have children involved in ministries at our church. They serve as ushers, greeters, choir members, and such. Some people complain that the children shouldn't be involved because they don't know what they're doing. But I contend that if they can understand and memorize the words of Ty, Tupac, Ludacris, and Kanye West, they can understand Matthew, Mark, Luke, and John.

We need to recognize what Jesus knew—that the kingdom "belongs to such as these." In Matthew 18:3, Jesus even said to His disciples, "I tell you the truth, unless you change and become like little children, you will never enter the kingdom of heaven." Let's not limit what God can do in and through the lives of our children.

God, help us not to overlook the children or wait for some later date to introduce them to Jesus and bring them into the kingdom and the life of the church. Remind us that the enemy will not wait to induct them into his kingdom efforts. Let us be faithful to them, O God, we pray, in the name of the One who called them unto Himself, Amen.

November 7

But he said to me, "My grace is sufficient for you, for my power is made perfect in weakness." Therefore I will boast all the more gladly about my weaknesses, so that Christ's power may rest on me.

—2 Corinthians 12:9

ONCE, WHEN I HAD BEEN INVITED TO preach at another church, one of the members of the congregation came to pick me up at the airport. During the drive to my hotel, he talked about the airport, about the streets, about the city, and about a recent storm there. He told me that God had been watching out for him, that he was the only person on his block whose power didn't go out during the storm. His neighbor across the street even came over to ask him how he still had power when everyone else had lost theirs. What the neighbor learned later on when he spoke with the utility repairman who was working on the lines was that this man's house was hooked up to a different power grid from his neighbors. Therefore, when the neighbors were disconnected from the source of their power, he was unaffected.

We need to remember that we don't have to lose the Source of our power, even when we're going through a storm. We can go through the same storms as our neighbors, but if we stay connected to Christ, we won't lose our power. In fact, as the verse today tells us, Christ's power is made perfect in our weakness, so the harder the storm hits, the more the power of Christ is released into our lives.

Lord Jesus, let us remember that You are the Source of our power and Your power never goes out. Thank You that even in the storms of life, we can shine brightly in our neighborhoods and our world. Let us remember that the darker the night, the brighter we shine. In Your precious name we pray, Amen.

November 8

The next day, the one after Preparation Day, the chief priests and the Pharisees went to Pilate. "Sir," they said, "we remember that while he was still alive that deceiver said, 'After three days I will rise again.'"
—Matthew 27:62-63

JESUS NEVER SPOKE OF HIS SUFFERING AND dying without also talking of His resurrection. Although He knew He had to go through the suffering and death, He also knew that His resurrection was assured.

The portion of scripture for today continues with the chief priests and Pharisees advising Pilate in verse 64, "So give the order for the tomb to be made secure until the third day. Otherwise, his disciples may come, steal the body, and tell the people that he has been raised from the dead. This last deception will be worse than the first." Not only were our Lord's enemies scheming about His death, but they also wanted to make sure that He never came back to life. But we know the rest of this story. On the third day, Jesus rose again! Even while our enemies are planning our persecution, God is planning our resurrection.

God, what an encouragement it is to us to know that no matter what our enemies do to us and not matter how elaborate and foolproof their tactics, You and You alone determine the course of our lives. Thank You that even when it seems that our enemies have won, on the third day, You prove otherwise! For those who are in the tomb right now, let them know that the third day is almost here. In Christ's name, Amen.

November 9

Yet the LORD longs to be gracious to you....

—Isaiah 30:18

ONCE, WHEN I WAS CHAPLAIN FOR THE Indiana Pacers, Mark Jackson hooked me up with tickets for a playoff game in Atlanta. I picked my two tickets up at the will-call window at the Georgia Dome, but in this huge football arena that had been revamped into a basketball stadium for these games, it was difficult to figure out the seating. We showed our tickets to an usher who guided us to some great seats mid-court in the sixteenth row. These were excellent seats, so when someone else came over and told us we had his seats, I was determined not to give them up. As we were looking at each other's tickets and trying to figure out who actually belonged in those seats, a security officer came by and offered to help resolve the issue. He looked at my tickets and said, "Man, what are you doing way up here? Your seats are down on the floor!" I had thought I was in the best seats I could get, and I was adamant about not giving them up. But better seats were awaiting me. I had to give up the good to get the best.

Some of us are hanging on to what we think is as good as it gets. We're hanging onto a dead-end job, a meaningless relationship, a five-year plan that failed after the first year, or a ministry within the church that we think is just perfect for us; and we are adamant about not giving up any of these things. All the while, God is waiting, even longing, to give us something abundantly above all we could ask or think. In *Sonnets from the Portuguese*, Elizabeth Barrett Browning wrote, "God's gifts put man's best dreams to shame." We need to give up what we consider good in order to get God's best.

God, we thank You that Your gifts far exceed even our desires. Thank You that when we let go of our trinkets, You give us priceless treasures in their place. Help us, God, to let go of what seems good to us in order that our hands are open to receive Your best. Amen.

November 10

"The son said to him, 'Father, I have sinned against heaven and against you. I am no longer worthy to be called your son.' But the father said to his servants, 'Quick! Bring the best robe and put it on him. Put a ring on his finger and sandals on his feet. Bring the fattened calf and kill it. Let's have a feast and celebrate. For this son of mine was dead and is alive again; he was lost and is found.' So they began to celebrate."

—Luke 15:21-24

THIS IS AN E-MAIL GENERATION. Many children today don't know how to address a letter; they don't even know about putting their own name and address on the envelope. They don't realize that if the addressee isn't located, the envelope can be stamped "Return to Sender" and sent back to the one who wrote the letter.

God had a destiny for each of our lives, but on our way to that destination, we got lost. When we gave our lives to Christ, He put His name on us, so we now belong to Him. That means we can always come back to Him.

God, sometimes even Your children get lost. You have provided guidance through Your written Word, the preached word, advice of godly friends, and in so many other ways. Yet, in spite of all that, we sometimes choose to head off in a direction in which You are not sending us. Some of us feel lost right now, at this very moment. Help us to know that we don't have to end up in a dead-letter file. You have placed Your name upon us, so we belong to You. Help us now to make our way home. Amen.

November 11

Early in the morning, as he was on his way back to the city, he was hungry. Seeing a fig tree by the road, he went up to it but found nothing on it except leaves. Then he said to it, "May you never bear fruit again!" Immediately the tree withered.

—*Matthew 21:18-19*

YEARS AGO, I WAS A MEMBER OF the leadership team for a particular conference. This was the first such conference, so the leaders were asked to attend every meeting and event to set an example. This meant that we started each day early and ended very late. One night I didn't get back to my hotel room until after one o'clock in the morning, extremely tired and very hungry. I called room service, but was told it would be about an hour-and-a-half before they could get some food to me. I replied that I would be asleep by then. Remembering the vending machines I had seen, I went to find something just to relieve the hunger pangs. I put my money into the machine, but nothing came out. Frustrated, I tried again and again, without success. Finally, I gave up and went to bed hungry. As I passed by the vending machine the next morning, I saw a sign that read, "Out of Order."

Whenever something should be working but isn't, it is out of order. Healthy adult children who do nothing when they should be working are out of order. If we are not serving in some capacity within our churches, we are out of order. If we are called into full-time ministry but are not ministering, we are out of order. We should be showing forth the love of Christ, but some of us, cranky and unkind, are out of order.

God, help us to get our lives in order. We know that in one area, or in several, we are not functioning as we are intended to function as Your people. We are like a fig tree that is not producing any fruit. Forgive us, God, and make whatever adjustments are needed within us so that we can again be faithful in doing what we have been born, and born again, to do. In Jesus' name, Amen.

November 12

My eyes are on all their ways; they are not hidden from me, nor is their sin concealed from my eyes.

—*Jeremiah 16:17*

WHEN OUR CHILDREN WERE SMALL, I GOT them a swing set. Our family spent a lot of time swinging, sliding, and playing together. One summer, a windstorm came through our community, causing a lot of damage. Our swing set was blown over. Some men came and helped me set it up again. In doing that, however, we noticed that some of the screws were loose and some of the wooden boards were warped. These weren't the *result* of the windstorm; they were only *revealed* by the windstorm. It took an act of God for me to see what was wrong.

Sometimes, God acts in our lives to show us things that are wrong that we aren't seeing. The storms in our lives don't *make* us miserable and hard to live with; but if we *are* miserable and hard to live with, the storms will certainly reveal that. If we are fearful, selfish, greedy, envious, or proud, a storm will reveal us for who we really are because there will be nothing to hide behind as the wind of the Spirit blows through our lives.

God, sometimes like that old swing set, we hide our flaws and weaknesses. But when a storm comes into our lives, we are vulnerable and exposed. That which is usually hidden is revealed, and we realize that some things need to be fixed. Thank You that You don't throw us away because of our faults or sins. In fact, You knew they were there all the time; You just wanted us to know it. Then, just as I worked to correct the problems on the swing set so that it again could become usable and a source of joy to my family, so You also work to correct us and again make us usable and a source of joy in Your kingdom. Thank You, God, for Your grace. Amen.

November 13

"See, I am sending an angel ahead of you to guard you along the way and to bring you to the place I have prepared."

—Exodus 23:20

I HAD LUNCH WITH MY FRIEND DR. Theron Williams, senior pastor of Mt. Carmel Baptist Church in Indianapolis, Indiana. He told me that he is buying a new house. It is a very nice older house in a well-established neighborhood with a big yard where he plans to have a pool installed. He kept going on and on about his house and how great it is. I was happy for him, but I didn't fully understand what he was feeling until he shared this story with me. He said, "When that house was built, I was only twelve years old. That year, I lived in Detroit in the projects. I always wondered then if I'd ever make it out of the projects and out of poverty. But at the very time that I was in Detroit, wondering and worrying about my future, God had someone in Indianapolis, Indiana, building a house for me!"

When we get to where God wants us, we will find that He has already been there and has things already prepared for us.

Father, it touches us deeply to know that You care so much for us. Thank You for preparing a place for us and guarding us in our paths so that we will arrive safely to the place of our blessing. Thank You for Your wonderful love and kindness. Amen.

November 14

So we make it our goal to please him....

—2 Corinthians 5:9

WHEN I WAS A KID, A GROUP CALLED B.T. Express performed a song that said, "Go on and do it, do it/Do it till you're satisfied/Whatever it is, do it, 'long as it pleases you...." The message in that song is so wrong.

My satisfaction does not come from doing whatever pleases me. I can't ignore God and avoid blessing other people and still think that I'm going to find satisfaction by doing what pleases me. While it may satisfy our carnal nature to do whatever pleases us, we will never truly be satisfied until we are living, not for ourselves, but for the glory of God and the welfare of others

O Lord, You told us, "'Love the Lord your God with all your heart and with all your soul and with all your mind.' This is the first and greatest commandment. And the second is like it: 'Love your neighbor as yourself.'" For us to do anything less will bring only dissatisfaction and a lust for more. We will forever be craving that which pleases us because that which pleases us temporarily does not satisfy us eternally. Help us to look for satisfaction in the only place we can find it—in You. Amen.

November 15

Jesus gave them this answer: "I tell you the truth, the Son can do nothing by himself; he can do only what he sees his Father doing, because whatever the Father does the Son also does.

—*John 5:19*

THE OTHER DAY, I CALLED A FRIEND of mine who used to be in the marketing field in corporate America. I had a question for him: I wanted to know why a company would stamp some products with "Satisfaction Guaranteed," but put nothing like that phrase on other items. I asked him how a company arrives at that conclusion. He said that at the company he worked for, the lawyers of the company had to approve the claim before that stamp could be put on the product. He told me that two criteria had to be verified before the lawyers would give their approval: 1) There had to be sufficient data to back up the product's claim—the product had to be tested and data collected to support the claim; and 2) Somebody must have already tried the product and found satisfaction in it. Upon confirmation of those two particular standards, they could guarantee satisfaction.

Today we can confidently guarantee satisfaction in Jesus Christ for those who put their faith in Him. We have two criteria for making that claim: 1) We have sufficient data from God's Word to back up the claim—time after time, it has been tested and proven true; and 2) We aren't the first ones to try Jesus. Others throughout history have been in a relationship with Him, and they found satisfaction too. We can confidently proclaim to others that in Christ, there is "satisfaction guaranteed."

God, we are so thankful that we have found satisfaction in our relationship with You. Not one of Your promises has ever failed. In test after test after test, You have proved Yourself trustworthy and faithful. And, Father, not only have we personally found genuine satisfaction in You, but ever since the very first days that Adam and Eve walked with You in the garden, humankind has found a deep satisfaction in knowing You. No one else can satisfy our souls like You. Amen.

November 16

Then he said to them, "Watch out! Be on your guard against all kinds of greed; a man's life does not consist in the abundance of his possessions."
—Luke 12:15

TIM MONTGOMERY, A WORLD-CLASS GOLD MEDALIST SPRINTER, was considered one of the fastest men in the world. He had popularity, prestige, and recognition worldwide. Soon after that, however, people would pay him just to run in a meet, whether he won it or not. Then, he started not only taking drugs but dealing them as well. He also was indicted for fraud and writing bad checks, and eventually he went to prison. While there, he was asked during an interview what happened. He said, "From the time I was a child, I was programmed wrong to go after money. For most of my adult life, I have been manipulating people by scheming and cheating. The reason I am in bondage right now is because it all caught up with me."

It all caught up with him? If greed can catch the fastest man in the world, what chance do we have? To avoid getting caught up in the continual lust for more, we need to stay close to Jesus, to embrace His value system, and to let Him live His life through us.

God, it's really sad when we hear about someone with so much potential losing everything because he or she became focused on the wrong thing. Please keep our eyes focused on You, our hearts tender toward You, and our minds dwelling on You. We pray this in Jesus' name, Amen.

November 17

What is more, I consider everything a loss compared to the surpassing greatness of knowing Christ Jesus my Lord, for whose sake I have lost all things. I consider them rubbish that I may gain Christ.

—Philippians 3:8

I'VE NEVER BOXED, SO I CALLED A friend of mine who has spent some time in the ring. I asked him what the apostle Paul meant when he said to fight the good fight of faith. I wondered how we can know the difference between what is a *good* fight and what is a *bad* fight. My friend said, "A good fight is when you have everything to gain and nothing to lose. A bad fight is when you have everything to lose and nothing to gain."

Those fighting a bad fight are living for the things of the world. They have no investment in the spiritual realm, so if they lose what they have on earth, they have lost everything. At the same time, they have nothing to gain because the most they can get is more of what they already have, which is not satisfying them anyway. But when we start fighting for the things of God instead of the things of the world, we will find ourselves fighting the good fight. We have everything to gain and nothing to lose. Like the old chorus goes, "Take this whole world, but give me Jesus."

We have spent too much time, Lord, fighting a bad fight. We have spent far too long trying to get more and more of what this world has to offer without ever being satisfied. We now want only You, Lord. What a relief we feel to be fighting the good fight of faith. Thank You, Jesus! Amen.

November 18

Christ redeemed us from the curse of the law by becoming a curse for us, for it is written: "Cursed is everyone who is hung on a tree."

—*Galatians 3:13*

IN "THE CURSE OF THE BLACK PEARL," the first *Pirates of the Caribbean* movie, Captain Barbossa and all his pirates were on a ship named *The Black Pearl*. As part of a plan to escape an ancient curse placed on them, they kidnapped the governor's daughter Elizabeth. Captain Barbossa made Elizabeth wear a certain dress, showed her all the wealth of the ship, and then laid out a huge spread for her. While she was devouring this feast, she realized Barbossa wasn't eating and began to think that the food and wine were poisoned. After assuring her that no one was trying to poison her, the captain explained to her that he and his men had captured a chest filled with gold that was said to be accursed. They didn't believe the curse and began to spend the money. He said the more they spent, the more they realized the chest actually was accursed because they couldn't stop spending it. None of the wine, the pleasure of women, or the money satisfied them; yet, they kept seeking more. The captain told her that the curse could only be lifted if they could find the blood of one righteous person and present that as a sacrifice.

This sounds like the way a lot of people live their lives today. They keep spending their money to get more and more things, but none of it satisfies them. They are under a curse but just don't know it. We all need the blood of one righteous Person to remove the curse that is upon us. Jesus redeemed us from the curse of the Law by taking our curse upon Himself.

O God, we thank You today that we are no longer under a curse because Jesus died to free us from that curse. We receive that salvation that He obtained for us by laying down His own life. He did not die in vain. We thank You for the cross. We thank You for the sacrifice. We receive the freedom that Jesus won for us. In His name we pray, Amen.

November 19

He got into one of the boats, the one belonging to Simon, and asked him to put out a little from shore. Then he sat down and taught the people from the boat. When he had finished speaking, he said to Simon, "Put out into deep water, and let down the nets for a catch." Simon answered, "Master, we've worked hard all night and haven't caught anything. But because you say so, I will let down the nets." When they had done so, they caught such a large number of fish that their nets began to break. So they signaled their partners in the other boat to come and help them, and they came and filled both boats so full that they began to sink.

—Luke 5:3-7

SIMON PETER WAS A FISHERMAN. FISHING WAS his business: he had invested in his boat in order to catch fish for his livelihood. He was willing, however, to let Jesus into his boat, into his means of making a living, in order that Jesus might reach out to others. When he first let Jesus into his boat, his boat was empty. After listening to Jesus and obeying Him, his boat became so full that he had to share with others in order to keep from sinking.

How full is your boat today? If we find that our boats are inadequately filled, we probably need to let Jesus into them. Whatever our job, our business, or our means of making a living, we need to let Jesus come in so that He can use that vessel to reach out to others. If we do that, we might just find our boats so full that we will have to share our overflow with others in order to keep from sinking.

God, You never do anything in a little way. You are a God of abundance and when You give, You give liberally—a good measure, pressed down, shaken together and overflowing! We invite You today into our workplaces. Reach out to others there so that they may know You. Show us all what it means, God, to have Jesus in our boats. We pray in Your holy name, Amen.

November 20

He must increase, but I must decrease.

—*John 3:30 (KJV)*

WHEN MY WIFE AND I WENT TO the Super Bowl in Miami the year the Colts won, we saw something at halftime that you don't get to see when you're at home watching the game on TV. The second the game went to halftime, people came from the four corners of the field and began setting up a stage so that Prince could come out and perform. The TV network played commercials during all this preparation; so if you were at home, one minute you were watching the game and after the commercials, there was Prince up on stage. But if it hadn't been for the people who came out to work behind the scenes to set up the stage for him, Prince could not have been seen by the millions of viewers.

We need to be willing to work in the background so that the Prince of Peace can be seen by others. If we try to get the spotlight to focus on us, we keep people from seeing Him. If we refuse to work behind the scenes and are only willing to work where we know that we will get the praise and acclaim that we think we deserve, we will find that the Prince doesn't need us after all. He will use the meek, the weak, and the insignificant of this world instead to showcase His glory.

God, let us always seek Your glory and not our own. Let no job be too small for us to do with joy and excellence. Let us remember the humility of our Lord and seek to work in the kingdom with that same spirit. In His name we pray, Amen.

November 21

This, the first of his miraculous signs, Jesus performed in Cana of Galilee.
He thus revealed his glory, and his disciples put their faith in him.

—*John 2:11*

I CALLED PASTOR WIGGINS THE OTHER DAY, and he answered, "Hello, Pastor Johnson." Then he told me that he had finally figured out how to know it was me calling, since my calls show up on caller ID as "Unknown Name, Unknown Number." He said that he set up his new phone so that my calls now have a special ring to let him know that it is me and not just some salesperson. But what he didn't know—and I had to fill him in on this—is that the reason he was able to tell that it was me was not because of what *he* did, but because of what *I* did. I have friends who had complained because they couldn't tell when it was me calling, so I did something at *my* end to reveal myself to them at *their* end. That's why Pastor Wiggins was able to know it was me.

It is what Jesus does that allows us to identify Him, not what we do. It is only by His grace that we can identify Him. He doesn't look like the pictures hanging on some walls. He doesn't always behave in ways we think He should, but He will reveal Himself to us in countless ways as we continue to walk with Him.

Lord Jesus, we thank You that You do not stay hidden from us. Thank You that You choose to identify Yourself to us. Thank You that we can know Your voice. Thank You that You have a way of letting us know deep in our spirits that the "Unknown Name, Unknown Number" calling us is You. With joy, we answer Your call. Amen.

November 22

He does not treat us as our sins deserve or repay us according to our iniquities. For as high as the heavens are above the earth, so great is his love for those who fear him.

—*Psalm 103:10-11*

I FLY WITH ONE PARTICULAR AIRLINE AS much as I can because over the past twenty-five years, we have developed a special relationship. This relationship allows me to buy a coach ticket that can be upgraded to first class. With this upgrade comes special perks, such as more individual attention and better-quality food—my peanuts turn into chicken cordon bleu. In first class, I am also closer to the pilot who is taking me to my destination.

If we got what we paid for, we would be going through life in coach—if we could afford to get on the plane at all. But because we have a special relationship with Jesus, He moves us up to first class. With that upgrade, blessings come to us that we don't deserve. But, most importantly, we can get closer to the One who is committed to taking us to our destination.

Thank You, God, that You have chosen to have a relationship with us—one that gives us blessings we don't deserve and allows us to stay close to You as you take us to our destination. We are so thankful that You don't treat us as our sins deserve, but You are gracious and You treat us with lovingkindness. Amen.

November 23

Consider him who endured such opposition from sinful men, so that you will not grow weary and lose heart.

—*Hebrews 12:3*

PASTOR CHARLES E. NESBITT JR., PASTOR OF Providence Baptist Church in College Park, Georgia, offers a great illustration. There once was a man who was an avid worker of jigsaw puzzles. He had such great patience with a particularly large and difficult puzzle. Day after day, he sat down at the table, painstakingly sorting the pieces and looking for pieces that connected with each other. After months of this tedious, careful work, his efforts paid off: the puzzle was finally completed. But barely was the puzzle finished when the man's dog came running through the room, hitting the table, and scattering the pieces of the puzzle all over the place. The man was feeling such a huge sense of frustration and despair when it dawned on him that he still had everything he needed to put the puzzle together again. It would take some more time and effort on his part, but all the pieces were still there, so he could do it. All was not lost.

You may have just gotten your "puzzle" together. Perhaps it was a relationship, a job, or your education. But a dog (in your relationship, in your workplace, or in your school) came by and ruined everything. But remember that if you still have your faith in Jesus, you have all that you need to put your life back together again.

God, You know how sad and frustrated we are about the area of our lives that has been damaged. We had worked and worked for such a long time to get to this point and then, when we finally reached the point of fulfillment and celebration, someone resembling a dog came by and ruined it. Help us, God, to have the strength and resilience to make a comeback. Restore what was upset and taken from us. Let us once again know joy and blessing in the very area in which we now feel defeated. We trust You, O God. Amen.

November 24

You were running a good race. Who cut in on you and kept you from obeying the truth? That kind of persuasion does not come from the one who calls you.

—Ephesians 5:7-8

IN 2007, THE MIAMI DOLPHINS WERE THE worst team in the NFL: they won only one game and lost fifteen. But the next year, they came back to win their division championship. One of the things they did differently was to change their offensive formation. Instead of handing off to the quarterback, they put him out of the picture and the center snapped the ball directly to the running back. When they got rid of the middleman, they were able to run to their goal.

There is no need for a middleman in our lives. A middleman is someone who makes calls that are not in keeping with what your Coach is actually instructing. God tells us to do *this*, but the middleman says, "Oh, you don't want to do *this* because…."; God tells us to do *that*, but the middleman says, "*That* just doesn't sound like God to me. I think you should…."; or God tells us that we can do all things through Christ who strengthens us, but the middleman says, "You can't do that. You don't have what it takes. Let someone else do it, and stick to what you know." Jesus can help us reach our goals when we are working directly with Him and hearing His voice for ourselves.

Thank You, God, that You work within us to help us to know and do what pleases You. You aren't telling us that we have no need of anyone in our lives or that we should never seek advice or help from others. You just want us never to substitute someone else in Your place. You want a personal relationship with us, not one that is always dependent upon someone else. Help us to hear and obey Your voice. In Jesus' name, Amen.

November 25

But let justice roll on like a river, righteousness like a never-failing stream!
—*Amos 5:24*

WHEN I WAS GROWING UP, WE DIDN'T have a lot of indoor gyms and other places to play as children have today. We went outdoors to a local park. It wasn't at all uncommon to see ten guys playing basketball on a court and fifty others hanging around hoping for a chance to get in the game. In those days, there was a magical system of "calling" that, for some unknown reason, children honored. It didn't matter how many guys were hanging around the court, the one who saw some action was the one who cried out, "I got next!"

I wonder today who's got "next." When we look back over history, we see folks who stood up for justice in our society. We think, for instance, of Sojourner Truth, Frederick Douglass, and Harriett Tubman in their day; we think of Rosa Parks, Malcolm X, and Martin Luther King Jr. in their day. But who's got next? When our children's generation and our grandchildren's generation look back at our day, who will stand out? Who will they point to with pride and say, "He didn't let us down," or, "She came through for us"? There are a lot of us hanging around today watching what's going on, but who is going to move into action? Who's got next?

Our Father, in Isaiah 61:8, You tell us that You love justice. Help us to love what You love. Let what matters to You matter to us. Help us not to be among those who simply stand around as onlookers in life, but help us to be those who call "next" and who step out in faith to proclaim Your justice in this world. Let us help keep justice rolling on. Let it not stop with our generation. Amen.

November 26

Being strengthened with all power according to his glorious might so that you may have great endurance and patience. . .

—Colossians 1:11

AT ONE OF OUR FAMILY GATHERINGS AT my cousin's house, we had a piñata for the children. A piñata is a paper mache figure of some sort that has been filled with candy and sweets. The children take turns being blindfolded, and using a stick (or in our case, a mop handle), they try to hit the piñata so that it will break and all the goodies fall out. As soon as the piñata breaks, all the children scramble on the floor or the ground to pick up the sweets that have fallen. This time, several of the children had taken whacks at the piñata before one of the younger cousins took his turn. The boy tried a couple of times but kept missing his target. He was about ready to take off his blindfold and give up, but his cousins were all cheering him on because they could see that the piñata had been damaged by earlier blows and was just about ready to break. The little guy wanted the thrill of breaking the piñata. The others encouraged him because they knew that if he broke it, that meant candy for everybody.

When we are frustrated and ready to quit before we reach our goal, we need to remember that our goal may be only seconds away. God has already put treasures within our reach, but we can't give them away to people until we achieve the goal. When we get *our* breakthrough, others will also be blessed.

God, help us not to give up. We're tired. We're tempted to stop. But You are giving us the power to press on. It is in Your name that we continue to press toward our goal. Amen.

November 27

They are the shoot I have planted, the work of my hands, for the display of my splendor.

—*Isaiah 60:21b*

ONE DAY MY BROTHER-IN-LAW STANLEY SAID THAT he had to go home and clean out his gutter because he had plants growing there. Now, I have seen dirt, mud, and leaves in a gutter, but I've never seen plants growing in a gutter, so I asked him how that was possible. He explained that he has a maple tree in his yard and that when the wind blows the seeds from that tree, they grow wherever they land. All the seeds need are soil and sunlight. Since even the gutter could provide soil and it was exposed to the sun, that's all the seeds needed to start taking root and growing. So Stanley had plants growing in his gutter.

We were designed for growth. When God created us, He put within us the capacity for life and growth. Some of us, however, imagined that we would be growing on a picturesque hillside or along a rippling brook, or in a beautiful park. But the circumstances of our lives have blown us into a gutter. We never intended to land in a failing marriage, or a financial disaster or a messy job situation, yet here we are. But that doesn't mean we can't grow! We were created for life! The light of the Son can reach us even in a gutter! Let's allow God to make of us what He intends for us to be. He can transplant us later. For now, let's just grow strong in Him.

God, when we were younger, we had hopes, dreams, and visions for our future. We never imagined that we would be in the gutter we find ourselves in today. But we are going to trust You right where we are. Rather than lying here lifeless, bemoaning the fact that we aren't somewhere else, we are going to do what we were created to do. We are going to start reaching up to the Son and letting His light bring life and growth to us. We trust You that at just the right time, You will come and transplant us to a better place. But for now, we are content to be the strongest, most beautiful plants we can be in this very place. Let our lives bring glory to You, O God. Amen.

November 28

It was he who gave some to be apostles, some to be prophets, some to be evangelists, and some to be pastors and teachers, to prepare God's people for works of service, so that the body of Christ may be built up.
—Ephesians 4:11-12

GOD'S WORD SAYS THAT HE *GIVES* US pastors. In my travels, I've encountered a number of churches without pastors. Sometimes the pastor has retired; or at times, he or she has simply chosen to move on; or perhaps the pastor has even been asked to leave. Naturally, my question for them is, "How long have you been without a pastor?" Sometimes it's six or seven years!

Sometimes a congregation will tell me that they are doing great without a pastor. We wouldn't think of flying in an airplane without a pilot, taking a cruise without a ship's captain onboard, or going to a hospital that doesn't have any doctors. Why then would we consider being in a church without a pastor? God *gives* us pastors.

God, we thank You for the pastors You have given us. Let us never take them for granted or feel we don't need them. You give them to us to prepare us to serve You. Let us show our appreciation to our pastors for the work that they do. Let us respect them and listen to them because You have given them to us for our good. Amen.

November 29

He heals the brokenhearted and binds up their wounds.

—Psalm 147:3

IF A LOVED ONE WERE SUDDENLY WOUNDED and began bleeding, we would instinctively apply pressure to that wound to try to stop the bleeding before he or she bled to death.

We shouldn't be surprised when God sometimes applies pressure in our lives to stop the bleeding of our wounds. He must first stop the bleeding so that the healing process can begin. Pressure is not usually pleasant, but it is often necessary. When a person's heart stops beating, a doctor will apply pressure—one compression after another—to get it to start functioning again. We so often think of pressure as a negative thing, but it can be a blessing when applied as needed by someone who cares and is skilled in its application.

God, thank You for applying pressure when we need it. Thank You for not leaving us wounded and bleeding; instead, You bind up our wounds and heal our broken hearts. You care so deeply for us, God, and You know best how to make us whole. We trust You, even in the midst of the pressure. If it is from Your hand, it is meant for our healing. Amen.

November 30

We do not want you to be uninformed, brothers, about the hardships we suffered in the province of Asia. We were under great pressure, far beyond our ability to endure, so that we despaired even of life. Indeed, in our hearts we felt the sentence of death. But this happened that we might not rely on ourselves but on God, who raises the dead.

—*2 Corinthians 1:8-9*

A MAN COMMITTED SUICIDE ON AN AIRPLANE flying from Los Angeles to New York. At thirty-five thousand feet, he went into a restroom and hung himself. You would have thought that he had risen to such a level that he would have been above his problems. Also, he had a destination; he knew where he was going. But the pressures he was facing brought depression that took over, so he ended his life. His plane was equipped to handle air pressure, but not pressure of the spirit.

We are all under a great deal of pressure these days. Time never slows down. The demands never let up. People are sometimes cruel. Money is often too scarce. Our bodies don't always work as they should. Many of us have felt pressure to the same degree as the man on that plane. As Paul expressed it in the scripture for today, "We were under great pressure, far beyond our ability to endure, so that we despaired even of life." So why don't we give up as the air traveler did? For the same reason that Paul indicated: because we rely on God and not on ourselves. In fact, he says that we face all of life's pressures so that we can learn to rely on God rather than ourselves. And, as a note of encouragement, he reminds us that this same God has the power to raise the dead.

God, You have raised people from the dead. Come now and help us in our dead situations. We are under great pressure, far beyond our ability to endure. We do despair even of life. But God, rather than giving up because we can't handle this ourselves, we know that we can rely on You to help us. We give our situation over to You, God. We believe that You can raise us up. Give us strength to endure, and empower us to deal with all that is weighing down upon us, O God. We pray this in the name of Jesus, Amen.

December 1

Now when I went to Troas to preach the gospel of Christ and found that the Lord had opened a door for me.

—2 Corinthians 2:12

A FEW YEARS AGO, WE OPENED A second church location in Fishers, Indiana, a suburb of Indianapolis. I have a wonderful office there, and I was given a passkey that unlocks all of the doors in the entire building. When we first moved in, I went from room to room, using my key to check out the new facility. I got in one room after another until I came to my own office; for that room, my key wouldn't work. After several futile attempts, I took my key to our staff engineer. A little while later, he gave it back to me. I asked if it was a new key, and he said no. I knew they hadn't put in a new door. So I asked him how it was going to work since it was the same key and the same door. He told me that he had put some oil on the key so it would help the tumblers in the lock fall into place.

We will find that the anointing of the Holy Spirit on our lives will also open doors. Just as God had opened a door for Paul in Troas, He will also open doors for us to minister for Him. We may sometimes be surprised at the doors God chooses to open for us.

Thank You, God, for Your anointing. Thank You for empowering us to do Your work. Thank You for the doors that You open for us. Amen and Amen!

December 2

The Spirit of the Sovereign LORD is on me, because the LORD has anointed me to....bestow on them a crown of beauty instead of ashes, the oil of gladness instead of mourning, and a garment of praise instead of a spirit of despair.

—*Isaiah 61:1, 3a*

WE CAN TELL A LOT ABOUT A person from the clothes he or she is wearing. We sometimes can tell what line of work the person is in, what sport he or she is involved in, where the person is going to hang out, or what activity the individual is going to do.

What we wear on the outside as Christians—our spirit, our attitude, our expression—should reflect that we hang out with God. Other people should see us clothed in a garment of praise because our God is worthy to be praised.

God, let our countenances reflect You and the beauty, gladness, and praise You have brought into our lives. Help people to see a difference in us. Help our attitudes and the expressions on our faces to be so attractive that others are drawn to You. Let what we "wear" be appropriate for those who are called by Your name. Amen.

December 3

Be very careful, then, how you live—not as unwise but as wise.
—Ephesians 5:15

IN JUNIOR HIGH SCHOOL, MRS. CRAWFORD TAUGHT us that during the days of industrialization, people migrated from the south to the north to get jobs in factories, foundries, and various industrial facilities. They worked ten to twelve hours a day with no breaks. But bosses noticed that even though the employees were working more hours, the production leveled off. In an effort to move on from that plateau, they introduced fifteen-minute breaks. It worked, and production went up again. They discovered that breaks help productivity, profit, and pay to go up.

I have noticed that when I stop to take a praise break, giving God praise for what He has done, my productivity goes up and I prosper more. It is too easy to get into the rut of taking for granted all that God has done. When that happens, nothing stirs us. Nothing blesses us. Nothing energizes us. When we stop, however, and praise God for what He has done, our spirit and God's Spirit meet. Then, we are refreshed and ready to again give a hundred percent.

Lord God, You are worthy of all praise. Make us ever mindful of that and ever grateful for all that You have done in our lives. We bless You, O God. We praise Your name. We worship You. We magnify You. You are good and Your mercy endures forever. We praise you, O God, for You are worthy of our praise. Amen.

December 4

They will be called oaks of righteousness, a planting of the LORD for the display of his splendor.

—*Isaiah 61:3b*

WE THINK OF TALL, MAJESTIC OAK TREES providing wonderful shade, but we often don't stop to think about the fact that they also provide acorns as well as shade. There would be no more oak trees were it not for the acorns. But an interesting fact is that oak trees can only produce acorns when they are full of water. Each tree can hold fifty gallons of water. So, when they are full, they produce; when they have insufficient water, they do not produce.

When we are filled with the Holy Spirit, we produce the fruit of the Spirit. But just like the oak trees, when we are empty, we are not productive.

Lord, help us to remain productive. Let us be filled with Your Spirit so that we might bear the fruit of the Spirit, so that others might also come to know You, and more Christians be produced as a result. Help us to be ever filled to overflowing with Your Spirit, we pray in Jesus' name, Amen.

December 5

As the rain and the snow come down from heaven, and do not return to it without watering the earth and making it bud and flourish, so that it yields seed for the sower and bread for the eater, so is my word that goes out from my mouth: It will not return to me empty, but will accomplish what I desire and achieve the purpose for which I sent it.

—Isaiah 55:10-11

VIAGRA BRINGS POTENCY AND POWER TO MEN who are impotent in a particular area of their lives. That was not, however, what researchers were originally looking for. I was told by a friend that scientists were actually trying to develop something that would grow hair on the heads of men who were bald. As part of the research study, the men taking Viagra were asked if they were noticing any new growth. The answer was yes, but not in the area they had anticipated.

God's Word blesses us in ways we never dreamed of when we take it into our spirits. We read it at times to learn more about God or to find the answer to a question, to become more knowledgeable about a doctrinal issue, or just because we think we should. But then, all of a sudden, it is as though a portion of scripture is written in neon lights. It exactly fits our situation and inspires us in a way that nothing else could.

Father, thank You for giving us Your Word. We realize that Your Word is not just a bunch of letters on a page, but it is alive and purposeful. Thank You that Your Word changes us and helps us to grow. In Jesus' name, Amen.

December 6

For the word of the LORD is right and true; he is faithful in all he does.
—Psalm 33:4

WHEN I ATTENDED CHURCH AS A YOUNG person, I often heard the statement: "God said it. I believe it. That settles it." Since I've been preaching myself, I've shortened the saying to, "God said it. That settles it."

In terms of it being true, it doesn't matter whether we believe God's Word or not. God isn't waiting for us to believe it before what He says proves true. The law of gravity isn't nullified if we don't believe it; it is still true. We can believe with all our hearts that the sun will not rise tomorrow; but when dawn comes, our belief will be proved false. God's Word is true, no matter what we think.

God, we do believe that Your Word is true. What You say, You will do. We know that what we believe doesn't change the veracity of Your Word, but we just want to tell You that we do believe. Amen.

December 7

Where there is no revelation, the people cast off restraint; but blessed is he who keeps the law.

—*Proverbs 29:18*

MY SONS AND I USED TO RIDE roller coasters together as we traveled around the country. But when I heard one day that someone had died while riding a roller coaster, I wanted to find out why. I needed to be sure the rides were safe before I would take my children on them again. I found out that the man died because he was riding without restraints. Roller coasters move quickly and go up, around, down, and even upside down; so there are restraints that hold the riders in to keep them safe. This man removed his restraints, and he died.

God's restraints are not intended to keep us from having a good time, but to keep us from killing ourselves *while* we're having a good time. Let's trust God that the restraints currently in place in our lives are for our own good. As we read the Word of God, we need to obey it.

God, You know that there are times we want to cast off our restraints. The fruit of the tree looks so good that we can't believe You really meant that we shouldn't eat of it. In those moments, help us to lean not unto our own understanding, but to obey You. Amen.

December 8

Honor the LORD with your wealth, with the firstfruits of all your crops; then your barns will be filled to overflowing, and your vats will brim over with new wine.

—Proverbs 3:9-10

GRAPE JUICE IS READY THE MINUTE THE juice is squeezed from the grapes, but wine takes time to produce. Wine-making requires a press, a channel, and a vat. It is the crushing of the grapes in the press that makes the new wine flow through the channels and into the vats. Even though grape juice and wine look a lot alike, wine tastes different, possesses greater value, and has greater influence.

In our world today, we have too many grape-juice Christians. Rather than recognizing that maturity is worth the wait, grape-juice Christians want everything immediately. It's maturity, however, that makes the difference. Some of us never experience the overflow of the Spirit because we don't want to undergo the crushing process. And we never become as valuable as we could be because we aren't willing to wait for God to mature us.

God, help us never to desire to be less than Your best. Help us not to be content to be grape-juice when we could be wine, or to be disobedient children when we could be mature adults. Give us the grace not to run from the crushing process, but rather be willing to embrace those things that will develop us. Thank You, God. Amen.

December 9

But just as you excel in everything—in faith, in speech, in knowledge, in complete earnestness and in your love for us—see that you also excel in this grace of giving.

—2 Corinthians 8:7

PASTOR JAMES JACKSON AND ANOTHER BROTHER WENT to a car wash. It was the type where you get out of the car, go inside, and pay your money while the attendants take care of getting the car through the car wash. On his way into the building, Jack saw a man hitting and kicking a vending machine. Endowed with southern friendliness, Jack stopped to talk to the man: "Why are you beating this vending machine?" he asked with a quizzical smile. The man responded, "I put in my money, but I can't get out of it what I'm supposed to get." He told Jack how much money he had put in. Jack read the sign on the vending machine, reached into his pocket, took out a dime, put the dime in the slot, pushed the button, and the item fell out.

Some of us stop one dime short of giving enough. Sometimes we expect to be getting something when we haven't put in enough of ourselves to get that sort of return. Rather than becoming angry at our circumstances, we need to stop and consider how much we have given. If we want a job that requires a college education, have we paid the price to get that education, or are we just angrily banging on employers' doors expecting something for nothing? If we want a happy and satisfying marriage, are we invested fully in meeting the needs of our spouse, or are we just waiting in expectation for that person to meet all of *our* needs?

God, help us to stop and take stock of ourselves, and what we are bringing into this life You have given us. Help us not to withhold what we need to give, whether that involves giving of our time in preparation for something you have in store for us, giving our money into a collection plate at church, giving ourselves to our spouse and children, or giving our talents to You in service to others. Whatever it is that we need to give, let us excel in this grace of giving. In Jesus' name, Amen.

December 10

After all, no one ever hated his own body, but he feeds and cares for it, just as Christ does the church.

—Ephesians 5:29

IN 2008, WE HEARD ABOUT A GROUP of four friends, including two NFL players, whose twenty-one- foot boat capsized in the waves while they were out fishing in the Gulf of Mexico. Nick Schuyler, a fitness trainer, was the only survivor. All four of them were alive and well, initially; but as darkness came, they couldn't see anything. They were cold; hypothermia set in. The waves were high and unrelenting. We can't imagine what was going on in their minds at that time. One of the men decided to let go of the boat and drifted out to sea; then, a second one did the same. A third man held on until daylight, when he thought he spotted a light and decided to try to swim toward it. Because he felt that the life jacket was impeding his swimming, he took it off. None of those three has been seen since they left the boat. The lone survivor was found wet, freezing, and exhausted—but alive. What saved him is that he stayed with the boat.

When some people are going through struggles, they leave the church and cast off what they consider to be restraints. They set out on their own and wander off, never to be heard from again. No matter how bad the situation seems, we need to stay with the boat, stay with the church. There is encouragement in the body of Christ. There is safety in the body of Christ. There is hope in the body of Christ. Jesus feeds and cares for His church: we need His nurturing *especially* when we are facing dark nights, cold situations, and weary times of waiting.

Lord, at the time when we most need to cling to the church, some of us have gone off searching for what we want on our own. We somehow think we can find on our own what we aren't yet experiencing within the confines of the church. Help us to know, Lord, that You love the church, You have laid down Your life for the church, and that we can expect You to find us in the church. Let us remain there as we wait for You to rescue us from our trials. In Your name we pray, Amen.

December 11

And we, who with unveiled faces all reflect the Lord's glory, are being trans-formed into his likeness with ever-increasing glory, which comes from the Lord, who is the Spirit.

—2 Corinthians 3:18

WHEN WE WERE GROWING UP, MY SISTER Tonette used to go to Momma's kitchen to get her hair done. Momma would pin a towel or a sheet around her and she would sit in a chair. Then Momma would take oil, apply it to Tonette's hair. After that, she picked up a hot comb and slowly combed it through her hair. (The comb had to be hot in order to work.) When the hot comb got close to Tonette's ear, she could feel the heat. Afraid that her mother was going to burn her, she started squirming, and Momma had to tell her to sit still. Our mother was not trying to burn her, but to better her. Tonette was a reflection of her mother, so her mother wanted her to look good.

We Christians are a reflection of who God is, so God wants us to look good. When we start feeling the heat that He is using to better us, we start squirming. We need to sit still and let God work because He has our best interests at heart.

How silly we are, God, to think that You don't know how to take care of us. You have created us, You have kept us, You have saved us, and You have supplied all of our needs. Yet, there are times when we cringe and say "Ow!" as though we think You are suddenly going to hurt us. We are sorry, God, for our foolish behavior. Help us to sit still as You work on us so that we can become a better reflection of You to this world. In Christ's name, Amen.

December 12

When Jesus reached the spot, he looked up and said to him, "Zacchaeus, come down immediately. I must stay at your house today." So he came down at once and welcomed him gladly.

—*Luke 19:5-6*

LUKE 19:1-10 TELLS US THIS STORY: "JESUS entered Jericho and was passing through. A man was there by the name of Zacchaeus; he was a chief tax collector and was wealthy. He wanted to see who Jesus was, but being a short man he could not see because of the crowd. So he ran ahead and climbed a sycamore-fig tree to see him, since Jesus was coming that way. When Jesus reached the spot, he looked up and said to him, 'Zacchaeus, come down immediately. I must stay at your house today.' So he came down at once and welcomed him gladly. All the people saw this and began to mutter, 'He has gone to be the guest of a *sinner*.' But Zacchaeus stood up and said to the Lord, 'Look, Lord! Here and now I give half of my possessions to the poor, and if I have cheated anybody out of anything, I will pay back four times the amount.' Jesus said to him, 'Today salvation has come to this house, because this man, too, is a son of Abraham. For the Son of Man came to seek and to save what was lost.'"

We are used to going to the Lord's house. We go there to worship, to praise, to fellowship, to learn, to serve, and to give our tithes and offerings. It's one thing to go to Jesus' house; it's quite a different thing to *take* Him to our house. When Peter took Jesus home, his mother-in-law was healed. When Matthew took Him home, his friends' lives were changed. When Jairus took Him home, his daughter was brought back to life. When Mary and Martha took Him home, their brother was raised from the dead. Things happen when we take Jesus home with us.

Lord, we are honored that You would want to come to our home. We gladly invite You in. Walk through each room and make Yourself at home. Let us know how we can serve You. Know that You are welcome. Amen.

December 13

As they approached the village to which they were going, Jesus acted as if he were going farther. But they urged him strongly, "Stay with us, for it is nearly evening; the day is almost over." So he went in to stay with them. When he was at the table with them, he took bread, gave thanks, broke it and began to give it to them. Then their eyes were opened and they recognized him, and he disappeared from their sight. They asked each other, "Were not our hearts burning within us while he talked with us on the road and opened the Scriptures to us?"

—Luke 24:28-32

MY WIFE AND I TOOK OUR SON Jordan to help get him settled into his dorm room at Tennessee State. While we were there, we began talking about his roommate who hadn't yet arrived. Jordie assured us that they wouldn't have any problems because they had known each other for years. He was convinced that it was going to be great. Sharon said to him, "Son, it isn't going to be the same. You don't really know a person until you live with him."

We never really know Jesus until He moves in and we live together. It's one thing to visit Him once a week at His house and do the things we are accustomed to doing while we are there. But it is another thing entirely when He comes to our house to *live* with us. We may begin to notice that our house isn't as clean as we thought it was. We might become more conscious of the clutter that we have allowed to accumulate there. We may pay more attention to what we watch on TV in the evening and to the reading material we bring under our roof. We may feel a need to make our conversations sound different and to relate to those around us in a kinder and gentler way. Jesus wouldn't have to say a whole lot; just His presence makes the difference.

Lord, as long as we kept You at a distance, we were cool. You didn't bother us, and we didn't bother You. We just went about our lives doing what seemed right in our own sight, and that was okay with us. But now, here You are, right in the middle of our lives; and everything looks different. We suddenly feel a need to change our behavior, our actions, our speech, and even our way of thinking. God, help us, change us. We need You. Amen.

December 14

Surely goodness and love will follow me all the days of my life....
                                                            —*Psalm 23:6*

INDIANA IS A STATE THAT LOVES BASKETBALL. Dr. James A. Jackson made an interesting observation one year during March Madness, the NCAA Men's and Women's Basketball Tournaments. He noticed that while the teams are playing, a lot of falling is going on. These players play hard, and in the course of the game, they fall. But he noticed that every time a player falls, there is someone who runs out on the court with a towel to clean up the mess. They do that to make sure the players won't slip and fall in the same place where they fell before.

When we get up from our falls in life, we don't have to go back and clean up the mess ourselves. God has arranged it so that goodness and mercy follow us. When we mess up—as we all do at times—goodness and mercy come along behind us and clean up our messes. That way, we don't keep slipping and falling in that same place over and over again.

God, You have thought of everything. Not only do You prepare the way before us, but You send goodness and mercy to follow us along our way. Thank You, God. It is comforting to know that, even though You don't want to see us fall, You have prepared in advance for that possibility. Thank You for goodness and mercy that follow us, cleaning up our messes so that we don't have to be afraid to pass by that same place again. If we mess up in our home, there's goodness and mercy following us. If we mess up at work, there's goodness and mercy again following us. If we mess up at church, even there, goodness and mercy follow us. Thank You, God, for Your goodness and Your mercy that will follow us all the days of our lives. Amen.

December 15

"Forget the former things; do not dwell on the past."

—*Isaiah 43:18*

"Do not worry about tomorrow, for tomorrow will worry about itself."

—*Matthew 6:34*

DR. THERON WILLIAMS HAS POINTED OUT THAT yesterday is the source of our guilt, tomorrow is the source of our stress, and today is the source of God's grace. God is a "very present help in trouble."

One thing that trips us up is our yesterdays. We remember our sins, our failures, our embarrassments, and our sorrows. If we dwell on those discouraging moments of the past, we will become depressed and unable to function in the present. We need to focus instead on today, because today is the day of salvation. If we continually think about the future, we will stress out because all that we have to do, all that we have to face, will seem overwhelming. We may be so frightened that we become paralyzed, unable to do anything. We need to stay focused on this day and this moment, and we will find that God's grace is sufficient.

How often, God, we have wasted time and have depleted our emotional reserves by dwelling on the past or contemplating the future. Help us, God, to focus our attention—to give ourselves fully—to this day. Help us to know how You want us to live in this moment of time. Amen.

December 16

When they came to the place called the Skull, there they crucified him, along with the criminals—one on his right, the other on his left. Jesus said, "Father, forgive them, for they do not know what they are doing." And they divided up his clothes by casting lots.

—Luke 23:33-34

IT WAS AT THE CROSS THAT JESUS taught us how to forgive. He didn't wait until the resurrection to forgive His enemies. He forgave while His abusers were still causing him pain: He was still experiencing physical and emotional agony from the spike in his feet, the nails in his hands, and the taunts and insults of those who hated him. It was then that He said, "Father, forgive them, for they do not know what they are doing." He forgave even when the people didn't ask Him for forgiveness.

Earlier, Jesus had taught us to pray, "Forgive us our sins, for we also forgive everyone who sins against us." We cannot be like Christ and live in a state of unforgiveness. Yes, we have been hurt. Yes, we have been treated unfairly. Yes, we have pain and anger because of what someone did to us. But we have to let it go. We have to let it go for our own sake. The people who hurt us have already moved on; we can't let their actions continue to hold us down. And we also have to let it go for Jesus' sake. For how can we glorify God with the same heart from which we curse our enemy?

Jesus, You know how hard it is for us to come to a place of willingness to forgive those who have deeply wounded—and perhaps even tried to destroy—us. You know how bad the situation is. You understand what we've gone through. Yet, You are not asking us to do something You were not willing to do. You set the example for us that we should follow in Your steps. Help us, God. Even now, we bring before You the person(s) we know we need to forgive. We see their faces in our minds, and we feel the pain they caused in our hearts. Not because they have asked us, not because we want to, and not because we feel like it, but in an act of love and obedience to You, we do forgive him/her/them. Help us now to let go of the feelings, the memories, and the attitudes we've been harboring. Let us focus on the fact that You have forgiven us. It humbles us, Lord, to think of Your grace and mercy to us. Thank You, God. Amen.

December 17

The Lord is my shepherd…

—*Psalm 23:1*

A YOUNG PREACHER WHO HAD JUST GRADUATED from seminary returned to his home church to thank the congregation for all their encouragement and all they had done for him along the way. The pastor of the church invited him to give remarks. At the close of his remarks, he quoted the 23rd Psalm. He did so with just the right voice intonation, and he articulated the words precisely. It was obvious that he was well educated, and his recitation sounded so beautiful that when he finished, the entire congregation stood and applauded. Later in the service, an old preacher got up and he, too, quoted the 23rd Psalm. He wasn't as articulate as the young man, he didn't have all the right inflections in his voice, and it was obvious that he had not had formal seminary training. But he continued on. When he finished, no one stood, and no one applauded. But the people sitting in their pews, were crying. The young man asked the pastor what had made the difference—why the congregation had responded so differently to this old preacher. The pastor told him, "It was obvious when you finished that you know the psalm, but the old preacher knows the Shepherd."

What is important to us? Do we care more about *what* we know or *Who* we know? Knowledge is a fine thing. I encourage all of the ministers I know to get a good education. But information about God cannot replace intimacy with God. Learning about God cannot replace loving God.

God, we thank You today for the opportunities we've had to get a good education. That is especially true for those of us who have had the privilege of attending Christian colleges and seminaries where we were able to increase our knowledge of You and of the Word of God. But, God, we know that none of our head knowledge can ever replace our heart-knowing. Help us to take advantage of all the opportunities we have for education, but help us at the same time to keep our focus on our relationship with You. Amen.

December 18

"What do you think? If a man owns a hundred sheep, and one of them wanders away, will he not leave the ninety-nine on the hills and go to look for the one that wandered off?"

—*Matthew 18:12*

A HEAVY SHEEP WEIGHED DOWN BY ITS fleece may lie down to rest, but sometimes it can inadvertently fall over on its back in an indentation of grass and cannot get up. This is referred to as a cast sheep or a cast-down sheep. No matter how much it kicks and flails its legs in the air, it stays on its back and cannot get up. Eventually, it will die. The shepherd has to come and help it right itself.

Some of us have been lying in places we don't belong for so long that we can't right ourselves. We need to have the Good Shepherd come to help restore us to our upright position. We want to move on, but we can't. We've fallen and we can't get up.

Yes, God, that's us You see kicking and flailing about, trying to stand up after we've fallen. We lay down in a pasture that we chose for ourselves, not one that You chose for us. It wasn't a safe pasture, and we have gotten ourselves stuck. Please, God, deliver us. We hear Your voice and want to follow You, but we can't unless You help us. Amen.

December 19

Even though I walk through the valley of the shadow of death, I will fear no evil, for you are with me...

—*Psalm 23:4*

SOME SCHOLARS SUPPORT THE NOTION THAT THERE is an actual "Valley of the Shadow of Death" in Israel. They say it has such steep cliffs on either side that the valley is in darkness whether it is day or night, except for high noon when the sun is directly overhead. They say it used to be a frightening place because there were caves and crevices in which thieves and robbers could hide and lie in wait for unsuspecting travelers. Even sheep were fearful as they walked through this valley, because there were so many places where they could get caught or even lose their footing and fall to their deaths.

Valleys in the Bible represent difficulty, hard times, and pain. Valleys are inevitable. Some think that if they live right, they won't go through valleys; but all of God's children, even Jesus Himself, have had to go through difficulties. The Shepherd will lead us even into the valley of the shadow of death, but we don't need to be afraid because He will be with us. He will take care of us. We can trust Him. We also should note that this verse speaks of walking through the valley of the *shadow* of death, not death itself. The shadow is not real; it's not going to hurt us. I'd rather be hit by the shadow of a truck than by a truck! But the shadow appears larger than it really is. We sometimes become afraid because the shadow we're facing looks bigger than the actual reality.

Lord, You know that we get afraid in the dark. We get afraid in the valley. We get afraid when we think of death. And yet, You, our Loving Shepherd, sometimes lead us into a place of darkness, steep inclines, and death. We may not understand why we're taking this route, but You know our destination, and You know why we need to go this way. The sheep never question the shepherd; they just follow. We don't want to question You either, our Shepherd. We trust You to lead us through the valley safely. In Christ's name, Amen.

December 20

When I am afraid, I will trust in you.

—*Psalm 56:3*

MY FRIEND COREY BROOKS, PASTOR OF NEW Beginnings Church in Chicago, says that the difference between a good day and a bad day is one phone call. One phone call telling us that our mother is in the hospital, our son is strung out on drugs, or our friend has been killed turns our good day into a bad day. Bad days are valley experiences.

There are three ways to deal with a valley: 1) *Eliminate* the valley—that is, pretend it isn't there; 2) *Expand* the valley—add to the drama to make it worse than it actually is; and 3) *Experience* the valley. If the Shepherd leads us into the valley, it's because He knows that's where the best pastures are, where the best grass is. There is always purpose in pain. So even on the bad days, we can trust in Him. Even when the phone call comes, we can trust in Him. Even when night sets in and we're still in the valley, we can trust in Him.

God, we know there are so many places in the Bible that we are told not to be afraid. But we are so thankful for this verse that says, "When I am afraid." It doesn't even say, "If I am afraid." Even though we should always trust and not be afraid, You included this verse to address those moments when we must acknowledge honestly that we are afraid. But we thank You, God, that when that happens, we can determine in our hearts that we "will" trust in You. Amen.

December 21

AFTER I GRADUATED IN DALLAS, I WANTED to stay there. It was a great city and had a lot to offer, so I tried hard to settle down there. But God closed one door after another, so I had no choice but to return to my hometown of Indianapolis and move in for six months with my parents. What I didn't realize then was that God was working on a plan. In the neighborhood where I grew up, there were a lot of great people, but there were also some haters. The haters took delight in telling me, "Your daddy was nothin', and you're not going to be nothin' either. Why are you going to school? You're not going to amount to anything." God brought me back here so that He could show my haters how He has taken care of me. He set a table before me in the presence of my enemies. They can continue to talk if they want to, but they can't get to me.

Tablelands are plateaus, flat areas found in an elevated place. When a shepherd fed his sheep on the tablelands, the sheep were visible to all sorts of enemies who wanted to attack them, but they couldn't do it because the shepherd would see them coming and get to them before they could get to the sheep. Our Shepherd knows how to take care of us. Even when we don't understand why He is leading us to a certain place, we can rest assured that He is doing what is best for us. We don't need to be concerned about our haters. Our Shepherd will get to them before they get to us. Our Shepherd will also let them know that we belong to Him, and they will see for themselves how God takes care of His own.

Thank you, God, that You do take care of us. Thank You that You see the enemy coming and are always there to protect us. Thank You that You deliver us from our enemies and that You even make sure that they see how You care for us. We praise Your precious name. Amen.

December 22

In the beginning was the Word, and the Word was with God, and the Word was God....The Word became flesh and made his dwelling among us.

—*John 1:1, 14*

SERENA WILLIAMS IS RANKED AS THE NUMBER one women's tennis player in the world. She was playing in a tournament one day in Miami against a younger player, and this other woman was killing her on the court. Her father, Richard Williams, was there that day. He was the one who taught her how to play the game and has coached her along the way. He was sitting up in the stands, watching. But as it became apparent that his daughter was getting beaten on the court, he got up, came down from the stands, and positioned himself courtside on the same level as Serena. Serena's game turned around. She was able to get the victory simply because she could see her father. After the game, she said, "I just felt like he was there really supporting me. I could feel it more when he was up close than when he was in the stands," she said. "I just felt like I could take it up to another level."

When humankind was being defeated by the enemy, God wrapped himself in flesh and came down to our level: "'. . .and they will call him Immanuel'—which means, 'God with us'" (Matthew 1:23). Because He is with us—God nearby, not far off—we can get the victory.

God, we are overwhelmed with gratitude to You for coming down to us. We could never have made it without Your presence. You are the One who gives us victory and helps us to conquer our enemies. Thank You for Your presence, Your very real presence, in our lives. We love You today. Amen.

December 23

And let us consider how we may spur one another on toward love and good deeds.

—Hebrews 10:24

WE HEAR ABOUT THIS HAPPENING MORE OFTEN these days, but I remember hearing one of the first news stories about someone who went through a drive-up window at a Starbucks and paid not only for his order but for the car behind him, too. That prompted the people in the next car to pay for the car behind them, and it kept going on all day. The reporter talked about the holiday cheer and the smiles this act of kindness had produced throughout the day. It was so unusual that the media even tracked down the person who started it all. A news reporter asked him, "Were you trying to spread the holiday cheer? To give joy and make people smile when you did that? To prompt others to do good to someone else?" The man replied, "No, I had no idea that would continue all day. I did it because when I was in line waiting for my coffee, the person in the car behind me kept blowing his horn, became belligerent, and was even gesturing me. This was really messing with me, but I'm into judo and karate, and I have learned in those situations to change my consciousness. This guy was bringing negativity into my situation, so to change my consciousness and turn it into something positive, I paid for his stuff. I didn't know it would keep going; I was just trying to deal with *me*."

No matter how negative the circumstances may get in your life, you can change your consciousness by blessing folks who are behind you. That way, when they get to the front, they will turn around and bless someone who is coming behind them. Just as the generation before you sacrificed to help you get to the front, you need to turn to those behind you and sacrifice for them so that they, too, can make it to the front.

God, help us to live our lives in such a way that we inspire others to want to be more generous and kinder to others. Let our lives be a living sermon that is beautiful and stimulating. Let us reach back and help those who are coming along behind us. Let us live for You and for others, not for ourselves. In Christ's name, Amen.

December 24

While they were there, the time came for the baby to be born, and she gave birth to her firstborn, a son. She wrapped him in cloths and placed him in a manger, because there was no room for them in the inn.

—*Luke 2:6-7*

A FEW YEARS AGO, ONE OF OUR members had been sick for awhile, so my assistant called ahead and a couple of the associate pastors and I went to visit her. When we got there, I was surprised by the incongruity I saw in her yard. There was Frosty the Snowman; Dasher, Dancer, Prancer and that crew; along with Rudolph and a bunch of other stuff. But alongside a big ol' Santa Claus, there was the Virgin Mary, Joseph, and the shepherds. I kept thinking, "If this is about Santa, why are you bringing in the Savior? But if this is about the Savior, why are you bringing in Santa?" I noticed, too, that there was no baby in the manger. I took all of this in during the few seconds it took to walk to the door where we knocked and knocked again, but got no answer. Thinking that perhaps she was sleeping, we left.

When I saw this woman a few weeks later at church, she said, "Pastor, you didn't come to visit me." I told her, "Yes, I came. Pastor Page and Pastor Jackson were with me. We knocked a couple of times, but no one answered." She said, "No, Pastor, that's not possible. I moved my bed into the living room when I was sick, and I know I wasn't sleeping because that was part of my problem: I wasn't able to sleep. I couldn't possibly have missed you." I replied, "I can prove that I was at your home. In your yard, you had a Santa Claus, Rudolph, the Virgin Mary. . ." and I named off all the things we had seen that day. She said, "Oh, Pastor, that wasn't my yard; that was my neighbor's yard. You were at the wrong house." I should have known I was at the wrong house when I saw that Jesus wasn't there.

God, let ours be the house where Jesus is. Let our hearts make room for Him this Christmas. May there be no incongruity, no question about the One whose day we are celebrating. In His name we pray, Amen.

December 25

Then the righteous will answer him, 'Lord, when did we see you hungry and feed you, or thirsty and give you something to drink? When did we see you a stranger and invite you in, or needing clothes and clothe you? When did we see you sick or in prison and go to visit you?' The King will reply, 'I tell you the truth, whatever you did for one of the least of these brothers of mine, you did for me.'

—*Matthew 25:37-40*

DR. SEUSS, A GREAT THINKER, TOLD THE story about the Grinch that stole Christmas. The Whoville people had beautiful trees with decorations, gifts, and big celebrations. The Grinch, however, couldn't stand them; so he stole Christmas by taking their gifts, decorations, trees, and everything he could to spoil their Christmas. Much to his chagrin, the next day he woke up expecting to hear weeping and lamenting over their loss; instead, he heard carols and songs, along with joy and laughter. He couldn't believe what he was hearing. In spite of his efforts to do away with it, Christmas came anyway. It came without packages, boxes, and bags. He learned that Christmas could not be purchased in a store: its meaning is much, much more.

Christmas is not about the presents under the tree; it's about the One who died on the tree. Our family and some of the others in our church have changed the way we look at Christmas. We are celebrating the day now for what it represents—the birthday of Jesus. We no longer give presents to each other—it isn't *our* birthday! Instead, we give food, clothing, and gifts to Jesus by giving these items to "the least of these." Our Christmases now are so much more joyful and meaningful than they ever were when we focused the day on us instead of Him.

Happy birthday to You! Happy birthday to You! Happy birthday, Dear Jesus! Happy birthday to You!

December 26

I know, O LORD, that a man's life is not his own; it is not for man to direct his steps.

—*Jeremiah 10:23*

TIM DUNCAN, WHO PLAYS FOR THE SAN Antonio Spurs, is a four-time NBA champion and a three-time MVP in the NBA Finals. But he didn't always dream of being a basketball star. As a child, he wanted to be an Olympic swimmer, and was training hard to achieve that goal. But when he was in the ninth grade, Hurricane Hugo hit the Virgin Islands and destroyed the only Olympic-size pool on the islands. Rather than giving up and spending the rest of his life talking about what he *could have done* if life hadn't treated him so unfairly, Duncan turned his talents to basketball. With the same hard work and determination he had applied to swimming, he now went in this new direction—and he succeeded. And he didn't just make a name for himself and buy more and more stuff. He established his own foundation that supports programs in education, youth sports, and health awareness. The storm redirected him in ways that proved best.

If we trust God, He will use the storms in our lives to guide us in directions that we would never have considered on our own—directions that are far better than those we *think* we want to go. Whether a storm is a good thing or bad thing depends on our attitude. There is always a rainbow after a storm, if we look for it.

Father, we do believe that You are in control, even when situations in our lives appear out of control. We used to think that a storm could only be bad because of the destruction it causes. But we understand now that all things work together for good to those who love You and are called according to Your purpose. So, God, we're going to look for the direction in which You are guiding us by the storms in our lives, knowing that You will bring us to a better place. We trust You, Father. Amen.

December 27

After forty days, Noah opened the window he had made in the ark and sent out a raven, and it kept flying back and forth until the water had dried up from the earth. Then he sent out a dove to see if the water had receded from the surface of the ground. But the dove could find no place to set its feet because there was water over all the surface of the earth; so it returned to Noah in the ark. He reached out his hand and took the dove and brought it back to himself in the ark. He waited seven more days and again sent out the dove from the ark. When the dove returned to him in the evening, there in its beak was a freshly plucked olive leaf! Then Noah knew that the water had receded from the earth. He waited seven more days and sent the dove out again, but this time it did not return to him.

—Genesis 8:6-12

IN SEPTEMBER 2008, I LEARNED THAT I had prostate cancer. In November, I underwent a two-and-a-half-hour operation. But it took six months for me to recover.

The aftermath of a storm takes longer to deal with than the actual storm. Some of us deal with the storm itself, but then we don't persevere through the aftermath of the storm. If Noah had said, "There has never been such destruction as this on the earth. There's no way the ground is ever going to dry out again," every person and animal on the ark would have suffered. If Noah had given up and stopped checking to see if the waters had receded, every person and animal on the ark would have died. Noah believed that God had a plan for *after the storm*; He had a purpose for *after the storm*. Can we believe that for our own lives?

Lord, when the devastation from the storm seems so great, it is easy to want to give up. When we've had to face a crisis of the magnitude we've never seen before, it is hard to see beyond the storm. But, God, today, we will begin checking to see what state our world is in now that the storm has stopped. We trust that You will help us to deal with the aftermath of the storm. We know that we can't expect life to be just as it was before the storm, but show us how to live with our new circumstances. Show us how to make our world beautiful again. Amen.

December 28

Let us throw off everything that hinders…

—*Hebrews 12:1b*

A SPACE SHUTTLE DOES NOT GO INTO orbit looking the same as it did sitting on the launch pad. When it starts toward its destination, it leaves the launch pad behind. A couple minutes into the launch, the rocket boosters that helped the shuttle to lift off begin to detach from the craft. A few minutes later, the external fuel tank that provided the fuel for the launch detaches as the shuttle soars higher. The shuttle is now unencumbered and free to press on to its destination.

If we are going to soar to the heights and reach our destinations, we are going to have to be prepared to have things, and even people, detach themselves from our lives. Some people would hold us back; we have to let them go. Some material goods would weigh us down; we have to let them go. Some attitudes would prevent us from soaring; we have to let them go. Some habits would keep us from taking off in the first place; we have to let them go.

Father, we acknowledge that there are people and things in our lives that do hinder us from going as deep, as high, and as far as You actually want us to go. God, we've been clinging to the things of this world as though we intend to stay here forever. But we really don't want to miss out on Your plans and purposes for our lives. Help us now, in this very moment, to throw off—even to lay at Your feet—all of the people and things that are keeping us from following You and serving You fully. We let them all go right now, in Your holy name. Amen.

December 29

"No one can serve two masters. Either he will hate the one and love the other, or he will be devoted to the one and despise the other. You cannot serve both God and Money."

—*Matthew 6:24*

IF MONEY BROUGHT PEOPLE JOY, THEN FORMER heavyweight champion Mike Tyson should be one of the most joyful persons alive. After all, he earned nearly four hundred million dollars in his career. But in a June 23, 2004 *New York Times* article, he said: "'When I had money, I was an animal. I was so belligerent, I was so cantankerous, so persistently disregardless. I wasn't that nice of a person. Just because you buy mansions and cars doesn't mean you know what money is worth. I lost all across the board. My life has been a total waste."

We need to be careful when we have the opportunity to gain wealth, change our status in society, and own some of this world's goods, that we don't expect those things to make us happy. We cannot serve both God and money. We have to make sure that we continue to *serve* God and *use* money. Otherwise, we will find ourselves *serving* money and *using* God. We have to keep our priorities straight.

Heavenly Father, we will have no other gods before us. We have so many examples before us of people whose minds and hearts have become warped because they began to serve money. Keep our minds and our hearts focused on You, O God. Let us recognize that all of our money belongs to You anyhow, so it is ours only to use as You wish, not as we want. Help us always to put You first, Lord God. In Your holy name we pray, Amen.

December 30

I will remain in the world no longer, but they are still in the world, and I am coming to you. Holy Father, protect them by the power of your name—the name you gave me—so that they may be one as we are one. While I was with them, I protected them and kept them safe by that name you gave me. None has been lost....

—*John 17:11-12*

THERE WERE NINE MEMBERS OF A CLIMBING group on Mount Hood. When one of them slipped, he took five others down the mountain with him. One of those who fell was a fourteen-year-old boy. He was climbing with his father, who was one of the four whose footing stayed firm. The ones who fell were covered with snow, and only this boy was found alive. When interviewed afterward, he was asked, "Were you afraid?" "Yes," he replied, "I was afraid." "Could you see anything?" "No, the snow had covered me, and I couldn't see anything." "Did you cry?" "Yes, I cried. It was very frightening and I cried." "Was there ever a time when you didn't think you were going to make it?" "No, because before we began climbing, my dad tied a rope around his waist and around mine; I was connected to him. When I fell, he didn't fall. I knew that no matter what, he would get me out."

We are protected by the power of the name of our Holy Father. When we fell into sin, our Father didn't fall, and we are bound to Him by the cords of His love. We can certainly be as trusting of our heavenly Father as this young boy was of his dad. We know that, "no matter what"—no matter how far we have fallen, no matter how much of a predicament we're in, or no matter what happens to others around us—He will get us out. It was Jesus who prayed for the Father to protect us. God *will* answer that prayer!

God, thank You for Your loving protection of us. We recognize our own vulnerability, our own fallibility, and our own unpredictability. Nevertheless, You, God, are all-powerful and perfect in every way. You are the same yesterday, today, and forever. We know we can trust You. Thank You for the cord of love with which You bind us to Yourself and to one another. Thank You that "no matter what," You will protect us and keep us. In Jesus' name, Amen.

December 31

The Lord is my light and my salvation—whom shall I fear? The Lord is the stronghold of my life—of whom shall I be afraid?

—*Psalm 27:1*

AGORAPHOBIA IS THE FEAR OF PUBLIC OR open places. If any of the people on Noah's ark had suffered from this disorder, they would not have been able to fulfill God's plan for them to multiply and replenish the earth. If they had stayed on the ark in their comfort zone, they would eventually have died without fulfilling their destiny.

We need to come out of our comfort zone if God is going to use us to fulfill His purposes. We need to overcome our fears. Whether it is fear of public speaking, fear of failure, fear of not being liked by everyone, or simply fear of the unknown, God does not want us to be controlled by our fears. We can simply cast our cares upon God.

Lord God, we are thankful that You are certainly a stronghold in our lives and in our families. Thank You so much for inspiring us to want to overcome our fears—of all sorts. Help us to know that You are our light and our salvation, so there is no need to be afraid. Help us, God, to trust You. In Christ's name, Amen.

How to Accept Christ as Your Personal Saviour

For those who are reading this and have never accepted Jesus as your personal Savior, salvation is available to you right now. Please read the following to find out how you can accept Him into your heart today.

"We have all sinned." Romans 3:23 – *For all have sinned and come short of the glory of God.*

"The penalty we pay." Romans 6:23 – *For the wages of sin is death; but the gift of God is eternal life through Jesus Christ our Lord.*

"God's love for us." Romans 5:8 – *But God commendeth His love for us, in that, while we were yet sinners, Christ died for us.*

"Salvation by Faith." Romans 10:9 – *That if thou shall confess with thy mouth the Lord Jesus and shall believe in thine heart that God hath raised him from the dead, thou shalt be saved.*

For whosoever shall call upon the name of the Lord shall be saved. Romans 10:13

For More Information About
Pastor Jeffrey A. Johnson's Ministry, Visit:

www.EasternStarChurch.org
www.KingdomWordMinistries.org